Putin's Olympics

President Vladimir Putin's Olympic venture put the workings of contemporary Russia on vivid display. The Sochi Olympics were designed to symbolize Russia's return to great power status, but subsequent aggression against Ukraine, large-scale corruption, and the doping scandal have become the true legacies of the games. The Kremlin's style of governance through mega-projects has had deleterious consequences for the country's development. Placing the Sochi games into the larger context of Olympic history, this book examines the political, security, business, ethnic, societal, and international ramifications of Putin's system.

Robert W. Orttung is the Research Director of the Sustainability Collaborative and Associate Research Professor of International Affairs at The George Washington University, USA.

Sufian N. Zhemukhov is a Senior Research Associate at The George Washington University and Lecturer at The University of Maryland Baltimore County, USA.

BASEES/Routledge Series on Russian and East European Studies

Series editor: Richard Sakwa

Department of Politics and International Relations, University of Kent

Editorial Committee:

Roy Allison, St Antony's College, Oxford

Birgit Beumers, Department of Theatre, Film and Television Studies, University of Aberystwyth

Richard Connolly, Centre for Russian and East European Studies, University of Birmingham

Terry Cox, Department of Central and East European Studies, University of Glasgow

Peter Duncan, School of Slavonic and East European Studies, University College London

Zoe Knox, School of History, University of Leicester

Rosalind Marsh, Department of European Studies and Modern Languages, University of Bath

David Moon, Department of History, University of York

Hilary Pilkington, Department of Sociology, University of Manchester

Graham Timmins, Department of Politics, University of Birmingham

Stephen White, Department of Politics, University of Glasgow

Founding Editorial Committee Member:

George Blazyca, Centre for Contemporary European Studies, University of Paisley

This series is published on behalf of BASEES (the British Association for Slavonic and East European Studies). The series comprises original, high-quality, research-level work by both new and established scholars on all aspects of Russian, Soviet, post-Soviet and East European Studies in humanities and social science subjects.

106. Georgia after Stalin
Nationalism and Soviet Power
Edited by Timothy Blauvelt and Jeremy Smith

107. The EU's Eastern Neighbourhood
Migration, Borders and Regional Stability
Edited by Ilkka Liikanen, James W. Scott and Tiina Sotkasiira

108. Freedom of Speech in Russia
Politics and Media from Gorbachev to Putin
Daphne Skillen

109. Putin's Olympics
The Sochi Games and the Evolution of Twenty-First Century Russia
Robert W. Orttung and Sufian N. Zhemukhov

Putin's Olympics
The Sochi Games and the Evolution of Twenty-First Century Russia

**Robert W. Orttung and
Sufian N. Zhemukhov**

LONDON AND NEW YORK

First published 2017 by Routledge

2 Park Square, Milton Park, Abingdon, Oxfordshire OX14 4RN
52 Vanderbilt Avenue, New York, NY 10017

Routledge is an imprint of the Taylor & Francis Group, an informa business

First issued in paperback 2018

Copyright © 2017 Robert W. Orttung and Sufian N. Zhemukhov

The right of Robert W. Orttung and Sufian N. Zhemukhov to be identified as authors of this work has been asserted by them in accordance with sections 77 and 78 of the Copyright, Designs and Patents Act 1988.

All rights reserved. No part of this book may be reprinted or reproduced or utilised in any form or by any electronic, mechanical, or other means, now known or hereafter invented, including photocopying and recording, or in any information storage or retrieval system, without permission in writing from the publishers.

Notice:
Product or corporate names may be trademarks or registered trademarks, and are used only for identification and explanation without intent to infringe.

British Library Cataloguing in Publication Data
A catalogue record for this book is available from the British Library

Library of Congress Cataloging in Publication Data
A catalogue record for this book has been requested.

ISBN: 978-0-415-82372-2 (hbk)
ISBN: 978-0-367-18598-5 (pbk)

Typeset in Times New Roman
by Florence Production Ltd, Stoodleigh, Devon, UK

For Nicole

Contents

Tables	ix
Notes on authors	x
Preface	xi
Abbreviations and acronyms	xiv

1	Introduction: how Putin's political system led to Olympic corruption, military adventurism, and state-sponsored doping	1
2	The 2014 Sochi Olympic mega-project and Russia's political economy	21
3	Political and civil society and the Sochi games	38
4	Security: fighting terrorism and strengthening the military	61
5	International issues: Circassians, the former Soviet countries, and the West	81
6	The legacy of the Sochi Olympics	104
	Index	130

Tables

1.1	Final medal count	12
4.1	Victims of terrorism and anti-terrorism in the North Caucasus, 2008–2015	63
4.2	Number of killed and wounded law enforcement officers before and after the 2014 Sochi Olympics	63
6.1	Tourism indicators in Krasnodar Krai	108
6.2	Distribution of tourists at hotels in Krasnodar Krai	110

Notes on authors

Robert W. Orttung is Research Director of the George Washington University Sustainability Collaborative and Associate Research Professor of International Affairs at the George Washington University Elliott School of International Affairs, USA.

Sufian N. Zhemukhov is Senior Research Associate at the Institute for European, Russian and Eurasian Studies at the George Washington University Elliott School of International Affairs, USA, and Lecturer in the History Department at the University of Maryland Baltimore County, USA.

Preface

The idea behind this book is to shed light on Putin's Russia through a case study of the 2014 Sochi Winter Olympics. The games highlight many of the triumphs and tragedies of contemporary Russia and we hope to use the nearly universal appeal of the Olympics to shine a light on an important aspect of international politics, namely the way Russia's political system works under President Vladimir Putin.

This book has been a long time coming. Our original plan was to publish it before the Olympics even took place, hoping to take advantage of the hype surrounding the games when people around the world would tune into the planet's greatest sporting extravaganza. However, we missed that deadline and many others. We finally finished more than two years after the closing ceremonies. Viewed from this vantage point, given the growing doping scandal surrounding Russia in summer 2016, the legacy of the games is beginning to evolve and new questions are starting to arise. It may be many years before we have the full account and can put the Sochi games into their proper context.

We certainly enjoyed the process of writing the book, which required many hours spent in the cafes of Washington, DC, discussing the vicissitudes of Russian politics over strong coffee and tasty pastries. Such things are the joys of life, as were reading a variety of other stories about the Olympics which mixed politics and sport. Among our favourites were David Maraniss's *Rome 1960: The Summer Olympics that Stirred the World* (2008), Daniel James Brown's *The Boys in the Boat: Nine Americans and Their Epic Quest for Gold at the 1936 Berlin Olympics* (2013) and Richard Askwith's *Today We Die a Little! The Inimitable Emil Zatopek, the Greatest Olympic Runner of all Time* (2016).

Even before the book was published, it received some attention when it was mentioned in Stephen Lee Myers' article about Sochi in *The New York Times Magazine* (Myers, 2014). This prominent citation gave us encouragement to keep going.

We met many new people in researching the Olympics and incurred numerous debts over the years to them and to old friends and colleagues who were also interested in various aspects of the Sochi games. We presented bits and pieces of this manuscript in numerous universities and conferences, including Grinnell College, Stetson University, Virginia Tech, 'Sochi 2014: (Geo) political, economic

xii *Preface*

and social dynamics', an international conference at L'Université libre de Bruxelles (ULB), 20–21 February 2014, a session of The George Washington University Institute for European, Russian, and Eurasian Studies' (IERES) Postcommunist Politics Social Science Workshop, 11 October 2011, the annual meeting of the Association of Slavic, East European, and Eurasian Studies in Boston, 21–4 November 2013, and a book incubator at IERES on 17 November 2015. A presentation at Johns Hopkins' School of Advanced International Studies on 12 September 2012, brought out three representatives of the Russian embassy in Washington; they kindly provided us with some useful fact sheets.

Among those we would like to thank are: Philip Alexiou, Richard Arnold, Harley Balzer, Henry Hale, Kathrin Hille, Eugene Huskey, Amy Kay, Charles King, Miriam Lanskoy, Danielle Lussier, Andrey Makarychev, Martin Müller, Stephen Lee Myers, Irina Olimpieva, Bruce Parrott, Margaret Paxson, Emil Persson, Bo Petersson, Elena Pokalova, David Segal, Ayesha Tanzeem, Gerard Toal, Christopher Walker, Julian Waller, Courtney Weaver, Cory Welt, and Jonty Yamisha. Of course, we are responsible for any errors of fact or judgement that remain in the text despite the best efforts of our colleagues.

We would like to thank Peter Sowden, our editor at Routledge, for everything but his patience. If we had a firm deadline, this book would have been done a long time ago. Since Peter never sent us threatening letters or accused us of being lazy bums and then, to make matters worse, assured us that 'these things take as long as they take,' we spent more time than is advisable sitting around Washington's aforementioned cafes discussing various topics, only some of which were relevant to the text presented here. While we are both democrats in all things, we would have preferred an editor with an iron fist to concentrate our thinking and motivate us to finalize the text. Ultimately, though, we must admit that perhaps there was some wisdom in Peter's tolerance. If we had published the book before the Olympics, as planned, it would have been completely different. Looking at the games with the benefit of hindsight allows us to better judge their place in history and measure their significance for Russia.

Finally, we wish to thank the publishers of the following articles for permission to include some of the material originally published there in the book:

Orttung, R.W. & Zhemukhov, S. (2013). The 2014 Sochi Olympics and Russia's Civil Society, *Euxeinos* 12: 26–35.

Orttung, R.W. & Zhemukhov, S. (2014). The 2014 Sochi Olympic Mega-Project and Russia's Political Economy, *East European Politics* 30 (2): 175–91.

Zhemukhov S. & Orttung, R.W. (2014). Sochi and the Circassian Issue. *Institute of Modern Russia*. February 27. http://imrussia.org/en/society/676-sochi-and-the-circassian-issue. (Accessed 10 October, 2016).

Zhemukhov, S. and Orttung, R.W. (2014). Munich Syndrome: Russian Security in the 2014 Sochi Olympics, *Problems of Post-Communism* 61(1): 13–29.

References

Askwith, R. (2016). *Today We Die a Little! The Inimitable Emil Zatopek, the Greatest Olympic Runner of All Time*. New York: Nation Books.

Brown, D.J. (2013). *The Boys in the Boat: Nine Americans and Their Epic Quest for Gold at the 1936 Berlin Olympics*. New York: Penguin Books.

Maraniss, D. (2008). *Rome 1960: The Summer Olympics that Stirred the World*. New York: Simon & Schuster.

Myers, S.L. (2014, January 22). Putin's Olympic Fever Dream. *The New York Times Magazine*.

Abbreviations and acronyms

CE	Caucasus Emirate
FIFA	International Federation of Association Football
FSB	Federal Security Service
FTP	Federal Targeted Program for the Development of Sochi in 2006–2014
IOC	International Olympic Committee
LGBT	Lesbian, Gay, Bisexual, and Transgender
MVD	Ministry of Internal Affairs
NGO	Non-Governmental Organization
OCOG	Organizing Committee for the Olympic Games
ROC	Russian Olympic Committee
RUSADA	Russian Anti-Doping Agency
UNEP	United Nations Environmental Programme
VEB	Vneshekonombank
WADA	World Anti-Doping Agency
WWF	World Wildlife Fund

1 Introduction

How Putin's political system led to Olympic corruption, military adventurism, and state-sponsored doping

Two puzzles stand at the centre of this book. The first examines what the 2014 Sochi Olympics tell us about the development of Russia. As Russia's leader and the individual who was the main driving force behind the games and the person most closely associated with them, President Vladimir Putin has chosen to cultivate Russia through a variety of mega-projects, of which the Sochi Olympics is the most important example. These mega-projects necessarily concentrate state and private resources for a specific purpose while assigning a lower priority to other goals. What are the consequences of such a development policy and what does it mean for Russia's future? Our argument here is that the path that Putin chose facilitated widespread corruption, the development of extensive security forces, and a crackdown on civil society. These are the defining features of the Putin era and key components of the Sochi games.

The second puzzle involves the legacy of the Sochi Olympics. As soon as the closing ceremonies were over, Russia invaded Ukraine and annexed Crimea in the first European land grab since the end of World War II. In the West, the two events did not fit together, and the Olympics were quickly forgotten. The ideal of the Olympics is to promote greater peace in the world through a coming together of young people for athletic competition. Invading your neighbour with military force seemed to be the antithesis of such idealistic objectives. By annexing Ukrainian territory immediately after the Olympics concluded, Putin erased any goodwill that he had earned in the international community from hosting the games.

We resolve this paradox by arguing that Russia's invasion of Ukraine was not a break with the Sochi Olympic effort, but a logical continuation of it from the Russian perspective. The nature of the Putin regime led to both the Sochi games in the corrupt, authoritarian form they occurred and the subsequent invasion of Ukraine. Sochi was not an anomalous event in Russian history, but deserves a central place in the narrative of Putin's Russia. Likewise, the hostilities were not a radical break with Putin's developmental model, but a logical continuation of it. Given this combination of corruption and aggression, the evidence that began to flow after the Olympics concluded that the Russian state had systematically organized doping among Russian athletes to ensure that they won the most medals fits the existing pattern. The corruption, aggression, and dishonesty were all part and parcel of the Putin system.

2   *Introduction*

Combining these two threads of analysis, we conclude that Putin's reliance on mega-projects led to a specific kind of Russian political development, the defining features of which were strict limits on civil society groups, a focus on increasing the state's repressive capacity, and, as a direct consequence of these policies, a flourishing of corruption and efforts to undermine all forms of fair competition. The quick evolution of events from Sochi to Crimea was not an about-face from peaceful development though mega-projects to aggressive military intervention, but an effort to achieve the same goal – Putin's vision of a Russia in which he was able to call the shots and direct resources to the projects that he personally considered the most important. The allegations of state-sponsored doping among many of Russia's athletes simply drew more attention to this state of affairs.

Were the Sochi Olympics a success or a failure? The 17 days of competition came off without a hitch and Russia was able to organize and host an international spectacle for a massive television audience of 2.1 billion people worldwide (International Olympic Committee, 2015). The coverage spilled across 412 channels, with 42,000 hours of reporting on television and 60,000 hours available on digital platforms. But beyond the two weeks of sporting displays, Russia did not boost its image in the international media or public perceptions; surveys by the Pew Research Center in spring 2015, one year after the games, found that most of the world's citizens held Russia and its leader in low regard (Stokes, 2015). The Kremlin's adoption of a 'conservative' ideology and attack on its sexual minorities showed that it was out of step with the Western countries that frequently serve as a reference point for Russian conceptions of its own identity, leading to a boycott of the games by Western leaders. Suffering from massive corruption, the games were badly mismanaged and came in considerably over budget. From Putin's perspective, they were probably not a success either since they did not really serve as a mechanism for uniting the country behind his leadership. It was only the invasion of Ukraine and the annexation of Crimea, resulting in a 'small victorious war', that seemed to cement Putin's role as the main arbiter of Russia's future and ensure that he would remain the paramount leader (Wood, 2015). We will return to the question of to what extent, and for whom, the games succeeded in much greater detail in considering the legacy of the Sochi Olympics in the book's final chapter.

Mega-events and mega-projects

In examining Russian development through the lens of sports mega-events and mega-projects, we seek to blaze a new conceptual path in the study of Russian politics. The literature on mega-events and mega-projects is growing rapidly, and while it typically addresses events like the Olympics and World Cup, we argue that such events can help shed light on the overall governance of centralized authoritarian countries like Russia. We start with definitions of the terms mega-events and mega-projects and then show how this lens is useful in explaining Russian developments.

Mega-events are typically defined in the academic literature as 'large-scale cultural (including commercial and sporting) events, which have a dramatic character,

Introduction 3

mass popular appeal and international significance' (Roche, 2000). Such events have long-lasing consequences for the host city, region, or country in which they occur and attract extensive media coverage (Horne & Manzenreiter, 2006, p. 2). While mega-events can be a good way of mobilizing capital for infrastructure investments, studies of past experience with mega-events suggests that the gains they produce can be offset by the way that they are organized and the particular interests behind them (Cornelissen & Swart, 2006, p. 110). In other words, mega-events can play an important role in a country's development, but their impact is not completely benign because their concentration of resources can help to facilitate the dispersal of state resources to corrupt actors. The Olympics are the largest and most significant mega-event in the world. Accordingly, they stimulate some of the most important mega-projects as well (Frawley & Adair, 2013, pp. 1, 2).

Mega-projects are massive infrastructure ventures, usually driven by public funding, which must be completed within defined time limits and with a constrained amount of resources (Frawley & Adair, 2013, pp. 3–4). Usually, they are worth more than $1 billion and seek to ambitiously change the structure of society (Flyvbjerg, 2014). They are different in kind than smaller projects, which fit into existing structures and do not attempt to transform them. In general, organizers claim that their mega-projects can create new jobs and provide for other forms of economic stimulus, such as increasing tourism and boosting sports participation in the host country (Hughes, 2012), though these initial optimistic hopes are not always borne out in practice (Müller, 2012; Owen, 2005; Shaw, 2008; Whitson & Horne, 2006). Nevertheless, economists have found that even just bidding for the Olympics is associated with a 20 per cent boost in exports for the host country (Rose & Spiegel, 2011).

Hosting a mega-event like the Olympics is a useful way of launching and carrying out mega-projects. The deadlines imposed by the need to complete the project before the opening ceremony help to ensure that the massive construction and infrastructure projects remain on schedule even if extra spending is required. The spectacle associated with the Olympics justifies the need for mega-projects.

Patriotic plans gone awry

Putin had long admired the Olympics and had worked since the 1990s to bring them to Russia as a way of demonstrating that the country had returned to its rightful place in the world. Putin planned to turn the mountains surrounding Sochi, where he regularly vacationed, into a winter resort that could rival anything in the Alps.

> For Putin, the projects were not investments in the purest business sense. In fact, they were economically dubious. Rather, they were patriotic endeavors carried out for the greater public good, which he believed he best understood and which he alone decided (Myers, 2015, p. 324).

The International Olympic Committee claimed that the original seed for Russia's winter games was a 'strategic vision to transform an entire region by creating a

4   Introduction

sports legacy that would benefit both elite and grassroots athletes' (International Olympic Committee, 2015). While Soviet leaders in the 1980s had considered proposing Sochi as a host of the Winter Olympics, the idea was audacious because Sochi did not have any world-class skiing facilities or the tourist infrastructure required to support the large crowds of spectators that the Olympics attracted. Building up Sochi to host the Olympics would also reshape Russia's centralized geography since it would develop a site outside of Moscow, the host of the 1980 Olympics and the focus for much of Russia's political, business, and cultural activity (Golubchikov, 2016).

But, whatever the lofty intentions at the origins of the 2014 Sochi Olympics, they quickly ran into the reality of Russia's deeply authoritarian and corrupt system. Even if Putin may have initially wanted the games to promote Russian greatness – we will never know what he was actually thinking – ultimately the Olympic project became symbolic of a system that excludes the public from decision-making and hands the most benefits to a select few. The Olympics provided a specific form of patrimonialism – Putin was willing to give large sums to his cronies, but they had to deliver results in terms of new sporting facilities and urban infrastructure to secure them. While this kind of corruption is certainly present in Western countries, it reached a peak in Russia.

In the case of the Sochi Olympics, Putin was the main organizer (Wood, 2015) and it was his favoured elites who benefitted most from them. Putin played the key role in securing the games for Russia and working to implement them. In contrast to typical mega-projects in Western countries that must operate within a constrained budget and with accountability to a broader public, Russia's income from oil and natural gas sales abroad and its centralized authoritarian leadership meant that Putin could essentially spend money without regard to rationality or public oversight, thinking only of maintaining the corrupt political system he had established since 2000. As Peter Pomerantsev put it 'The USSR built mega-projects that made no macroeconomic sense but fitted the hallucinations of the planned economy; the new hyper-projects make no macroeconomic sense but are vehicles for the enrichment of those whose loyalty the Kremlin needs to reward' (Pomerantsev, 2014, p. 206).

Although the Russian government does not refer to mega-projects in the most prominent strategic economic planning documents, such as Strategy 2020, published in March 2012 (Connolly, 2013; Strategiya 2020, 2012), in practice, it has invested in numerous such projects in addition to the Olympics. Among them are the $20 billion reconstruction of Vladivostok for the 2012 APEC summit (Kalachinsky, 2010) and the even more expensive plans ($42 billion) to develop the Far East in general (Medetsky, 2013); the $6.9 billion Universiade Games held in Kazan in July 2013 (ITAR-TASS, 2013); the 2018 World Cup; the $15.2 billion Skolkovo innovation centre (Ulyukaev, 2013); the Gazprom tower in St. Petersburg (Reshetnikov, 2011); and the various energy pipeline projects – South Stream, for example, was expected to cost $39 billion before Putin abruptly cancelled the project at the end of 2014[1] (Hill, 2010).

Introduction 5

Russia has effectively begun to use such mega-projects as de facto regional development tools because it has been unable to come up with a coherent regional development policy that can provide a firm answer to the question of how to balance between the competing priorities of promoting equality among all regions and developing the most advanced regions as locomotives driving economic growth for the rest of the country (Kinossian, 2013). Effectively, regardless of what leaders claim their policy is, inequality is increasing across Russia in the absence of a redistributive social policy (Remington, 2011), while the federal state spends investment funds on high cost and high-profile projects that increase differentiation and resource concentration (D. Black, 2007, p. 274). The focus on mega-projects means that large federal investments go into regions that host the events, while other regions do not gain such benefits. Along these lines, one rationale for investing in Vladivostok and Sochi, and not other parts of Russia, was that big projects in those place would help hold the country together (Shchukin, 2014).

Such mega-projects can drive urban redevelopment plans (Altshuler & Luberoff, 2003; Gold & Gold, 2008). Since 1984, the Olympics have become a method for achieving large-scale urban infrastructural modernization (Essex & Chalkley, 2007, pp. 55–7). Barcelona's 1992 games have become the model for what can be achieved in terms of urban rejuvenation and planning (Coaffee, 2007, p. 155). During the 1960s and 1970s, the IOC did not support major urban investments, but its attitude evolved as it assimilated ideas of urban sustainability and began to view the Olympics as a driver to stimulate environmentally friendly urban transformation (Pitts & Liao, 2009, pp. 19–20), though investment in urban infrastructure varies greatly from city to city (Liao & Pitts, 2006, pp. 1240–11).

Most Olympics require at least some development of the host city's infrastructure. Tokyo spent 97 per cent of its budget on urban improvements, while Barcelona spent 67 per cent (Liao & Pitts, 2006, p. 1247) and Beijing spent approximately 65 per cent (Smith & Himmelfarb, 2007). Of course, in all Olympic projects, questions arise as to whether the funds used preparing for the games are well spent and if better infrastructure could have been built without the need to host a massive sports party (Shaw, 2008). Research on previous Olympics has found that the organizers oversold the benefits (Flyvbjerg, 2006; Whitson & Horne, 2006). There are also considerable opportunity costs to directing investment to only one city (Whitson & Horne, 2006) and evidence that infrastructure costs can be particularly burdensome in developing countries (Matheson & Baade, 2004).

The cost of the games was a politically volatile topic in Russia in the year before the opening ceremony. In the beginning of February 2013 Nizhny Tagil blogger Yegor Bychkov lit up Russia's blogosphere by calculating that the approximately 1.5 trillion rubles ($45 billion) then planned to be spent on the Olympics could better promote sport in Russia by using the same money to build a swimming pool, ice rink, soccer stadium, and health centre in every city of Russia, as well as buying ice and roller skates, a soccer ball, volleyball, and basketball for every resident between the age of 5 and 25 (Bychkov, 2013). A June 2013 Levada Center poll found that 65 per cent believed that Olympic money was not used effectively

6   *Introduction*

or simply stolen (Levada Center, 2013). Ultimately, the key to success in urban renewal schemes depends on how effectively the host city can integrate the infrastructure investments into the larger economy and it remains to be seen how well Sochi can do this after the Olympians have left, a topic addressed in the final chapter of this book.

Putin had personal reasons to be interested in the Olympics. During his time working in the St. Petersburg mayor's office under Anatoly Sobchak, the future president helped his boss prepare a bid for the city to host the 2004 Summer Olympics. The effort did not reach the final round of the competition however, and the IOC ultimately selected Athens as the host (Myers, 2015, p. 94). Similarly, Putin also saw the effort to host the games in Sochi as a way for Russia to regain the lost glory of the 1980 Moscow Summer Olympics, which were the target of a Western boycott after the Soviet Union invaded Afghanistan (Myers, 2015, p. 323).

Why did Putin choose to hold the Olympics in Sochi rather than another Russian city? At first glance, the location does not seem to be a logical pick since it does not have reliable snow and is known as a sub-tropical beach resort in an area near some of Russia's most violent conflicts. When Russia bid for the winter games, it did not have any world-class ski resorts, but the possibility of hosting the Olympics offered a chance to build one. While the idea for launching the resort likely came from oligarch Vladimir Potanin and the location of Sochi from Krasnodar Krai Governor Aleksandr Tkachev (Weiss & Khvostunova, 2013), the main force behind the games was Putin, an avid sportsman, who particularly liked to vacation in Sochi. The first time he went to Sochi was with his wife as a young man, so he had a strong personal connection. He likely saw the city and the surrounding natural beauty as a resource for the nation and the state. The historic sanatoria already built there for the lower middle class helped him legitimize the area as a place that served ordinary people as well as the Russian elite.

Nevertheless, the decision to choose Sochi as an Olympic city was made in secret without public discussion. While Putin certainly does not control every decision in Russia, he took a special interest in this issue. Finally, the fact that all the facilities and much of the city infrastructure had to be built from scratch had a perverse sort of appeal. During the 2000s, the IOC liked cities with little existing sports infrastructure because that meant that they would have to build new, state of the art facilities (Large, 2012, p. 32). In proposing Sochi, Putin built on earlier efforts – in 1995, Yeltsin's government had made a bid for Sochi to host the 2002 Winter Olympics, but that effort had gained little traction (Myers, 2015, p. 324).

Soviet history is replete with gigantic ventures, including Magnitogorsk (Kotkin, 1995), the Belomor Canal (Ruder, 1998), the Moscow metro system (Taubman, 2003, pp. 93–4), the Virgin Lands Campaign, and the Baikal-Amur Mainline Railway (Ward, 2009). Of course, the purpose of the Soviet mega-projects differed depending on the Stalinist, Khrushchevite or Brezhnevist context. However, they all were implemented in a system defined by corruption, with the Communist Party's monopoly on power, state control of the economy and the extensive use of informal networks at all levels of society (Karklins, 2005, p. 75). Typical also of Soviet projects was an exclusion of any public input, a policy that Putin continued in the efforts surrounding Sochi (Graham, 1998, p. 100). As the Soviet system evolved from Stalinism to Brezhnevism, the leader was no longer free to act independently and had to ensure that he exercised power in the interest of all the elites who controlled power, leading to 'stability of cadres' in which elites and masses alike generally were guaranteed to hold on to their jobs, thus spreading the benefits of the system (Jowitt, 1983, p. 286). But even as the nature of Russia's political system transformed radically through both the Soviet and post-Soviet eras, the focus on the use of mega-projects as a development tool remained in place.

Evolution of Putin's Russia

Putin's reliance on mega-projects to develop the country had a number of consequences in determining the way that Russia has evolved under his leadership. First, the Olympics helped maintain in power a centralized authoritarian regime. Second, they facilitated and perpetuated the extensive corruption that was already prevalent in Russia. Third, they helped the state crackdown on civil society groups. And, finally, they helped build up a strong security apparatus.

Sochi produced clear benefits for Russia's leaders. While Western cities, prodded by local business interests, typically host the Olympics as a way of expanding tourism and directing resources to specific development goals, in Russia the situation was different. The initiative for the Olympics came from the top, with Putin seeking to host the games as a way of maintaining his grip on power over the long term. The Olympics provided a goal for the overall society where none had really existed before. Rather than implementing a far-reaching series of economic reforms that would reduce Russia's dependence on natural resources such as oil and gas, Sochi 2014 focused popular attention on a new goal: developing the resources required to host the world's most prestigious mega-event. The idea of the Olympics served as a camouflage for a lack of other development goals. The development of Sochi came to stand in for the development of the whole system. After Sochi, Putin turned to an invasion of Ukraine and then deployed Russian forces in Syria, relying on those adventures as new distractions to divert attention away from Russia's lack of broader development goals.

Events like the Sochi Olympics contribute to Russia's image-building efforts (Alekseyeva, 2013). The Olympics and a handful of other events make it possible to reach a global television audience that is both large in size and includes viewers willing to interrupt their daily routine for the event (Spa, Rivenburgh, & Larson, 1995, p. 209). Putin presented Russia's bid in terms of promoting Russia's national identity and global image, in which hosting the games allowed the world to recognize Russia's growing international status and prestige (Cha, 2009, p. 37). Putin regards the ability of his administration to organize the Olympics as proof of the fact that he managed to transform and stabilize the economic situation in Russia in the 2000s and overcome the instability he perceived during the 1990s (Persson & Petersson, 2013). In contrast to the 1936 Berlin games, which the Nazis used in an effort to demonstrate the superiority of their ideology, or the Soviet

8　*Introduction*

use of the Olympic movement, which, beginning in 1952, sought to employ the games to promote the international appeal of socialist political, economic and social systems (Shaikin, 1988, p. 31), the Sochi games were planned to show that Russia could excel in the modern age of capitalism, like the advanced Western countries (Tsygankov, 2012), and did not seek to promote a particular ideology. Russia's efforts were more similar to Japan's use of the 1964 Olympics to return to the international community after WWII (Pound, 1994). Like other semi-peripheral countries, Russia has sought to use mega-sport events to boost its marketing power and regime legitimacy (D. R. Black & Westhuizen, 2004; Hopf, 2012). Recent studies have shown that hosting sports mega-events can effectively build pride among a country's population, rebrand the country's image, and help to bestow a greater sense of legitimacy on the government that organized them (Dowse, 2012; Westhuizen, 2004). Of course, the games have an inherent risk, as the Germans discovered in 1972, when a terrorist attack marred the peaceful image that West Germany was trying to project to the world in the Munich games (Large, 2012) or the numerous technical glitches that inflicted derisive headlines on the 1996 Atlanta games (Dobson & Sinnamon, 2001). Similarly, the Beijing 2008 Olympics did not produce the image boost that the Chinese leaders hoped for. In fact, surveys show that the number of people with positive impressions of China fell in other countries after the games concluded (Finlay & Xin, 2010).

Russia's mega-projects provide large amounts of state funding that open the door for numerous corruption opportunities. The logic for these large construction and event projects is the same as it is for the state weapons procurement programme (Bryce-Rogers, 2013) and the numerous energy development projects, which also concentrate resources and facilitate extensive corruption (Hedlund, 2014). To develop Sochi, Putin relied on a small number of close associates who received contracts to make the preparations for Sochi. Using his cronies to develop the infrastructure made it possible for Putin to deliver keys assets from the state budget to central allies. The massive corruption surrounding the games helped these groups amass additional resources throughout the seven-year buildup to the opening ceremony. The focus on mega-projects facilitated the corruption through the large-scale nature of the projects, the reliance largely on state funding and the great speed with which everything needed to be accomplished. Putin's previous crackdowns on the media and public oversight through elections and civil society made it possible to build the infrastructure through corrupt transactions without obstacle or delay.

In the Russian context, mega-projects play a strong political role in maintaining the current regime in power by preserving the loyalty of the masses and elites in the ruling coalition. In an age of 'ideological emptiness' (Popescu, 2006), hosting mega-events provides a replacement for the ideology of communism or democracy by imbuing media discussions with a larger idea. Similarly, by providing entertainment and a set of developmental goals, mega-events feed into what Ivan Krastev calls 'zombie authoritarianism' (Krastev, 2011) in which people passively accept the status quo even if they are not necessarily satisfied with it. The Olympics, and other mega-events, offer the host population a sense of pride in their country

Introduction 9

and, by extension, its leadership. The preparations for the games generate extensive compelling content for Russian television, which can help convince the mass domestic audience that the country is progressing well and that there is no need to engage in the kind of political protests advocated by the opposition (Spa *et al.*, 1995, p. 231).

The games make it possible for the elites to engage in rent distribution, giving key regime allies strong incentives to maintain the current leaders in power. In Russia, a coalition of ruling elites manipulates the economy to produce rents while maintaining the kind of stability that makes normal forms of social life possible (North, Wallis, Webb, & Weingast, 2007; North, Wallis, & Weingast, 2009). The factions involved in this process are identified in various ways (Sakwa, 2011), but typically include *siloviki* (members of the Federal Security Service, military, and police) (Taylor, 2011) and the oligarchs (Minchenko Consulting, 2012). Within this system, the ability to form state corporations are among the most valuable sources of elite rents, the flows of public money that enrich the top members of the ruling coalition. The ability to generate and distribute rents through state-controlled entities makes it possible to discipline elites and keep the ruling coalition intact (North *et al.*, 2009, p. 20). In other words, dividing up the rents among the elites, prevents them from engaging in a 'war of all against all' (Yakovlev, 2012). Mega-projects play a key role in this process of trading economic rewards for loyalty, which is the central feature of Putin's kleptocracy (Dawisha, 2014).

Maintaining an authoritarian kleptocratic regime in power requires repressing individuals and groups in Russian society that reasonably protest against the nature of the country's leadership and the particular policies that the leaders implement. Russia's political opposition sought to use the Sochi Olympics as a platform for seeking greater democracy within the political system as a whole. They also sought to block specific policies, such as the construction of sporting facilities in areas that had been designated as national parks. The Olympic organizers used a variety of repressive tools, from manipulating elections to imprisoning activists, to ensure that they could pursue their intentions without making concessions to the democratic and environmental activists. The authoritarian nature of the Olympic enterprise fit in well with Russia's authoritarian culture and helped to perpetuate it.

Finally, the Olympics led to the buildup of Russia's security services and military forces. The state budget provided additional revenue to these groups in the run-up to the games, creating additional capacity that could be used for purposes that the leaders defined beyond the Olympics. The Olympics stimulated the development of new military units, provided additional training and concentrated resources as part of an effort to ensure that no terrorist groups would be able to attack the games and use access to the media surrounding the event for their own purposes. To ensure that Russia could indeed place a 'ring of steel' around Sochi, the Kremlin gave the security forces the ability to develop an elite group of special forces that furnished the regime with capacities that it had not possessed in the past (Barabanov, 2014).

10 *Introduction*

The preparations of the military in advance of Sochi certainly had some impact on Putin's ability to invade Ukraine and capture Crimea with military force as quickly and effectively as he did. But what was more important than simply sending in the troops was the parallelism of the spectacle itself. Both Sochi and Crimea are instances of a state-managed display to mobilize patriotic feelings. Crimea was much more successful than Sochi because it galvanized the Russian population in support of Putin and his system of government.

Both Sochi and the Crimean War were used to demobilize opposition to Putin's regime. War could be used to flatfoot the opposition; in effect, the war tranquilized the opposition, to use Andrew Wilson's term (Wilson, 2014). Blocking critics of the Olympics and the invasion from the public sphere and driving popular opinion against them had the parallel effect of ensuring that there would be no one to point out the costs of the actions that the Russian leadership had taken.

The political spectacle in Sochi was a rationale for the Russian leadership to allow kleptocratic accumulation of resources by favoured elites. In Crimea the Russian invaders and their local sponsors were basically in the position of stealing what they could easily get their hands on.

If Russia had not won the right to host the Olympics in 2007, it would still have faced endemic corruption throughout the period afterwards. Additionally, it would have most likely invaded Ukraine after the removal of Yanukovych from power. Looking at this counterfactual – the absence of the Olympics – suggests that the Olympics were not crucial for Russia to develop the way that it has under Putin, but the games provided a focal point under Putin that shaped the nature of the corruption in ways that would not have made sense without them. Russia would not be less corrupt without the games because corruption is an integral part of Putin's 'patronal politics' (Hale, 2014).

The Sochi Olympics: From the successful bid to extinguishing the flame

Russia won the right to host the 2014 Sochi Olympics in 2007, when Putin famously flew to Guatemala to address the International Olympic Committee in English and French, while also using his personal charm to lobby the voting members who had the power to decide which country would have the right to spend the next seven years preparing for the games. As is often the case, the initial euphoria after being chosen led to a long period when journalists and activists questioned the ability of the host to make the necessary preparations and ponder whether it even made sense to do so.

Russia faced considerable scepticism from the Western media in its ability to serve as a competent host (Taras, 2013). Beyond the usual questions of whether the facilities would be ready in time and whether the host could provide effective levels of security, Russia faced questions about the way it handled human rights, including key vulnerable sectors of its population. Putin's decision to promote his return to the Kremlin for a third presidential term as an advocate of 'traditional values' put him on a collision course with Western publics and leaders. When

Introduction 11

Russia in June 2013 passed a law banning propaganda of 'nontraditional sexual relations', a thinly disguised effort in which the Kremlin sought to build its popularity by exploiting homophobic attitudes widespread among the Russian population, many activists in the West sought to use the Olympics as a platform to force the Kremlin leaders to change their policies (Lenskyj, 2014). While the campaign had little impact on Moscow's policy, it convinced Western leaders not to attend the opening ceremonies, delivering a humiliating rebuke to the Russian leader. Although there had been talk of another Olympic boycott, repeating the experience of the 1980 Moscow summer games when most Western countries refused to participate in protest over the USSR's 1979 invasion of Afghanistan, all the athletes showed up. Instead of President Barak Obama, the US sent a delegation that pointedly included outspoken homosexual sports stars. Many European leaders also decided not to participate.

The games themselves achieved the most that the host could have expected. Despite warm temperatures, snow covered the ski slopes. The 'ring of steel' security preparations held and there were no terrorist attacks even though Russia suffered a scare when there were explosions in Pyatigorsk and Volgograd in December 2013, leaving 37 dead and hundreds of casualties just six weeks before the opening ceremony (Markedonov, 2014). And, even if the organizers relied heavily on migrant labour and hurried, last minute efforts to prepare the facilities, none of the new stadiums collapsed because of shoddy construction. The main failings were mushy snow due to excessive sunshine, which caused some difficulties for skiers and snowboarders, and heavily publicized hotel rooms that suffered from unfinished bathrooms.

In fact, Putin's Russia had demonstrated that it could deliver a world-class event, with a spectacular opening ceremony, thrilling sports competitions, and a friendly face as personified by a group of volunteers who welcomed the spectators to the newly refurbished Black Sea resort. Russians who followed the course of the competition and commented about it on the country's popular social media sites praised the Olympics' ability to give the country's citizens a shared public event that they could be proud of.

Even the sporting results were a boon for Russia. Demonstrating Russia's ability to win glory at the games was a key aspiration of the leadership (Gorokhov, 2015, p. 276). Although the Russian hockey team, led by superstar Alexei Ovechkin, exited early from the Olympic tournament, Russia won the most medals of any country, 33, and the most gold medals, 13, as well, an excellent accomplishment after having performed disastrously in the Vancouver games in 2010 (See Table 1.1). Such national tallies have been important for propaganda purposes and rallying nationalism since journalists started keeping track of them in 1928 (Schwartz, 1998). Even if hockey is by far the most popular sport in Russia and the results were disappointing, there was plenty to cheer among the figure skaters and other competitors. Russia could even pride itself in being a country that attracts talent from elsewhere, since two of its gold medal winners had been born abroad – American snowboarder Vic Wild won two golds for Russia, leaving the US after the US Ski and Snowboard Association closed its alpine snowboard programme

12   *Introduction*

and Wild had married his Russian girlfriend in 2011, while South Korean Viktor Ahn, who became a Russian citizen in 2011 because he thought the training conditions were superior to those in his own country, won three golds and a bronze in short track speed skating. In the paralympic games, which were largely overshadowed by the simultaneous drama of Russia's invasion of Crimea, Russia won a record 73 medals, besting the achievement of Austria at the 1984 Innsbruck games by three. Russia's effective use of foreign coaches even raised the question among some commentators about whether Russia needed a special path of its own or could simply be another member of the world community (Orekh, 2015). The Russians graciously shared the stage with others as well. The Dutch dominated the speed skating competitions, while the Americans performed well in the new slopestyle snowboarding competitions.

But even as the Olympic events were successfully unfolding in Sochi, revolution was brewing in Ukraine, immediately next door to Russia. After President Viktor Yanukovych had refused to sign the Association Agreement with the European

Table 1.1 Final medal count

Country	Gold	Silver	Bronze	Total
Russia	13	11	9	33
United States	9	7	12	28
Norway	11	5	10	26
Canada	10	10	5	25
Netherlands	8	7	9	24
Germany	8	6	5	19
Austria	4	8	5	17
France	4	4	7	15
Sweden	2	7	6	15
Switzerland	6	3	2	11
China	3	4	2	9
Korea	3	3	2	8
Czech Republic	2	4	2	8
Slovenia	2	2	4	8
Japan	1	4	3	8
Italy	0	2	6	8
Belarus	5	0	1	6
Poland	4	1	1	6
Finland	1	3	1	5
United Kingdom	1	1	2	4
Latvia	0	2	2	4
Australia	0	2	1	3
Ukraine	1	0	1	2
Slovakia	1	0	0	1
Croatia	0	1	0	1
Kazakhstan	0	0	1	1
Totals	99	97	99	295

Source: www.nytimes.com/interactive/2014/02/23/sports/100000002726250.app.html

Introduction 13

Union, as he had promised to do, in October 2013, protesters began to fill Kyiv's central square. When the police sought to remove the demonstrators with force, they only angered many in the Ukrainian population and brought more activists out into the streets. Quickly the protests evolved from backing a trade deal with the West to demanding an end to Yanukovych's corrupt rule. Even though he had been democratically elected to Ukraine's highest office in 2010, Yanukovych had broken many of the country's laws as he concentrated power in his hands and stole as much of Ukraine's wealth as he could. On February 21, after the crowds had stood on the street during four months of winter, with some groups throwing Molotov cocktails at the regime's snipers, Yanukovych finally accepted the end of his rule and fled to Russia, taking as much of his ill-gotten gains as he could carry.

Following Putin's decision to send Russian forces into Ukraine on the heels of the revolution, the central question is why Putin invaded after spending seven years and more than $50 billion on an international image-building campaign? For Putin, Yanukovych's exit was a strategic loss because he had backed the Ukrainian leader since his failed attempt to win the presidency in 2004, when his dirty tricks triggered Ukraine's Orange Revolution. Far more importantly, however, was the spectre of a crowd of pro-democracy, anti-corruption demonstrators filling up Red Square in Moscow and removing Putin's regime, whose own popularity had been sliding since the end of 2011, when Putin and his assistant Dmitry Medvedev had announced that Putin was going to return to the Kremlin for a third term after the formality of Russia's 2012 presidential elections were completed. While Putin claimed that he invaded Ukraine in February 2014 in order to protect ethnic Russians living there and prevent a takeover by NATO, the most likely explanation was that he did not want to allow Ukraine to serve as a model for Russians to remove him from power.

Putin's decision to send in soldiers with no identifying insignia, known as 'little green men' to the outside world and 'polite people' to Kremlin spin doctors, proved to be a brilliant tactical manoeuvre. While Ukraine reeled from more than 20 years of allowing its military to decay and months of revolutionary upheaval in Kyiv and other cities, Russia was able to occupy the Crimean Peninsula nearly without firing a shot. This formal act of war quickly and decisively put an end to whatever belief idealists may have harboured in the Olympic peace formally declared by the United Nations only a few days earlier. In fact, Putin's decision to unleash his superior military force at a time when Ukraine had just removed a deeply corrupt president demonstrated that he was willing to take risks in certain situations, and plunged the world into its most dangerous crisis since the end of the Cold War (Menon & Rumer, 2015).

Whatever Putin's original intentions in seeking to sponsor the Olympics, the event ended as everything during his rule does – mired in corruption and leading to increased power and resources for Russia's security forces and military. These are the sectors of the economy that the organizers understood best and where they eventually devoted their energy. In order to protect the games from the potential of a terrorist attack, Putin rebuilt and mobilized Russia's elite forces instead of

14 *Introduction*

relying on the semi-civil, semi-militarized units that had been part of the original plan. In the run-up to the games, there were secret relocations of military units to the North Caucasus, just as there would eventually be secret relocations of soldiers to eastern Ukraine, as Putin sought to expand on his success in Crimea, but ran into the armed resistance of a quickly reorganizing Ukrainian army. Mothers protested the use of their young sons for these operations, just as they would begin to protest the use of force in Ukraine as Russian soldiers began to die when the Ukrainian military sought to protect its homeland. The logistical organization that was developed for the Olympics did not simply go away after the closing ceremonies. Rather Putin found a new purpose for Russia's increased capability in trying to quell the anti-corruption revolution in Ukraine. Likewise, by moving the assets of Olympstroy to Crimea, Putin was able to use the resources concentrated for the Olympics to start rebuilding the infrastructure of the peninsula.

The 2014 Sochi Olympics were immediately followed by war not because of an original plan in the Kremlin, but because the basic methods that Putin mobilized for the Olympics ended up being useful for Crimea. Building up the security forces, crushing civil society, and concentrating resources for urban development projects served perfectly for the invasion and annexation of Crimea and subsequent efforts to reconstruct its dilapidated infrastructure. If there had been no Olympics, Putin would not have had so many security forces concentrated in one place. His military reforms and preparations over many years allowed him to take advantage of the degeneration of the Ukrainian military during the previous years. The experience of rebuilding Sochi gave him confidence that he could do something similar in Crimea.

Plan for the book

The book proceeds in the following way. The next chapter focuses on the political economy of the games. It examines the overall structure of the Russian economic and political systems. Then it examines how the games are financed, lays out a method for understanding the expenses of the games and shows how the Russian state provided almost all of the funding for Sochi despite promises to tap private sources. It explains how the use of the state corporation Olympstroy made the Sochi Olympics even more opaque than their Western counterparts. Finally, it examines some of the most egregious examples of cost overruns associated with the games and the corruption mechanisms facilitating them. We argue that the Olympics ultimately fed into the centralization of financial flows through state-guided development without effective public oversight that encouraged the existing extensive corruption within Russia.

The games also reflected the Russian authorities' treatment of domestic civil society organizations in terms of the way they dealt with opposition political parties, the environmental movement, housing rights, and the LGBT community. This is the topic of Chapter 3. Such issues are complicated in any society; here we show how the organizers were able to use state resources to achieve their goals while blocking effective public input into the policymaking process. While the various protest movements had little tangible impact, the activists were able to gain valuable experience and raise awareness of their issues.

The fourth chapter examines the extensive security Russia imposed to ensure that no terrorist attacks would disrupt the games. Given the ongoing insurgency in the North Caucasus, such concerns were prominent worries for both the planners and the athletes who attended the games. The Olympics reinforced Putin's existing preferences for a strong reliance on deploying overwhelming force in terms of intelligence, military, and law enforcement personnel, as well as extensive efforts to collect information about all people who attended the games. While no terrorist attacks occurred, the use of such overwhelming security measures helped to shape Russia's approach to domestic and international problems moving forward. The chapter examines the anti-terror activities, the military build up surrounding the games and the specific measures taken during the games. It argues that the increased Russian capabilities achieved during the seven years leading up to the games provided a basis for Russia's subsequent incursion into Ukraine.

The fifth chapter, examining the international aspects of the games, looks at the contrasting ways Russia dealt with domestic issues, relations with former Soviet countries, and ties to the West. Typically, the Kremlin used repression domestically, aggression with its closest neighbours, and sought accommodation with the West. It denied a voice or platform to the indigenous Circassian people who sought to gain recognition of their history through the games. The invasion of Georgia in 2008 marked the kind of aggression the Kremlin displayed with its neighbours. During the games, Russia showed some restraint with the West and tried to retain good ties, though its poor human rights record at home made that difficult. The invasion of Ukraine and annexation of Crimea ultimately destroyed Russia's relationship with the West and upset the balance that Putin had tried to maintain between repression at home, aggression toward Russia's neighbours, and businesslike ties with the West.

The final chapter addresses the legacy of the 2014 Winter Olympics for the city of Sochi, Russia and the international Olympic movement. For the city, the Olympics created a huge amount of new infrastructure, but it remains to be seen if this new development will actually stimulate future economic growth. For the country, the Olympics simply reinforced the existing political system without bringing any changes to it. Internationally, the Olympics did little to burnish Russia's image. Following the games, the international Olympic movement had to adopt reforms to prevent huge cost overruns, discrimination against the LGBT community and doping at future games.

Our central argument in the following analysis is that the 2014 Sochi Winter Olympics reflected larger processes shaping Russia's political and economic system, but also had an autonomous impact. The games sharpened the nature of regional development policies in a way that concentrated extensive resources, through corrupt mechanisms, in the construction of infrastructure that is not likely to provide a sound basis for future development in Sochi or the rest of the country. The safety arrangements prevented terrorist attacks for this extraordinary event, but also helped generate an offensive military capacity that Putin had new

16 *Introduction*

confidence in deploying in Ukraine. Finally, the games only enhanced the Russian state's ability to crack down on its civil society rather than allowing citizens to hold their government accountable. Ultimately, future historians are unlikely to consider the vast resources invested in the 2014 Sochi Olympics to have provided commensurate benefits.

Note

1   www.upstreamonline.com/live/article1315361.ece

References

Alekseyeva, A. (2013). Discourse vs. Reality: The Rhetoric of a New Russia in the Sochi Olympics. In B. Petersson & K. Vamling (Eds), *The Sochi Predicament: Contexts, Characteristics and Challenges of the Olympic Winter Games in 2014*. Newcastle upon Tyne, UK: Cambridge Scholars.

Altshuler, A., & Luberoff, D. (2003). Mega-Projects: The Changing Politics of Urban Public Investment. Washington, DC: Brookings.

Barabanov, M. (2014). Changing the Force and Moving Forward after Georgia. In C. Howard & R. Pukhov (Eds), *Brothers Armed: Military Aspects of the Crisis in Ukraine*. Minneapolis, MN: East View Press.

Black, D. (2007). The Symbolic Politics of Sport Mega-Events: 2010 in Comparative Perspective. *Politikon*, *34*(3), 261–276.

Black, D.R., & Westhuizen, J.V.D. (2004). The Allure of Global Games for 'Semi-Peripheral' Polities and Spaces: A Research Agenda. *Third World Quarterly*, *25*(7), 1195–1214.

Bryce-Rogers, A. (2013). Russian Military Reform in the Aftermath of the 2008 Russia-Georgia War. *Demokratizatsiya: The Journal of Post-Soviet Democratization*, *21*(3), 339–368.

Bychkov, Y. (2013). Vmesto Olimpiada v Sochi, http://egor-bychkov.livejournal.com/2013/02/02/. (2 February). http://egor-bychkov.livejournal.com/2013/02/02/ (Accessed 10 October 2016).

Cha, V. (2009). *Beyond the Final Score: The Politics of Sport in Asia*. New York: Columbia University Press.

Coaffee, J. (2007). Urban Regeneration and Renewal. In J.R. Gold & M.M. Gold (Eds), *Olympic Cities: City Agendas, Planning, and the World's Games, 1896–2012* (pp. 180–93). London: Routledge.

Connolly, R. (2013). Economic Growth and Strategies for Economic Development in Russia. *Russian Analytical Digest* (133), 5–9.

Cornelissen, S., & Swart, K. (2006). The 2010 Football World Cup as a Political Construct: The Challenge of Making Good on an African Promise. In J. Horne & W. Manzenreiter (Eds), *Sports Mega-Events: Social Scientific Analyses of a Global Phenomenon* (pp. 108–24). Malden, MA: Blackwell Publishing.

Dawisha, K. (2014). *Putin's Kleptocracy*. New York: Simon & Schuster.

Dobson, N., & Sinnamon, R. (2001). A Critical Analysis of the Organisation of Major Sports Events. In C. Gratton & I.P. Henry (Eds), *Sport in the City: The Role of Sport in Economic and Social Regneration* (pp. 63–77). London: Routledge.

Dowse, S. (2012). Exploring the Political and International Relations Dimensions of Hosting Sports Mega Events Through the Lens of the 2010 FIFA World Cup in South

Africa. In R. Shipway & A. Fyall (Eds), *International Sports Events: Impacts, Experiences, and Identities* (pp. 27–41). London: Routledge.

Essex, S.J., & Chalkley, B.S. (2007). The Winter Olympics: Driving Urban Change, 1924–2002. In J.R. Gold & M.M. Gold (Eds), *Olympic Cities: City Agendas, Planning, and the World's Games, 1986–2012*. London: Routledge.

Finlay, C.J., & Xin, X. (2010). Public Diplomacy Games: A Comparative Study of American and Japanese Responses to the Interplay of Nationalism, Ideology and Chinese Soft Power Strategies Around the 2008 Beijing Olympics. *Sport in Society, 13*(5), 876–900.

Flyvbjerg, B. (2006). Design by Deception: The Politics of Megaproject Approval. In W. S. Saunders (Ed.), *Urban Planning Today* (pp. 131–51). Minneapolis, MN: University of Minnesota Press.

Flyvbjerg, B. (2014). What You Should Know About Megaprojects and Why: An Overview. *Project Management Journal, 45*(2), 6–19.

Frawley, S., & Adair, D. (2013). The Olympics Games: Managerial and Strategic Dimensions. In S. Frawley & D. Adair (Eds), *Managing the Olympics*. Basingstoke: Palgrave Macmillan.

Gold, J.R., & Gold, M.M. (2008). Olympic Cities: Regeneration, City Rebranding and Changing Urban Agendas. *Geography Compass, 2*(1), 300–18.

Golubchikov, O. (2016). The 2014 Sochi Winter Olympics: Who stands to gain? In G. Sweeney (Ed.), *Global Corruption Report: Sport* (pp. 183–91). London: Routledge and Transparency International.

Gorokhov, V.A. (2015). Forward Russia! Sports Mega-Events as a Venue for Building National Identity. *Nationalities Papers, 43*(2), 267–82.

Graham, L.R. (1998). *What Have We Learned About Science and Technology from the Russian Experience?* Stanford, CA: Stanford University Press.

Hale, H.E. (2014). *Patronal Politics: Eurasian Regime Dynamics in Comparative Perspective*. New York: Cambridge University Press.

Hedlund, S. (2014). *Putin's Energy Agenda: The Contradictions of Russia's Resource Wealth*. Boulder, CO: Lynne Rienner.

Hill, F. (2010). *Dinner with Putin: Musings on the Politics of Modernization in Russia*. Washington, DC: Brookings Institution.

Hopf, T. (2012). The Evolution of Russia's Place in the World: 1991–2012. *Demokratizatsiya: The Journal of Post-Soviet Democratization, 20*(3), 274–81.

Horne, J., & Manzenreiter, W. (2006). An Introduction to the Sociology of Sports Mega-Events. In J. Horne & W. Manzenreiter (Eds), *Sports Mega-Events: Social Sceintific Analyses of a Global Phenomenon* (pp. 1–24). Malden, MA: Blackwell.

Hughes, K. (2012). Mega Sports Events and the Potential to Create a Legacy of Increased Sport Participation in the Host Country. In R. Shipway & A. Fyall (Eds), *International Sports Events: Impacts, Experiences, and Identities* (pp. 42–54). London: Routledge.

International Olympic Committee. (2015). *Factsheet: Sochi 2014 Facts & Figures*. Lausanne, Switzerland: International Olympic Committee.

ITAR-TASS. (2013). Ob"em investitsii na podgotovku k Universiade-2013 sostavlyaet 228 mlrd rublei. *Kommersant Volga-Ural*. Retrieved from www.kommersant.ru/doc-rss/2150967 (Accessed 10 October 2016).

Jowitt, K. (1983). Soviet Neotraditionalism: The Political Corruption of a Leninist Regime. *Soviet Studies, 35*(3), 275–97.

Kalachinsky, A. (2010). Putin Is Turning Vladivostok into Russia's Pacific Capital. *Russian Analytical Digest, 82*.

18 Introduction

Karklins, R. (2005). *The System Made Me Do It: Corruption in Post-Communist Society*. Armonk, NY: M.E. Sharpe.

Kinossian, N. (2013). Mega-Projects as a Solution to the Challenges Facing Russia's Arctic Cities., from www.gwu.edu/~ieresgwu/assets/docs/KINOSSIAN_WashingtonConference%20(2).pdf

Kotkin, S. (1995). *Magnetic Mountain: Stalinism as a Civilization*. Berkeley, CA: University of California Press.

Krastev, I. (2011). Paradoxes of the New Authoritarianism. *Journal of Democracy*, 22(2), 5–16.

Large, D.C. (2012). *Munich 1972: Tragedy, Terror, and Triumph at the Olympic Games*. Lanham: Rowman & Littlefield.

Lenskyj, H.J. (2014). *Sexual Diversity and the Sochi 2014 Olympics: No More Rainbows*. Basingstoke, UK: Palgrave Macmillian.

Levada Center. (2013). www.levada.ru/2013/06/27/obshhestvennoe-mnenie-ob-izderzhkah-olimpiady/ (Accessed 9 October 2016).

Liao, H., & Pitts, A. (2006). A brief historical review of Olympic urbanization. *International Journal of the History of Sport*, 23(7), 1232–52.

Markedonov, S. (2014). *The 2014 Sochi Olympics: A Patchwork of Challenges*. Washington and Lanham: Center for Strategic & International Studies and Rowman & Littlefield.

Matheson, V.A., & Baade, R.A. (2004). Mega-Sporting Events in Developing Nations: Playing the Way to Prosperity? *The South African Journal of Economics*, 72(5), 1085–96.

Medetsky, A. (2013, 17 January). Plan for Far East Development Unveiled. *Moscow Times*.

Menon, R., & Rumer, E. (2015). *Conflict in Ukraine: The Unwinding of the Post-Cold War Order*. Cambridge, MA: A Boston Review Book, The MIT Press.

Minchenko Consulting. (2012). Vladimir Putin's Big Government and the 'Politburo 2.0'. http://minchenko.ru/netcat_files/File/Big%20Government%20and%20the%20Politburo%202_0.pdf (Accessed 10 October 2016).

Müller, M. (2012). Popular Perception of Urban Transformation through Mega-Events: Understanding Support for the 2014 Winter Olympics in Sochi. *Environment and Planning C: Government and Policy*, 30(4), 693–711.

Myers, S.L. (2015). *The New Tsar: The Rise and Reign of Vladimir Putin*. New York: Alfred A. Knopf.

North, D. C., Wallis, J.J., Webb, S.B., & Weingast, B.R. (2007). Limited Access Orders in the Developing World: A New Approach to the Problems of Development. WPS 4359, Washington, DC: World Bank.

North, D.C., Wallis, J.J., & Weingast, B.R. (2009). *Violence and Social Orders: A Conceptual Framework for Interpreting Recorded Human History*. New York: Cambridge University Press.

Orekh, A. (2015, 9 January). Itogi goda. Sport: Zhizn' posle Sochi, ili rubl' kak glavnyi igrok. *Ezhednevnyi zhurnal*. Retrieved from http://ej.ru/?a=note&id=26761 (Accessed 10 October, 2016).

Owen, J.G. (2005). Estimating the Cost and Benefit of Hosting the Olympic Games: What Can Beijing Expect from its 2008 Games? *The Industrial Geographer f* 3(1), 1–18.

Persson, E., & Petersson, B. (2014). Political Mythmaking and the 2014 Winter Olympics in Sochi: Olympism and the Russian Great Power Myth. *East European Politics*, 30, 192–209.

Pitts, A., & Liao, H. (2009). *Sustainable Olympic Design and Urban Development*. London: Routledge.

Pomerantsev, P. (2014). *Nothing is True and Everything is Possible*. New York: Public Affairs.

Popescu, N. (2006). Russia's Soft Power Ambitions. *CEPS Policy Brief* (115), 1–4.

Pound, R.W. (1994). *Five Rings Over Korea: The Secret Negotiations Behind the 1988 Olympic Games in Seoul*. Boston, MA: Little, Brown and Company.

Remington, T.F. (2011). *The Politics of Inequality in Russia*. Cambridge: Cambridge University Press.

Reshetnikov, A. (2011). Russia's 'Great Project' Politics. *Demokratizatsiya: The Journal of Post-Soviet Democratization, 19*(2), 151–75.

Roche, M. (2000). *Mega-Events and Modernity*. London: Routlege.

Rose, A.K., & Spiegel, M.M. (2011). The Olympic Effect. *The Economic Journal* (121), 652–77.

Ruder, C.A. (1998). *Making History for Stalin: The Story of the Belomor Canal*. Gainesville, FL: University Press of Florida.

Sakwa, R. (2011). *The Crisis of Russian Democracy: The Dual State, Fractionalization, and the Medvedev Succession*. Cambridge: Cambridge University Press.

Schwartz, S. (1998). Olympics Games. In R. Cole (Ed.), *International Encyclopedia of Propaganda* (pp. 544–48). Chicago: Fitzroy Dearborn.

Shaikin, B. (1988). *Sport and Politics: The Olympics and the Los Angeles Games*. New York: Praeger.

Shaw, C.A. (2008). *Five Ring Circus*. Gabriola Island, Canada: New Society Publishers.

Shchukin, A. (2014). Nauchilis' delat' megaproekty. *Expert, 7*(886).

Smith, C.J., & Himmelfarb, K.M.G. (2007). Restructuring Beijing's social space: Observations on the Olympic Games in 2008. *Eurasian Geography and Economics, 48*(5), 543–54.

Spa, M.d.M., Rivenburgh, N.K., & Larson, J.F. (1995). *Television in the Olympics*. London: John Libbey.

Stokes, B. (2015). Russia, Putin Held in Low Regard Around the World. *Pew Research Center*, (August 5). Retrieved from www.pewglobal.org/2015/08/05/russia-putin-held-in-low-regard-around-the-world/ (Accessed 10 October 2016).

Strategiya 2020. (2012). *Strategiy-2020: Novaya model' rosta-novaya sotsial'naya politika*. Retrieved from http://2020strategy.ru/data/2012/03/14/1214585998/1itog.pdf. (Accessed 10 October, 2016).

Taras, R. (2013). Snow, Ice, and Vertical Drops: What Is Different about the Sochi Winter Games? In B. Petersson & K. Vamling (Eds), *The Sochi Predicament: Contexts, Characteristics and Challenges of the Olympic Winter Games in 2014* (pp. 20–40). Newcastle upon Tyne, UK: Cambridge Scholars.

Taubman, W. (2003). *Khrushchev: The Man and His Era*. New York: W.W. Norton.

Taylor, B. (2011). *State Building in Putin's Russia: Policing and Coercion after Communism*. Cambridge: Cambridge University Press.

Tsygankov, A.P. (2012). *Russia and the West from Alexander to Putin: Honor in International Relations*. Cambridge: Cambridge University Press.

Ulyukaev, A. (2013). *O gosudarstvennoi programme Rossiiskoi Federatsii 'Ekonomicheskoe razvitie i innovatsionnaya ekonomika'*. Retrieved from http://government.ru/news/3490#ul.(Accessed 10 October 2016).

Ward, C.J. (2009). *Brezhnev's Folly: The Building of BAM and Late Soviet Socialism*. Pittsburgh, PA: University of Pittsburgh Press.

Weiss, M., & Khvostunova, O. (2013, 17 June). Whose Idea Was It to Build a Winter Resort in the Warmest Part of Russia? *The Atlantic*.

20 *Introduction*

Westhuizen, J.V.D. (2004). Marketing Malaysia as a Model Modern Muslim State: The Significance of the 16th Commonwealth Games. *Third World Quarterly*, *25*(7), 1277–91.

Whitson, D., & Horne, J. (2006). Underestimated Costs and Overestimated Benefits? Comparing the Outcome of Sports Mega-Events in Canada and Japan. In J. Horne & W. Manzenreiter (Eds), *Sports Mega-Events: Social Scientific Analyses of a Global Phenomenon* (pp. 73–89). Malden, MA: Blackwell.

Wilson, A. (2014). *Ukraine Crisis: What It Means for the West*. New Haven, CT: Yale University Press.

Wood, E. A. (2015). A Small Victorious War? The Symbolic Politics of Vladimir Putin. In E.A. Wood, W.E. Pomeranz, E.W. Merry, & M. Trudolyubov (Eds), *Roots of Russia's War in Ukraine* (pp. 164–213). Washington, DC: Woodrow Wilson Center Press and Columbia University Press.

Yakovlev, A. (2012). In Search for a New Social Base or Why the Russian Authorities Are Changing Their Relations with Business. *Russian Analytical Digest* (121).

2 The 2014 Sochi Olympic mega-project and Russia's political economy

Introduction

This chapter seeks to illuminate key aspects of Russia's contemporary political economy by focusing on the role of mega-projects in the system. We show that mega-projects form a central feature of Putin's policymaking and management style and that this aspect of Russia's political economy opens the door to extensive corruption in the country. Mega-projects also played a major role in economic development during the Soviet era, but they have continued on even as the system of government has radically changed. The 2014 Sochi Olympics are a useful case study of this larger phenomenon, as well as being interesting on their own.

Centralized mega-projects in an authoritarian context serve a number of the regime's political and economic goals. First, mega-projects offer a platform for improving Russia's international image and winning external recognition of its latest accomplishments. Second, in an age when Russia lacks a coherent development plan for its disparate regions and urban areas, mega-projects provide a de facto policy for defining spending priorities. Third, mega-projects help main-tain mass and elite loyalty by providing a national purpose in an era defined by the lack of a clear ideology, distracting the attention of the population from pressing problems facing society, and helping to distribute rents to key elite players who are crucial to maintaining the stability of Russia's current political and economic system.

This combination of political and economic purposes, pursued in an authoritarian atmosphere in which there is little electoral accountability or financial oversight, opens the door to extensive cost overruns and corruption. The desire to promote Russia's image at home and abroad make it justifiable to spend enormous sums. One year before the opening ceremonies, the Sochi Olympics won the dubious distinction as the most expensive Olympics in history, with a price tag estimated at the beginning of 2013 of $50 billion. Estimates conducted after the game put the total bill at $55 billion (Müller, 2015). Of these expenses, about $51 billion went to infrastructure development, nearly $2 billion for security, and the rest for operational expenses for the games.

The first section of the chapter places the Sochi Olympics into the broader context of scholarly works examining Russia's political economy. The second section

22 *The 2014 Sochi Olympic mega-project*

examines mega-project financing. The third section looks at cost estimates of the Olympics in Sochi. The fourth section looks at the source of the funds. Then we examine the management of the Olympic mega-project and what it tells us about its role in Russia. The conclusion lays out the implications of mega-projects for Russia's political and economic development.

Conceptions of Russia's political economy

Recent studies of the Russian political economy stress the personalization of Russian leadership in President Vladimir Putin and the corrupt nature of the inner circle around him (Hill & Gaddy, 2013); the influence of weak institutions (Mendras, 2012) and failed efforts at state building (Taylor, 2011). Other scholarly works emphasize the importance of the oil and natural gas sector on the overall political and economic systems, again emphasizing the high levels of corruption (Goldman, 2010; Gustafson, 2012). Studies of Russia's media and the overall information space of ru.net highlight the cynicism of television audiences regarding what they see on their screens (Mickiewicz, 2008) and the inability of the internet, so far at least, to generate extensive political activism (Oates, 2013). Broader examinations focus on the intersection of formal and informal politics in hybrid regimes (Ledeneva, 2013; Robertson, 2009; Sakwa, 2011) and emphasize the personal connections inherent in neo-patrimonialist systems like those in Russia (Hale, 2012, 2014; Laruelle, 2012).

Of course, each of these interpretations is highly contested and often they are Western readings of the situation in Russia. They cannot be accepted uncritically. Nevertheless, an analysis of mega-projects in Russia builds on these previous studies. Mega-projects serve to maintain the existing regime, despite its weak institutions, by emphasizing Russian state accomplishments in a way that fills the ideological void created by the collapse of Communism. As the discussion in this book details, such projects do give citizens a genuine sense of pride in their country. At the same time, mega-projects provide corruption opportunities that facilitate the informal networks needed to keep the system running while distributing oil rents to key elite groups crucial for maintaining the regime in power. In other words, mega-projects provide some of the ideological and financial glue that allows 'Putinism' to remain in office.

By 'Putinism' we mean a system in which power is highly personalized, but constrained by the prevalence of weak institutions that limit the leader's ability to implement many of his decisions. While Putin is not accountable to free and fair elections, the institutional checks and balances provided by an independent legislature and judiciary, or investigative journalism in the traditional media, especially the country's television networks, his power is ultimately limited by the extensive corruption that pervades the system. For example, as the president, Putin could make the decision that Russia should seek to host the Olympics, but he then had to rely on weak and corrupt state institutions to prepare Sochi's municipal infrastructure and sport facilities for the actual event.

Previous Olympic financing

Historically, there has been a sharp contrast in the economic performance of different Olympic games, and only an exceptional few have produced a profit. The 1976 Montreal games were considered extremely expensive at the time they were held and left the city saddled with debt that took 28 years to pay off. The original estimate for the cost of the games was $125 million, but the final price tag was closer to $2 billion. The Montreal case was unusual because the city had to bear most of the costs, whereas usually, the city, regional, and national governments share the burden (Whitson & Horne, 2006). Fearing another deficit, Los Angeles Mayor Tom Bradley said that his city would bear none of the costs for the 1984 games, in violation of the Olympic Charter's Rule 4, which required the host city to guarantee all expenses as the funder of last resort. Bradley was able to impose his will on the IOC because there were no other bidders for the games that year, and a private group ultimately organized them (Shaikin, 1988, p. 39). Only the spartan 1984 Los Angeles and 1988 Calgary games were able to cover their costs, though even in LA some agencies, such as the local transportation authority, sustained losses (Kitchin, 2007, p. 116; Whitson & Horne, 2006).

While Los Angeles demonstrated that it was possible to boost the city's image without spending large sums of public money, other hosts put less emphasis on expenses and primarily used the games to promote their image on the global stage, with the 1936 Berlin, 1964 Tokyo, and the 1980 Moscow games the most prominent examples. Similarly, the 2008 Beijing and 2014 Sochi Olympics emphasized a nationalist narrative to a much greater extent than the commercial goals epitomized by the 1984 Los Angeles games, with the idea of promoting Chinese and Russian greatness, respectively, on the international arena (Müller, 2011; Tomlinson, 2010). While turning a profit can demonstrate a form of international prowess, pursuit of more intangible goals focused on image-building can, in part, explain the willingness of the state to spend lavishly on a two-week sporting event.

Estimating the costs of the games

This section lays out the cost of conducting the Sochi Olympics, relying on public information. It demonstrates that the price tag for the games grew significantly between 2007, when Russia won its bid, until the actual event seven years later. Looking at the costs in cross-national perspective shows that Russia's expenses are the highest ever for the games and that the cost overrun is much larger than usual for the games in recent years, though not unprecedented. The discussion examines the reasons for the overruns that have applied in other countries and argues that those explanations do not work in terms of explaining what happened in Russia.

Estimating the costs of the Olympics is difficult in all cases, regardless of where they are held, because the International Olympic Committee (IOC) itself does not provide a public accounting of the expenses and host countries are reluctant to publish detailed explanations of their spending and revenues (Shaw, 2008, p. 183).

24 The 2014 Sochi Olympic mega-project

Journalistic reporting about the Olympics usually includes vaguely defined figures for the cost of the games. Figuring out what these numbers mean is often a difficult task because usually it is not clear what components of the games are included in them and what components are left out (Horne & Whannel, 2012, p. 4). Therefore, it is helpful to break the spending down into the main categories:

> operating expenses for the 17 days of the events (technology, transportation, administration, workforce, catering, ceremonies), the construction of Olympic event facilities (in the case of Sochi, stadium, ski runs, cross country ski trails, bobsled and luge runs, indoor ice arena, the Olympic village, international media center), urban infrastructure to facilitate the holding of the games (in Sochi – airport, roads, railroads, auto and train tunnels, water supply and sewer systems, new electricity power plants, natural gas lines, and private business investment, such as in hotels), and security.

Estimates of the overall cost for the Sochi Games, including all of the items listed above, increased dramatically after Russia won the right to hold them from $12 billion to $55 billion, a jump of more than 400 per cent. The cost estimate included in the 2007 bid submitted to the IOC was 314 billion RUR, approximately $12 billion (Sochi 2014, 2007). At the end of 2011, the Accounting Chamber claimed that the overall costs were well above expectations at 1.316 trillion rubles ($41.3 billion) (Schetnaia palata Rossiiskoi Federatsii, 2012, p. 52). At the beginning of 2013, the media began reporting a figure of $50 billion (von Twickel & Filatova, 2013). Opposition politician Alexey Navalny put the figure at $45.8 billion (Anti-Corruption Foundation, 2014). Post-game estimates by University of Zurich scholar Martin Müller reached $55 billion (Müller, 2015). Müller's analysis is by far the most authoritative to be produced in the wake of the games and stands unchallenged.

Drawing on these figures, the total cost overrun for the Sochi Olympics is more than 450 per cent. The cost overrun for Kazan's Summer 2013 Universiade were of a similar scale. The initial budget was $1.5 billion (Government of the Republic of Tatarstan, 2006), but, ultimately, the cost was $6.9 billion (228 billion rubles), according to Tatarstan President Rustam Minnikhanov (ITAR-TASS, 2013). For that event, the cost overrun reached 460 per cent and demonstrates that what happened in Sochi was by no means an anomaly within Russia.

Cost overruns are common for mega-events and mega-projects around the world. Accordingly, some might suggest that the cost overruns in Russia are typical for what happens in other countries. An analysis of this evidence suggests that is not the case, however. Every Olympiad in the last 50 years has gone over budget and the average overrun for sports related expenses, at 179 per cent, was worse than for any other kind of mega-project, according to an analysis by Bent Flyvbjerg and Allison Stewart (Flyvbjerg & Stewart, 2012). The average cost overrun for the Winter Olympics was 135 per cent. By comparison, industrial mega-projects – private sector projects that were worth more than $1 billion on 1 January 2003 ($1.7 billion in nominal 2010 dollars) and focus on the production of natural resources for profit – are considered a failure if their costs overruns are more than 25 per cent (Merrow, 2011, p. 15).

Budget overruns during the Olympics have different causes. In democratic societies, Olympic promoters consciously underestimate expenses in the early stage of the process in order to make the idea of hosting the Olympics more appealing to the government and citizens of the potential host city and country. Once the city is committed to holding the games, the figures are inevitably recalculated upwards, when it is no longer feasible to simply cancel the project and the public is already on the hook for the expenses (Flyvbjerg, 2006). This scenario is likely what transpired in London, where the actual expenses for the 2012 summer games were much higher than the original cost estimates (Flyvbjerg & Steward, 2012). Given Russia's centralized, authoritarian government, where there is little public oversight of how state money is actually spent, officials' attention to public criticism regarding expenditures is less relevant than in developed democracies. Putin and his colleagues never had to worry that they would face serious challenges on the state-controlled television networks (Mickiewicz, 2008) or be held accountable in the country's heavily manipulated elections (Fish, 2005; Myagkov, Ordeshook, & Shakin, 2009; Sakwa, 2011, p. 258).

A second problem is that the cost of construction rises due to inflation in the price of construction materials and real estate. In Russia, the rate of inflation was 11.9% in 2007, 13.3% in 2008; 8.8% in 2009; 8.8% in 2010; 6.1% in 2011; and 6.6% in 2012, making it a significant cost factor (Bank of Finland Institute for Economies in Transition, 2012), but not high enough to explain the enormous jump in costs for the games. Certainly, the cost of property and housing in Sochi rose dramatically before the games and was a cause of concern among local citizens who complained that the influx of outside capital drove prices up (Müller, 2012). However, while prices went up between 2007 and 2010, by 2013 they had largely returned to their 2007 level due to new construction, especially at the lower end of the market (Zharkov, 2013). The main Olympic sites were located in the Imeriti Lowlands and the authorities confiscated land in this area from private owners in order to build the Olympic stadium and other facilities. The process was highly contentious with many of the residents complaining that the compensation they received was not adequate (see Chapter 3). According to Russian legislation, Olympstroy, the state corporation in charge of Olympic construction, had the right to pick the company that determined the price of the property and made sure that the prices the state paid were below market value (Karbainov, 2013, p. 126). Given this situation, rising land values were likely not a major driver of cost overruns.

In the following sections, we lay out the evidence that cost overruns associated with the Sochi Olympics grew out of the corruption associated with mega-projects in Russia and the rent redistribution to maintain the loyalties of the elites. So far, we have ruled out two plausible alternative explanations for the overruns, namely the idea that the costs were underestimated to build public support and the role of inflation. In the next section, we show that most of the Olympic money came from public sources and that the ruling elites sought to avoid oversight as much as possible.

The source of the funds

The vast majority of the funds for the Olympics ultimately came from the Russian state budget. Müller calculates that Russian public sources provided 96.5 per cent of the funds to prepare for the Olympics (Müller, 2015). In Russia, the state typically controls sufficient funds to carry out investments while the business community lacks autonomy (Müller, 2011). In Sochi, as in previous projects, like the development of Kazan, the dominant role of the federal state leaves little room in practice for public-private partnerships or autonomous actions by city-level officials (Kinossian, 2012).

The project for the 2014 Olympic Winter games was embedded in the Federal Targeted Program for the Development of Sochi in 2006–2014 (FTP) (Russian Federation Government, 2006). The aim of the FTP was to modernize the region by creating new rail, road, telecommunications, energy and hospitality industry infrastructure and through the construction of sports venues. Initially, the FTP was to be funded 60 per cent by public sources and 40 per cent by private investment (International Olympic Committee, 2007).

In reality, however, the state budget provided almost all of the financing. Various federal, regional, and state budgets contributed 58 per cent of the costs (Müller, 2015). The FTP identified

> US$12 billion of programmed investments, guaranteed by the federal government, to provide for the development and funding for all venue, environmental, transport, technology, accommodation and many other projects necessary for the 2014 Winter games and the long-term advancement of Sochi. (Sochi 2014 Candidature File, p. 17)

This investment dramatically increased over the years as the cost estimates grew. In cases where corporate investors were supposed to contribute, the corporations were not private companies, but mostly state-owned and controlled entities, such as Gazprom and Russian Railroads. These corporations provided 22.5 per cent of the overall financing (Müller, 2015).

Even where private investors were supposed to kick in, Vneshekonombank (VEB), a state corporation like Olimpstroy (discussed in detail below), provided much of the financing. Navalny estimates that the bank provided $7.6 billion and, even before the games, had written off 76 per cent as bad debt (Anti-Corruption Foundation, 2014, p. 4). Müller similarly calculates the VEB share as 16 per cent of the overall costs. Putin was a member of the supervisory board of the bank and helped direct its loans to support contracts for his friends (Myers, 2015, p. 365). Ultimately, the state bank was the main creditor for the Olympic construction (Fedorova, 2014). In April 2012, the VEB board of directors agreed to allowing the state to cover up to 90 per cent of the costs of Olympic construction (Tkachenko, Kanaev, & Chernoivanova, 2012).

The reason that the bank had to step in and provide more funding was that many of the private investors felt that they would not recoup their investments in the Olympic projects and therefore were reluctant to put their own money at risk.

The key beneficiaries of the VEB loans were Vladimir Potanin's Interros, Oleg Deripaska's Basic Element, and the state-owned corporations Sberbank and Gazprom, Russia's largest bank and natural gas monopoly respectively (Anti-Corruption Foundation, 2014, p. 10). To cite just one example, the Olympics required a large number of new hotel rooms, but it was not clear that these accommodations would be needed after the games finished. In fact, as the concluding chapter shows, Sochi now has more hotel rooms than it needs during much of the year.

Olimpstroy: An opaque manager for Olympic preparations

Most Olympic games are managed by an Organizing Committee for the Olympic Games (OCOG), which is accountable to the IOC. The Sochi case was different. Rather than empowering the OCOG to run the games, Putin put infrastructure development under the control of a less accountable and more opaque state corporation. Accordingly, the method that the Russian state used to manage preparations for the Olympics provided numerous opportunities for corruption. Understanding the specifics of these opportunities is crucial to determining the causes of corruption (Kostadinova, 2012, p. 28).

The central player in the story was Olimpstroy, the special state corporation set up to manage the preparations for the games. In all countries, the organizations that run sports mega-events are often described as undemocratic, non-transparent, and cloaked in secrecy (Horne & Manzenreiter, 2006, p. 13), and Putin sought to include an extra layer of protection for the Sochi games. Other cities, like Munich in the late 1960s also set up special corporations to handle the extensive construction associated with the games, but the German corporation working on the 1972 games was subject to clear local, regional, and federal oversight (Large, 2012, p. 53).

Putin created the State Corporation for the Construction of Olympic Venues and the Development of Sochi as a Mountain Resort (commonly known as Olimpstroy) on September 30, 2007, on the basis of a federal law, to oversee the design and construction of the sporting venues, transportation, electricity, tourism, and security buildings; organize their functioning; hold tenders; and monitor the progress of Olympic construction and the performance of related activities (Russian Federation Federal Law, 2007). This organization effectively replaced the OCOG, which 'receives instructions' from the IOC, and is usually entrusted with organizing the games, including building the sporting facilities, lodging the athletes, solving transportation problems, and meeting the requirements of the mass media, according to the IOC website.[1]

The OCOG budget was the most detailed part of the Russian application submitted in 2007 because the OCOG traditionally is considered the most important institution to organize and manage the games and the IOC requires extensive detail on its operations. The Sochi OCOG proposed a revenue and expenditure budget in two tables with a total amount of $2.6 billion. However, those detailed spending plans were dwarfed by the actual infrastructure expenditures once the preparations got underway.

28 The 2014 Sochi Olympic mega-project

Olimpstroy was not mentioned in the original application, but received the right to manage the entire non-OCOG budget, initially estimated at $12.272 billion (International Olympic Committee, 2007, p. 16), and which grew substantially over time. One of the explanations why the organizers of the Sochi Olympics did not trust the Russian OCOG with the massive construction projects required to prepare Sochi for the games may be that the OCOG's transparency to the IOC would not work for the prevailing conditions in the Russian construction industry, which is considered one of the most corrupt sectors in the Russian economy (Tyuryukanova & Kostyrya, 2008, pp. 14, 21). The organizers may not have wanted to be held accountable for expenditures in this area.

In contrast to the OCOG, as a 'state corporation', Olimpstroy benefitted from a special status in the Russian legal system that made its financial dealings even more opaque than a typical private corporation or government agency (Urnova, 2009). Political Scientist Richard Sakwa traced this type of corporation to Putin's June 1997 doctoral dissertation and the 2004 law on non-commercial organizations, pointing out that 'the creation of the industrial state corporations was as much about control over cash flow as it was about development' (Sakwa, 2011, p. 152). Russian critics point out that state corporations are more likely to produce corruption than modernization because they combine small managerial structures with little public transparency and accountability (Delyagin, 2008). State corporations are not required to provide detailed annual financial reports even though they have access to state budget funds. In effect, Olympstroy's status as a non-profit state corporation made it possible to control state money with a minimum of bureaucratic interference (Volkov, 2008). Ultimately, seven state corporations were created: Olympstroy, Rosatom, Russian Technologies, Rusnano, Vneshekonombank, the Mortgage Lending Agency and the Housing and Utilities Reform Fund. President Vladimir Putin personally monitored the work of Olimpstroy (Sakwa, 2011, p. 154), and Deputy Prime Minister Dmitry Kozak served as the head of the board of directors until 2012, when he was replaced by Igor Slyunyaev, Russia's minister for regional development, though Kozak still oversaw the Olympic project until its completion as deputy prime minister.

During his presidency, Dmitry Medvedev criticized the state corporations and seemed interested in subjecting them to greater oversight. On November 10, 2009, Procurator General Yury Chaika delivered to President Medvedev a report which described the state corporations as using state funds both ineffectively and for purposes other than intended (Granik, 2009). Chaika recommended increasing oversight of the state corporations. Medvedev backed this approach during his 12 November 2009 address to the parliament. However, any plans to rein in the state corporations came to an end when Putin objected. During his annual call-in show on 3 December 2009, in which Putin answered questions carefully selected from the viewing audience, the then prime minister said that state corporations 'are neither good nor bad. They are necessary' (Putin, 2009).

The Russian government had the duty of appointing the president of Olimpstroy, according to the law creating the corporation, and there was little stability in the position in the beginning. During its first five years, the corporation saw four presidents – Semyon Vainshtok (2008), Viktor Kolodyazhnyi (2008–9), Taimuraz Bolloev (2009–11), and Sergei Gaplikov (since 2011). The rapid turnover in the leaders of the organization was an indicator of poor management and, the short-term time horizons of the groups in charge, creating fertile grounds for the ineffective use of the funds entrusted to the corporation (Sokolov, 2012). On July 22, 2013, Medvedev included the head of Olympstroy on a list of Russian officials who must officially declare their income, expenses, and property holdings as part of a broader effort to crack down on government corruption (Russian Federation Government, 2013). By contrast, in organizations that by their nature were more transparent, the jobs of Aleksandr Zhukov, the president of the Russian Olympic Committee, and Dmitri Chernyshenko, the head of OCOG, were more stable.

The results of the Olympic project clearly reflect the classic consequences of high-level corruption (Rose-Ackerman, 1999, p. 38): serious distortions in the way that the government operates (with the creation of Olympstroi), huge state-funded cost overruns in large-scale procurements, and apparent large rents for insiders at the cost of distorted public policy (as documented in the next section).

Examples of corruption and overspending associated with Sochi

In the run-up to the games, several researchers and activists laid out some of the most egregious abuses. An early study by Russian graduate student Aleksandr Sokolov detailed the cost overruns. Closer to the Olympics, opposition politician and anti-corruption crusader Alexey Navalny released hardhitting reports detailing the corruption. (Boris Nemtsov and his colleagues also released several reports and they are detailed in Chapter 3, which covers civil society efforts to protest the games). Here we examine some of the claims levelled by Sokolov and Navalny.

Sokolov's study of Olympstroy spending showed that the cost of building a stadium, road, or bridge in Russia was much more expensive that constructing a similar structure in other countries (Sokolov, 2012). His examination of seven key Olympic projects found that the Russian projects cost 57.4 per cent more than projects built in other countries and claimed that the difference in costs had gone to insider rents. In looking at specific projects connected with the games, the average cost overrun for seven key objects was 171 per cent. In the most egregious cases, the main stadium cost grew three times, while cost estimates for the railroad and road connecting Adler to the Krasnaya Polyana ski resort jumped 2.5 times (Sokolov, 2012). The study concluded with a *cri de coeur* for improved oversight over Olympstroy and holding its leaders responsible for the results of their work. Sokolov's criticisms fell on deaf ears because no one in the Russian leadership wanted to hear them. Moreover, just two days before the games began, 10 police came crashing through Sokolov's door,[2] seeking to harass the grad student for speaking out against the extensive corruption in Sochi.

Navalny's Anti-Corruption Foundation published an extensive report about the cost of the Olympics on the eve of the games (Anti-Corruption Foundation,

30 *The 2014 Sochi Olympic mega-project*

2014). The report provided a detailed overview of the spending, and identified the main beneficiaries of the corruption and the mechanism by which they received money. It also compared the Russian projects to comparable projects implemented outside of Russia. The report gave Arkady Rotenberg the gold medal for 'classic stealing'. Along with his brother Boris, Arkady Rotenberg was a childhood friend of Putin. Between them, they received more than $7 billion worth of Olympic contracts. Nemtsov pointed out that their 21 no-bid contracts accounted for 15 per cent of the total budget for the games (Dawisha, 2014, p. 93). When the US Treasury Department imposed sanctions on key Russian elites as part of the West's response to the invasion of Ukraine, it specifically targeted the Rotenberg brothers and mentioned their Olympic connection, noting as well that their personal wealth had increased by $2.5 billion in the previous two years.[3] This increase came at the same time that the Russian government was cutting spending on health care for the population (Dawisha, 2014, p. 315).

The Adler-Krasnaya Polyana car and rail link was the most expensive Olympic infrastructure project, costing $8.7 billion in Navalny's calculation and providing income to key Putin cronies Russian Railroads CEO Vladimir Yakunin, Putin friend Gennady Timchenko, and Rotenberg (Anti-Corruption Foundation, 2014). Most of the funding came from the federal government and the state-owned rail company. The new transportation links can move 20,000 people per hour, but following the games, there was almost no demand for them.

Navalny's report sought to show what the money could have been spent on if not for the Sochi Olympics. For example, instead of building the Adler-Krasnaya Polyana road, the same funds could have purchased every resident of Krasnodar Krai a new refrigerator.[4] In terms of cost per Olympic event, the Sochi games were 5–10 times more expensive than all the previous Olympics, including games in China and Greece, where cost problems were much greater than in places like London or Salt Lake City (Anti-Corruption Foundation, 2014, p. 13).

Corruption opportunities in Olympstroy

Understanding corruption's role as a structural characteristic of mega-projects in Russia in general and in the Olympics in particular is important to making sense of the political economy of the games. Corruption is a useful tool for the regime leaders. It helps the regime establish control over business since corrupt companies become vulnerable and therefore obedient (Ledeneva, 2006, p. 13). But it is not simply a matter of holding everyone in line with compromising information. Corruption and the neo-patrimonial ties that it fosters also provides positive incentives to support the existing authorities by offering a way to pay off the different groups the regime needs to maintain its power (Hale, 2012; Karklins, 2005; Sajo, 2002; Voslensky, 1984).

Anti-corruption efforts in Russia have not been effective (Levin & Satarov, 2012). Russia under Putin is an authoritarian and not a totalitarian system and the contradictory nature of the system, consisting of various components that fight each other, means that the system regularly suffers from leaks of information

The 2014 Sochi Olympic mega-project 31

describing corruption at the highest levels of the political and business worlds (Szilagyi, 2002). The corruption scandals that play out in the Russian media reflect battles among different groups jockeying for power and resources (Coulloudon, 2002, pp. 200–201), rather than serious efforts to combat abuse of office.

Some of the biggest corruption scandals related to the preparation for the Olympic games involved high-ranking officials. However, leaders like Putin, Medvedev, and Kozak were never implicated directly. The most prominent corruption scandals against powerful officials most likely were initiated by their equally powerful rivals who used their influence over law-enforcement institutions to redistribute resources and positions. The Krasnodar Krai branch of Russia's Investigative Committee (*Sledstvennyi Komitet*) initiated 19 legal cases in 2009 and 27 in 2010, according to the head of the Sochi Branch of the Committee (Kavkazsky uzel, 2011). However, none of the targets of these investigations was ever put on trial. When in 2012, the Ministry of Internal Affairs made a statement about two legal cases in connection with the Sochi Olympics, it characterized them as 'the first legal cases that are directly linked to violations in the construction of venues for the 2014 Olympics' (BBC, 2012). Kozak also stated, apparently without irony, that 'this is happening for the first time in the history of law-enforcement agencies, in the operation of the construction business in Russia' (Gladunov, 2012).

In some cases, Putin and his team sought to limit the amount of corruption surrounding the Olympics, but they only followed through on the threats in a symbolic manner. In March 2011, then President Medvedev ordered General Procurator Yury Chaka and Prime Minister Putin to address the problem of cost overruns, but no criminal cases resulted. In May 2012, Putin again sought to impose greater discipline on Olympic contractors, though there is no evidence of his order having a major impact (Podrez & Mertsalova, 2012). The only major figure who lost his job for corruption related to Olympics preparations was Akhmed Bilalov, the vice president of the Russian Olympic Committee and director of the North Caucasus Resorts state-controlled company. The firing took place on 7 February, 2013, one day after Putin had inspected the Olympic sites Bilalov was responsible for building. In addition to his other duties, Bilalov was the 'main beneficiary' of the Krasnaya Polyana company that was responsible for building the ski jump and other facilities, which were two years behind schedule and whose cost had jumped from 1.2 billion rubles to 8 billion (Protsenko, 2013). After the Ministry of Internal Affairs opened an investigation, Bilalov left Russia. The generally reliable newspaper *Vedomosti* claims that Bilalov was part of Medvedev's team, had no direct access to Putin and therefore became a scapegoat (Tovkailo, 2013). Moscow formally closed Bilalov's North Caucasus Resorts on 18 June, 2014, when Deputy Prime Minister Alexander Khloponin announced their demise in a speech to the Federation Council, the upper chamber of Russia's parliament.

Ultimately, corruption mechanisms associated with the Sochi Olympics took four identifiable forms. First, in cases of fictitious employment, firms received extra compensation from the state by claiming that they had paid salaries to employees who did not actually exist. Second was kickbacks on state contracts (*otkaty*), with

32 *The 2014 Sochi Olympic mega-project*

the case of Valery Morozov, a contractor who claimed that he had paid off presidential administration officials but did not receive the favoured treatment that he had expected and later fled the country, being the most prominent (Anin, 2010; Leppard & Franchetti, 2010; Muradov & Rubnikovich, 2012). Third was overbilling for supplies used in the construction process. And, a fourth type of corruption involved transferring abroad money that should have been spent for construction in Sochi. While all these forms of corruption were discussed in the Russian press, it is impossible to document the extent to which they took place given the secrecy surrounding the state budgets and the firms' records.

Conclusion

Mega-events provide a useful prism for examining the most salient features of Russia's political economy. Mega-projects define development policy priorities for the Russian economy. Russia needs to expand and upgrade cities outside of Moscow to take the current migration pressure off the capital. But policy-makers have not articulated a strategy for how best to achieve this goal. Rather, the massive urban renewal investments associated with the Sochi Olympics and the future World Cup host sites pick a small number of Russian cities for development and concentrate many of the state's resources on these areas. It is not at all clear that the sports-driven development will best serve the needs of the citizens in these urban areas or that planners have considered the opportunity costs. Hosting sports events focuses spending on stadiums, airports, and hotels, when increased and better housing for city residents, more parks, and popularly accessible sports facilities might have been a more effective investment.

At the same time, the games help to promote regime stability by providing a sense of national pride for the masses and a source of rent distribution for key elites whose support is crucial for the leadership to maintain the status quo. The Olympics bolster a sense that under the current leadership the country is moving forward and gaining international recognition for its advances. The Kremlin uses the games to show that Russia is capable of hosting an international mega-event that demonstrates its independence from the West and the capacity of its state to carry out complex tasks. Similarly, the games promote sport as part of a healthy lifestyle in Russia. In this sense, Russia's leaders can promulgate an ideology based on the idea of a capable state that works in close collaboration with a fit and strong population.

At the same time, the games emphasize the central role of corruption in the Russian political economy. While underestimated initial budgets and eventual cost overruns are typical for mega-events in all countries where they take place, in the Russian case they were more extreme due to the centralized authoritarian nature of the political system. Organizing the games through the opaque Olimpstroy, a state corporation with special status under Russian law that made it less accountable than ordinary state institutions and private corporations, allowed spending on the games to take place outside typical forms of scrutiny. The result was that the games became corrupted by Russia's existing system and helped to add to this corruption. In other words, the way the Olympic mega-project was organized in

Russia detracted from its ability to deliver effective development to the citizens of Sochi. Most importantly, the Olympic construction is unlikely to increase overall productivity and stimulate GDP growth, which was flagging in Russia even before the collapse of oil prices in 2014 (Kaznacheev, 2014).

The implications of this analysis for Russia's future development suggest that the emphasis on mega-projects like the Sochi Olympics concentrates state resources in projects that are conceived and implemented largely by a small group of people with little outside input. As with many mega-projects, the extent to which society as a whole, rather than a small group of insiders, will benefit remains an open question.

Notes

1 www.olympic.org/ioc-governance-organising-committees?tab=mission and www. olympic.org/ioc-governance-organising-committees?tab=main-tasks, accessed July 17, 2013.
2 http://igpr.ru/sochi_2014_repression, accessed June 18, 2016.
3 US Department of the Treasury, 'Treasury Sanctions Russian Officials, Members of the Russian Leadership's Inner Circle, and an Entity for Involvement in the Situation in Ukraine', 20 March 2014. www.treasury.gov/press-center/press-releases/Pages/jl23331.aspx
4 http://sochi.fbk.info/en/place/14/ (Accessed 8 October 2016)

References

Anin, R. (2010, July 28). D.A. Medvedev – Yu. Ya. Chaika: 'Razberites' i dolozhite'. *Novaya gazeta.*
Anti-Corruption Foundation. (2014). *Sochi 2014: Encyclopedia of spending The Cost of Olympics Report.* Moscow: Anti-Corruption Foundation.
Bank of Finland Institute for Economies in Transition. (2012). Russia Statistics (accessed July 17, 2013). www.suomenpankki.fi/bofit_en/seuranta/venajatilastot/Pages/default.aspx
BBC. (2012, August 9). MVD zayavilo o moshennichestve na olimpiiskoi stroike v Sochi. *BBC Russian Service.* Retrieved from www.bbc.co.uk/russian/rolling_news/2012/08/120809_rn_sochi_2014_embezzlement.shtml (Accessed 20 October 2016).
Coulloudon, V. (2002). Russia's Distorted Anticorruption Campaigns. In S. Kotkin & A. Sajo (Eds), *Political Corruption in Transition: A Sceptic's Handbook* (pp. 187–206). Budapest: CEU Press.
Dawisha, K. (2014). *Putin's Kleptocracy.* New York: Simon & Schuster.
Delyagin, M. (2008). Goskorporatsii: Modernizatsiia ili korruptsiya? *Nash Sovremennik* (11), 201–4.
Fedorova, M. (2014, December 17). Postolimpiiskii Sindrom [Post-Olympic Syndrome]. *Kommersant.* Retrieved from www.kommersant.ru/projects/sochi (Accessed 7 October 2010).
Fish, M.S. (2005). *Democracy Derailed in Russia: The Failure of Open Politics.* Cambridge: Cambridge University Press.
Flyvbjerg, B. (2006). Design by Deception: The Politics of Megaproject Approval. In W.S. Saunders (Ed.), *Urban Planning Today* (pp. 131–51). Minneapolis: University of Minnestoa Press.

34 *The 2014 Sochi Olympic mega-project*

Flyvbjerg, B., & Stewart, A. (2012). Olympic Proportions: Cost and Cost Overrun at the Olympics 1960–2012 *Working Paper*. Oxford: Oxford University Saïd Business School.

Gladunov, O. (2012, September 9). Ugolovnye rekordy Olimpiady-2014. *Svobodnaya pressa*. Retrieved from http://svpressa.ru/economy/article/58466/ (Accessed 7 October 2016).

Goldman, M.I. (2010). *Petrostate: Putin, Power and the New Russia*. Oxford: Oxford University Press.

Government of the Republic of Tatarstan. (2006). *Byudzhet Universiady-2011 v Kazani sostavit bolee milliarda dollarov*. Kazan, Russia: Portal pravitel'stva Respubliki Tatarstan.

Granik, I. (2009, November 11). Sud'ba goskorporatsii reshitsya 12 noyabrya. *Kommersant*. Retrieved from www.kommersant.ru/doc/1272565 (Accessed 7 October 2016).

Gustafson, T. (2012). *Wheel of Fortune: The Battle for Oil and Power in Russia*. Cambridge: The Belknap Press of Harvard University Press.

Hale, H.E. (2012). Two Decades of Post-Soviet Regime Dynamics. *Demokratizatsiya: The Journal of Post-Soviet Democratization, 20*(2), 71–8.

Hale, H.E. (2014). *Patronal Politics: Eurasian Regime Dynamics in Comparative Perspective*. New York: Cambridge University Press.

Hill, F., & Gaddy, C.G. (2013). *Mr. Putin: Operative in the Kremlin*. Washington, DC: Brookings Institution Press.

Horne, J., & Manzenreiter, W. (2006). An Introduction to the Sociology of Sports Mega-Events. In J. Horne & W. Manzenreiter (Eds), *Sports Mega-Events: Social Sceintific Analyses of a Global Phenomenon* (pp. 1–24). Malden, MA: Blackwell.

Horne, J., & Whannel, G. (2012). *Understanding the Olympics*. London: Routledge.

International Olympic Committee. (2007). 2014 Evaluation Commission Report. Belmont-sur-Lausanne, Switzerland.Retrieved from www.olympic.org/Documents/Reports/EN/en_report_1187.pdf (Accessed 7 October 2016).

ITAR-TASS. (2013). Ob''em investitsii na podgotovku k Universiade-2013 sostavlyaet 228 mlrd rublei. *Kommersant Volga-Ural*. Retrieved from www.kommersant.ru/doc-rss/2150967 (Accessed 7 October 2016).

Karbainov, N.I. (2013). Kak izymayut sobstvennost' v olimpiiskikh stolitsakh: Olimpiada v Sochi v sravnitel'noi perspektive. *Mir Rossii*(1), 106–29.

Karklins, R. (2005). *The System Made Me Do It: Corruption in Post-Communist Society*. Armonk, NY: M.E. Sharpe.

Kavkazsky uzel. (2011, January 31). Sledovateli zayavili o korruptsii v 'Olimpstroe' posle otstavki Bolloeva. *Kavkasky uzel*. Retrieved from www.kavkaz-uzel.ru/articles/180375/ (Accessed 7 October 2016).

Kaznacheev, P. (2014, February 26). Sochi Olympics Boost Morale but Not Economy. *Moscow Times*.

Kinossian, N. (2012). 'Urban entrepreneurialism' in the Postsocialist City: Government-led Urban Development Projects in Kazan, Russia. *International Planning Studies, 17*(4), 333–52.

Kitchin, P. (2007). Financing the Games. In J.R. Gold & M.M. Gold (Eds), *Olympic Cities: City Agendas, Planning, and the World's Games, 1896–2012* (pp. 103–19). London: Routledge.

Kostadinova, T. (2012). *Political Corruption in Eastern Europe: Politics After Communism*. Boulder: Lynne Rienner.

Large, D.C. (2012). *Munich 1972: Tragedy, Terror, and Triumph at the Olympic Games*. Lanham: Rowman & Littlefield.

The 2014 Sochi Olympic mega-project 35

Laruelle, M. (2012). Discussing Neopatriomonialism and Patronal Presidentialism in the Central Asian Context. *Demokratizatsiya: The Journal of Post-Soviet Democratization, 20*(4), 301–24.

Ledeneva, A.V. (2006). *How Russia Really Works: The Informal Practices That Shaped Post-Soviet Politics and Business.* Ithaca, NY: Cornell University Press.

Ledeneva, A.V. (2013). *Can Russia Modernise? Sistema, Power Networks, and Informal Governance.* Cambridge: Cambridge University Press.

Leppard, D., & Franchetti, M. (2010, May 30). Kremlin Bribery Whistleblower Flees to UK. *The Sunday Times.* Retrieved from www.timesonline.co.uk/tol/news/uk/article 7140175.ece

Levin, M., & Satarov, G. (2012). Korruptsiy v Rossii: Klassifikatsiya i Dinamika. *Voprosy Ekonomiki, 10*, 4–29.

Mendras, M. (2012). *Russian Politics: The Paradox of a Weak State.* New York: Columbia University Press.

Merrow, E. W. (2011). *Industrial Megaprojects: Concepts, Strategies, and Practices for Success.* Hoboken, NJ: John Wiley and Sons, Inc.

Mickiewicz, E. (2008). *Television, Power, and the Public in Russia.* Cambridge: Cambridge University Press.

Müller, M. (2011). State Dirigisme in Megaprojects: Governing the 2014 Winter Olympics in Sochi. *Environment and Planning A, 43*(9), 2091–2108.

Müller, M. (2012). Popular Perception of Urban Transformation through Mega-Events: Understanding Support for the 2014 Winter Olympics in Sochi. *Environment and Planning C: Government and Policy, 30*(4), 693–711.

Müller, M. (2015). After Sochi 2014: costs and impacts of Russia's Olympic Games. *Eurasian Geography and Economics, 55*(6), 628–55. doi: 10.1080/15387216.2015. 1040432

Muradov, M., & Rubnikovich, O. (2012, May 15). SKR vosstanovil olimpiiskoe spokoistvie, Prekrashcheno delo o korruptsii v upravgelami prezidenta PF. *Kommersant.* Retrieved from http://kommersant.ru/doc/1934098 (accessed 7 October 2016).

Myagkov, M., Ordeshook, P.C., & Shakin, D. (2009). *The Forensics of Election Fraud: Russia and Ukraine.* Cambridge: Cambridge University Press.

Myers, S.L. (2015). *The New Tsar: The Rise and Reign of Vladimir Putin.* New York: Alfred A. Knopf.

Oates, S. (2013). *Stalled Revolution: The Political Limits of the Internet in the Post-Soviet Sphere.* Oxford: Oxford University Press.

Podrez, T., & Mertsalova, A. (2012, June 1). Olimpiiskie zastroishchiki dozhdalis' natsionalizatsii. *Izvestiya.* Retrieved from http://izvestia.ru/news/526193 (Accessed 7 October 2016).

Protsenko, N. (2013, February 7). Krakh politicheskogo kapitalista. *Ekspert on-line.* Retrieved from http://expert.ru/2013/02/7/krah-politicheskogo-kapitalista/ (Accessed 7 October 2016).

Putin, V. (2009). Razgovor s Vladimirom Putynym. Prodolzhenie. from http://top.rbc.ru/ politics/03/12/2009/351083.shtml (Accessed 7 October 2016).

Robertson, G.B. (2009). Managing Society: Protest, Civil Society, and Regime in Putin's Russia. *Slavic Review, 68*(3), 528–47.

Rose-Ackerman, S. (1999). *Corruption and Government: Causes, Consequences, and Reform.* Cambridge: Cambridge University Press.

Russian Federation Federal Law. (2007). O gosudarstvennoi korporatsii po stroitel'stvu olimpiiskikh ob"ektove i razvitiyu goroda Sochi kak gornokolimticheskogo kurorta.

36 The 2014 Sochi Olympic mega-project

Federal Law no. 238. http://pravo.gov.ru/proxy/ips/?docbody=&nd=102117698&rdk= &backlink=1 (Accessed 9 October 2016).

Russian Federation Government. (2006). *Federal'naya tselevaya programm 'Razvitie g. Sochi kak gornoklimaticcheskogo kurorta (2006–2014 gody). Utverzhdena postanovleniem Pravitel'stva Rossiiskoi Federatsii ot 8 iunya 2006 g. No. 357'.* Retrieved from http:// fcp.economy.gov.ru/cgi-bin/cis/fcp.cgi/Fcp/ViewFcp/View/2006/231/. (7 October 2016).

Russian Federation Government. (2013). *Postanovlenie No. 613.* Retrieved from http:// government.ru/media/files/41d47b4b141cf877a41e.pdf. (Accessed 7 October 2016).

Sajo, A. (2002). Clientelism and Extortion: Corruption in Transition. In S. Kotkin & A. Sajo (Eds), *Political Corruption in Transition: A Sceptic's Handbook* (pp. 1–21). Budapest: CEU Press.

Sakwa, R. (2011). *The Crisis of Russian Democracy: The Dual State, Fractionalization, and the Medvedev Succession.* Cambridge: Cambridge University Press.

Schetnaia palata Rossiiskoi Federatsii. (2012). *Itogi raboty schetnoi palaty Rossiiskoi Federastii v 2011 godu i osnovnye napravleniia deiatel'nosti v 2012 godu.* Moscow: Schetnaia palata. Retrieved from http://audit.gov.ru/upload/uf/778/7786553d0878ab186 afd4de5e2fac37d.pdf (accessed 9 October 2016).

Shaikin, B. (1988). *Sport and Politics: The Olympics and the Los Angeles Games.* New York: Praeger.

Shaw, C.A. (2008). *Five Ring Circus.* Gabriola Island, Canada: New Society Publishers.

Sochi 2014. (2007). Sochi Candidature File 'Sochi 2014 Candidate City: Gateway to the Future'. http://web.archive.org/web/20100103043040/http://sochi2014.com/sch_question naire (Accessed 7 October 2016).

Sokolov, A. (2012). Insider Control and Investments of GK 'Olympstroy'. *Naukovedenie* (4).

Szilagyi, A. (2002). Kompromat and Corruption in Russia. In S. Kotkin & A. Sajo (Eds), *Political Corruption in Transition* (pp. 207–31). Budapest: CEU Press.

Taylor, B. (2011). *State Building in Putin's Russia: Policing and Coercion after Communism.* Cambridge: Cambridge University Press.

Tkachenko, E., Kanaev, P., & Chernoivanova, A. (2012, April 25). Natsionalizatsiya olimpiiskikh vidov riska. *Gazeta.ru.* Retrieved from www.gazeta.ru/business/2012/04/25/ 4563725.shtml (Accessed 7 October 2016).

Tomlinson, R. (2010). Whose Accolades? An Alternative Perspective on Motivations for Hosting the Olympics. *Urban Forum, 21*, 139–52.

Tovkailo, M. (2013, June 17). Kak tratyat den'gi Olimpiady. *Vedomosti.* Retrieved from www.vedomosti.ru/library/news/13145811/pryzhki_s_tramplinom (Accessed 7 October 2016).

Tyuryukanova, E., & Kostyrya, E. (2008). The Socio-Economic and Criminal Effects of Contemporary Migration in Large Russian Cities. In R.W. Orttung & A. Latta (Eds), *Russia's Battle with Crime, Corruption, and Terrorism* (pp. 11–35). London: Routledge.

Urnova, A. (2009). Russian State Corporations: A Stabilizing Economic Force or a Drag on Growth? www.wilsoncenter.org/publication/russian-state-corporations-stabilizing-economic-force-or-drag-growth (Accessed 7 October 2016).

Volkov, V. (2008). Russia's New 'State Corporations': Locomotives of Modernization or Covert Privatization Schemes? *PONARS Eurasia Policy Memo, 25.*

von Twickel, N., & Filatova, I. (2013, February 3). Sochi Olympics Most Expensive in History. *The Moscow Times.* Retrieved from www.themoscowtimes.com/news/ article/sochi-olympics-most-expensive-in-history/474951.html#ixzz2PsrOpVqU (Accessed 7 October 2016).

The 2014 Sochi Olympic mega-project   37

Voslensky, M. (1984). *Nomenklatura: The Soviet Ruling Class*. Garden City, NY: Doubleday.

Whitson, D., & Horne, J. (2006). Underestimated Costs and Overestimated Benefits? Comparing the Outcome of Sports Mega-Events in Canada and Japan. In J. Horne & W. Manzenreiter (Eds), *Sports Mega-Events: Social Scientific Analyses of a Global Phenomenon* (pp. 73–89). Malden, MA: Blackwell.

Zharkov, S. (2013). Nedvizhimost' v Sochi posle Olimpiady: perspektivy vyzhivaniya regiona. *Indikatory rynka nedvizhimosti*. www.irn.ru/articles/35084.html (Accessed 7 October 2016).

3 Political and civil society and the Sochi games

What is the relationship between opposition political parties, civil society groups, and the organizers of mega-events such as the Olympics? Activists in the field, and academics investigating them, have come to mutually contradictory conclusions. One side focuses on how opposition and civil society groups can use the massive investment made in the Olympics by others as a platform through which they can hijack the international media spotlight to promote progressive change that the event organizers did not plan (Price, 2008). Along these lines, the Olympics present a political opportunity in the sense that Sidney Tarrow has in mind that, unlike money or power, 'can be taken advantage of by even weak or disorganized challengers (Tarrow, 2011, p. 33)'. The other side argues that mega-events work in just the opposite way – allowing states and corporations to limit the input of civil society while they take advantage of the scale and limited time frame afforded by Olympic planning to act with little public oversight or scrutiny (Lenskyj, 2008).

Efforts by political opposition and civil society groups to exploit the Olympics to promote their own agendas take advantage of the fact that the games stand at the nexus of a country's domestic and foreign policy. Olympic hosts decide to bid for the games, in part, because they are interested in boosting their international image (Burbank, Andranovich, & Heying, 2001), which makes them susceptible to pressure from the international community. The most celebrated example of an Olympic event encouraging democratization was the end of military rule in South Korea just before the 1988 Seoul Games. Political protests in the summer of 1987 called into question Korea's ability to host the games the next year and the unprecedented international media attention on the country facilitated the declaration of military ruler President Chun Doo Hwan on 29 June 1987 to step down and call direct elections in December 1987 (Pound, 2008). With an eye to such global leverage, international non-governmental organizations (NGOs), such as Human Rights Watch, regularly seek to capture the media attention of the Olympics to affect change on a wide range of issues, including labour abuses, media repression, religious freedom, and civil liberties (Worden, 2008). The games are also seen as a mechanism for promoting environmental awareness and developing a green lifestyle in the host countries and among those who attend or view the competition on television. Even if efforts to promote such causes are not immediately successful, the Olympics provide a rallying point around which

Political and civil society 39

opposition and civil society organizations can develop experience to use in future campaigns (Fors, 2009).

While the Olympics may provide civil society groups with a platform to promote their causes, they also hand the state and corporations tools for limiting society's ability to exercise oversight and hold the officials accountable. Researchers like Bent Flyvbjerg and his colleagues describe a world of 'design by deception', in which mega-projects are frequently approved even though their sponsors underestimate costs, overestimate benefits, overvalue local development effects, and undervalue environmental impacts (Flyvbjerg, 2006). Once a city wins a bid for the Olympics, it has seven years to prepare the event facilities and the urban infrastructure supporting them. Since there is no flexibility in the schedule – the opening ceremony must take place at the appointed time – officials often shortcircuit ordinary accountability processes as they determine resource allocations in democratic countries (Lenskyj, 2008) and use the Olympic cloak to legitimize their actions in authoritarian countries, where there is little public accountability even under normal conditions. One recent study concluded:

> There is, in other words, a well-established pattern here, spanning mega-events, continents, and regime types. The pattern is one where corporate profit and effective delivery are valued more highly in event hosting than the values of participatory democracy or social justice. (Hayes & Karamichas, 2012, p. 21)

This chapter sorts out these contesting versions of the relationship between civil society and mega-events in authoritarian conditions using our case study of the 2014 Sochi Olympics. When does 'platforming' work, allowing opposition and civil society groups to change the narrative of the games that was designed by state and corporate Olympic organizers for other purposes? When do states and corporations prevail in using mega-events in ways that limit the role of civil society and the political opposition? We examine examples including the 2009 Sochi mayoral elections, the environmental movement, housing issues, and LGBT issues.

Ultimately, this chapter argues, mega-events provide a way for state-business alliances to impose their development preferences on society with little oversight or accountability. Political opposition and environmental groups, in particular, find few opportunities to influence decisions. Nevertheless, activism is not completely futile because, in some cases, groups can use events like the Olympics as a platform to score small victories and to develop experience that can be applied in subsequent confrontations. Additionally, mega-events expand the repertoire of Russian organizations by giving them a central focus around which they can organize.

The Olympic mega-event and state-society relations in Russia

Having defined mega-events and mega-projects in the introduction, we now turn to civil society. Our definition of civil society distinguishes it from the state and

40   *Political and civil society*

corporations (Cohen & Arato, 1994). In particular, we focus on the organizations that serve as intermediaries between citizens, on one side, and state and corporations, on the other (Henry, 2010). This definition of civil society is particularly useful in authoritarian Russia, where the individuals who control the state frequently work closely with chosen corporations in a manner that does not take into account broader public interests. We follow the conventional wisdom in dividing the political opposition from citizen groups focused on ostensibly non-political goals, such as protecting the environment. Of course, in an authoritarian environment, all actions may be perceived as political, especially at a time when the Kremlin is suspicious of all independent activities. In fact, as Vladimir Gel'man has pointed out, the refusal of the authorities to meet the demands of Russia's evolving society have only encouraged its politicization (V. Gel'man, 2012, p. 102).

Typically Russia's society organizations did not have anywhere near the resources or organizational infrastructure of the Olympic backers, making their interaction asymmetrical (McCarthy & Zald, 1977). Groups opposing the Olympics are engaged in contentious politics because they lack access to representative institutions and they are challenging the authorities to make claims that they do not accept (Tarrow, 2011, p. 7). People engage in contentious collective action because such behaviour is the only way that they can press their claim against a stronger opponent. The Olympics add to the conventional repertoire of the protest movement in Russia and benefit civil society because the games deliver a specific event around which organizations can mobilize. Moreover, the Olympics provide a set of ideals that the Russian authorities claim to support and the members of civil society can hold them to these ideals.

In contrast to the relatively resource-deprived civil society organizations, the Russian state has an extensive tool kit that it can use in responding to citizen-led initiatives. These responses range from repression (arresting the key activists, forcing their emigration, or using violence against them), harassment (intrusive legal or regulatory investigations, hacker attacks on their websites), cooption (inducing groups to support regime preferences), ignoring, and even incorporating their input into the decision-making processes (Robertson, 2009, pp. 537–47).

For Russia's civil society, a central question is to decide whether to play by the regime's rules and work inside the system or instead to devote their resources to pressuring the regime from outside, using street protests and other means (Kozlovsky, 2013). Participating within the system is difficult because the regime elites have stacked the rules in their favour, making it extremely hard for the opposition to win a contested election or gain access to meaningful decision-making processes (Henry, 2010, p. 33). Past research has shown that the openness of Russian regional and local administrations to NGOs can have a big impact on their activeness (Sundstrom, 2006). Even established democracies have blocked access by environmental groups. In several Olympic cities, the organizers set up consultative bodies to work with civil society groups and incorporate their input. However, it is not clear whether these groups had any real power to make changes in the ways the games were organized or were just designed to neutralize unwanted

Political and civil society 41

public criticism. In fact, some activists charge that the authorities' motivation behind establishing such groups is to prevent the opposition from having any impact on the management of the games (Shaw, 2008, p. 11). Given the small chance of success, it is difficult to mobilize Russian citizens to participate in such 'systemic' activities. Protests, on the other hand, can be dangerous for participants since they risk being beaten by police or arrested, making it difficult to turn out people in numbers that will make a difference in the political system. Given the choice between these poor alternatives, most Russian citizens decide not to participate at all (Howard, 2002).

Russian critics of the Sochi Olympics represented a rich and varied set of proposals designed to change official plans on how to organize and conduct the games. The civil society activists sought to use the Olympics to protest against immediate issues, such as those discussed above, as well as to highlight the existing problems of the state more broadly and to present an alternative view of what state policy could be. Over the course of the preparations for the Olympics, they worked in the areas of politics, the environment, housing and LGBT rights (we will examine issues related to Circassian protests in Chapter 5.)

Politics and elections

The 2009 Sochi mayoral elections provided a perfect opportunity that Russia's opposition could exploit to lay out its critique of the Putin regime. The elections were held on 26 April 2009. The balloting initially seemed like an opportunity for the authorities simply to place their preferred candidate in the office, but given the Olympic spotlight, the campaign quickly attracted national and international attention. The result of this attention meant that the Kremlin was more constrained in the use of its repressive apparatus.

Sochi is located in Krasnodar Krai and during the entire Olympic period was firmly under the control of Aleksandr Tkachev, the krai's powerful governor who had been in office since 5 January 2001. Tkachev ultimately served as the regional leader until 22 April 2015, when he was appointed minister of agriculture in Prime Minister Dmitry Medvedev's cabinet. As is typical for powerful governors in Russia, Tkachev sat at the nexus of business and politics forcing all major decisions to go through him (Lussier, 2002; Sharafutdinova, 2009; Stoner-Weiss, 1997). Moreover, his family controlled one of the largest agribusinesses in the region (R. Orttung, 2016). Although governors are formally elected, in Russia's authoritarian system, the Kremlin selects only governors who will be able to maintain stability in their regions and deliver votes for the important presidential and parlimantary elections. Under this system of personnel management, stable economic development is not a priority when picking regional leaders (Reuter & Robertson, 2012).

The mayoral elections became necessary following a strange string of resignations. After Mayor Viktor Kolodyazhnyi left the office to take over Olimpstroy for a short-lived tenure (see Chapter 2) on 29 June 2008, 85 per cent of Sochi voters cast their ballot for his replacement, Vladimir Afanasenkov, a close ally

42   Political and civil society

of the governor. Afanasenkov had been in charge of road construction in the region, one of the most notoriously corrupt enterprises in Russia, from 2001 until 2008. Beginning in 2007 he led efforts to implement the federal targeted programme for developing Sochi as a mountain resort as well. Voters were initially disappointed that the new leader chosen for them was not from Sochi, but apparently liked his promises to end traffic jams in the city within five years and threw their support behind him (Pavlovskaya, 2009).

However, Afanasenkov resigned just four months after his election, on 31 October 2008, again creating an opening in the mayor's office. Although he cited health reasons for his quick exit, the media asserted a variety of alternative explanations for the mayor's resignation, ranging from Deputy Prime Minister Dmitry Kozak's unhappiness with his oversight of the Olympic preparations (Titov, 2008) to concerns that his efforts to adopt a new general plan went against the interests of local developers and investors or even that he was not up to the job of condemning and seizing existing private land for the construction of Olympic objects (Perevozchikov, 2008). In the run-up to his resignation, municipal, regional, and federal authorities accused each other of causing delays in the construction of the Olympic sites. Nevertheless, the resignation was unexpected because Dzhambulat Khatuov, the mayor of Armavir, was appointed acting mayor, but was quickly replaced when it became clear that he would have trouble winning even a controlled election due to his lack of popularity. Ultimately, the krai authorities settled on Anatoly Pakhomov, the mayor of Anapa and considered to be a competent administrator. They appointed him acting Sochi mayor in 2009 and he became the officially-backed candidate in a new election set for 26April 2009.

The individual who saw the opportunity to use the elections in the Olympic capital to advance his agenda most clearly was prominent opposition leader Boris Nemtsov. Nemtsov's political star had risen quickly through the 1990s with the backing of President Boris Yeltsin, when he served in the Soviet-era Russian Supreme Soviet, as reform-minded governor of Nizhny Novgorod Oblast, and then deputy prime minister for energy issues in the Russian government. However, as part of Russia's economic team, he took the blame for the 1998 financial crisis. Although he won a seat in the State Duma in the 1999 elections, he did not hang on to it in the 2003 voting (Mommen, 2016). During the 2000s, he actively criticized Putin's governance, becoming one of the most well-known leaders in an opposition movement that has minimal influence over policy and little traction with the broader public in Russia (Gel'man, 2005; March, 2009; A. Wilson, 2007). Nemtsov, who was born in Sochi, announced on March 12, 2009, that he would run for the mayor's office in the elections then about six weeks away.

Nemtsov sought to use the 2009 Sochi mayoral campaign as a way to bring more attention to his criticism of Putin's overall governing record as well as his conduct of the Sochi games. Nemtsov's campaign used the media attention focused on the election to highlight a variety of corrupt deals surrounding the Olympics and the authorities' abuse of power to push the Olympics forward. Most of these accusations were included in the publication Nemtsov and his colleague

Political and civil society 43

Vladimir Milov (2009) wrote entitled 'Sochi and the Olympics', one of several pamphlets they produced criticizing the Putin leadership.

The main topics included in the pamphlet repeated many of the themes that had been discussed in other Olympic host cities. The text, which was distributed on city buses and via the Internet, warned that conducting the winter games in Sochi would have catastrophic consequences for the city by putting an incredible strain on the local transportation, sewage, and electricity infrastructure. The authors also claimed it would hurt the future tourist potential of the area by polluting the environs and turning some of the best beaches into cargo ports. Such an outcome would have a catastrophic effect on the local economy since many local residents make their living from serving tourists who mainly visit the city for its warm weather resorts. It complained that the authorities were inappropriately moving residents from their houses and not providing fair compensation in order to make room for the new infrastructure. The report described extensive corruption connected with Olympic facilities construction, noting that its main goal was to allow the elites to steal more money from the state budget. And the document warned of the high potential for violent conflict in the restive North Caucasus surrounding Sochi, including the possibility of renewed military confrontation with Georgia, given that memories of the 2008 war were still fresh at that time.

Nemtsov and Milov confirmed that they supported the idea of holding the Olympics in Russia, but they proposed an alternative approach to the one adopted by Putin and his team. They described the idea of holding the games in a 'seaside town with a sub-tropical climate' where the 'infrastructure had not been modernized since Soviet times' to be a 'senseless adventure' (p. 5). The situation was especially difficult given that construction would start in 2009, just as the effects of the global economic crisis were starting to be felt. They proposed 'decentralizing' the Olympics by sending the various events to cities that had the necessary sporting and tourist infrastructure. This proposal picked up on an idea that had been promoted by Ivan Starikov, a prominent member of the opposition who had served in the State Duma and Federation Council, and the Committee for Citizen Oversight, which produced a manifesto entitled 'SOS: Save the Doomed Sochi Olympics' criticizing the Olympic preparations that had been published in the opposition newspaper *Novaya gazeta* on 4 July 2008 (Committee for Citizen Oversight, 2008). The plan called for leaving the opening and closing ceremonies and the five major alpine events in Sochi, but spreading the other winter sports events to other parts of Russia that either already had the necessary infrastructure or would be able to use it after the games were over. Starikov argued that the 1980 Moscow Olympics, as well as the recent games in China and Canada, took place in a variety of different locations, as do the World Cup soccer championships.

Nemtsov also ran a populist campaign that sought to win the voters' support through various promises. These included a promise to freeze the level of municipal fees, cut the number of bureaucrats in the city, stop the practice by which contractors build new structures all over the city without first receiving permission or going through legislative hearings, and put an end to the practice of allowing

44 *Political and civil society*

Krasnodar deputy governors to rule the city by returning power to the locals.[1] In short, Nemtsov stressed that he wanted to make the games a good deal for the residents of Sochi.

While the authorities did not feel comfortable simply preventing Nemtsov from participating in the campaign, as frequently happens in Russian regional elections, they took active measures to ensure that he could not win by turning the elections into a circus, thereby distracting attention away from the key issues that Nemtsov sought to highlight. The list of candidates and potential candidates included ballerina Anastasia Volochkova, famously fired from the Bolshoi for being too heavy in 2003; oligarch Alexander Lebedev, a former KGB agent who grew rich as a banker and then teamed up with former USSR President Mikhail Gorbachev to back Russia's most outspoken opposition newspaper, *Novaya gazeta*, while maintaining close ties to the Kremlin despite criticizing the Olympic expenditures as 'idiotic'; and Andrei K. Lugovoi, a Duma member who was wanted by British authorities for the radiation attack that killed KGB defector Alexander Litvinenko in London. Ultimately, the authorities had to remove these candidates when it became clear that in such a crowded field their preferred candidate would not win the 50 per cent of votes required to avoid a runoff, but they let Nemtsov remain on the ballot. The scandalous nature of the campaign reached a peak on March 23, when a man dressed as a woman threw ammonium chloride at Nemtsov's face just as he was entering his campaign headquarters. Although a few drops of the chemical landed in his eyes, the candidate was not injured. Nemtsov claimed that the Kremlin instigated the attack due to his criticism of the Olympics (Gutterman, 2009). At a press conference in Sochi that day, Putin seemed to warn Nemtsov to curtail his activities by declaring that 'I hope that Sochi residents will not allow anyone to use the Olympic project to realize their own ambitions, which have nothing in common with the interests of citizens' (Kuzmin, 2009).

The authorities' media blackout on Nemtsov was far-reaching, making it difficult for him to campaign even though he remained in the race. They tried to make him invisible by blocking his access to federal and local television and newspapers and the acting mayor refused to debate him. First Deputy Presidential Chief of Staff Vladislav Surkov, the Kremlin's main ideologist, called NTV, Russia's third largest network, and told it not to air an episode of the 'Main Hero' show in which journalist Anton Khrekov had filmed Nemtsov, Pakhomov and other candidates individually answering questions and then assembled the film in such a way so that it appeared that the candidates were debating with each other, according to information Nemtsov included in his blog.[2] Local TV regularly accused Nemtsov of 'selling the Olympics to the Koreans', who had actively bid for the games, coming in second place to Sochi, and 'working for the Americans', while praising Acting Mayor Pakhomov. On March 11, local journalists received calls from the city's Directorate of Information and Analysis which informed them of 'Mayor Pakhomov's personal request' to ignore Nemtsov's campaign and even his presence in Sochi. Journalists said Pakhomov's campaign manager Galina Snimshchikova was behind the move (Glanin, 2009). The chief editor of the newspaper *Business Sochi* had to resign under pressure from the paper's owner immediately after announcing that he was supporting Nemtsov (Titov, 2009). Additionally, Nemtsov faced intense opposition from local construction companies that were making large profits from their Olympic contracts; they did not appreciate the opposition candidate's efforts to draw attention to the expensive nature of the event.

Ultimately, Acting Mayor Pakhomov, with the strong support of the Kremlin, won 77 per cent of the vote and Nemtsov took only 13.5 per cent, with just 39 per cent of the voters participating in the elections. Pakhomov's election ended a period of chaos in the city – over the course of the previous year, Sochi had had four different mayors. Pakhomov brought a sense of stability to the city and served through the Olympic games.

Nemtsov protested the validity of the election results, but in June 2009 a Sochi court declared that the elections had been lawful (No author, 2009b). While the authorities scored a resounding victory on the basis of their overwhelming institutional advantage and administrative resources, Nemtsov did show that there nevertheless was a resilient opposition in Russia, including one that was critical of the official conduct of the games. Nemtsov did not oppose the Sochi Olympics per se, but argued that they should be held in a manner that better served the interests of Sochi residents. Many locals feared that all the profits from the games would end up in the hands of Moscow elites and other outsiders, while they had to bear all the costs.

Nemtsov's efforts showed that it was possible to use the Olympics as a platform to promote the cause of raising questions about the authoritarian and corrupt nature of the Putin regime. His campaign activities in Sochi, though ultimately unsuccessful, presaged the wave of protests that swept Russia after the December 2011 parliamentary elections, bringing more than 100,000 demonstrators onto the streets in Moscow and sparking smaller protests in other cities (Gel'man, 2012; Greene, 2013; Robertson, 2013). He also provided a model of how to conduct an opposition electoral campaign in authoritarian conditions that influenced the efforts of Alexei Navalny's campaign for Moscow mayor in 2013. Navalny was able to build on Nemtsov's efforts to reach out directly to the voters despite the lack of access to the state-influenced media (Orttung, 2013). Nemtsov was assassinated on 27 February 2015, just steps from the Kremlin, in a murder that remained unexplained more than a year after it happened (Mommen, 2016).

The environmental movement in Sochi

Environmental issues present a useful test of whether the Olympics serve as a platform for civil society groups to promote progressive causes or a mechanism for states and corporations to circumvent such input. The IOC had little interest in environmental issues before the 1990s, but the 1992 Albertville Games were considered to pay little attention to environmental issues, prompting the 1996 Lillehammer hosts (Case, 2012), in particular, and the Olympic movement more broadly to revise their policies and add the environment as the movement's third pillar, along with sport and culture. There was some anticipation that having

46 *Political and civil society*

environmental standards could promote international norms diffusion and raise expectations among domestic constituencies of a cleaner environment (Hayes & Karamichas, 2012).

The environmental stakes for the Sochi Olympics were high because the infrastructure construction associated with the winter Olympics has a greater impact on the natural setting than the construction associated with the summer games, even though the summer games usually have a higher profile and more participants. The winter games take place in mountainous areas that are more ecologically fragile than the urban locations where summer events are held and usually require the construction of a man-made setting that is more difficult to manage (Dansero, Corpo, Mela, & Ropolo, 2012). Likewise, the winter events concentrate large numbers of people in small places, which can put severe stresses on the surroundings. Sochi's ecological footprint is bigger than for most games because its bid proposed an ambitious plan that would deliver all new sporting facilities and extensive infrastructure construction, including a new airport terminal, construction of railway and roads from coast to mountains, roads in the mountain area linking the sites, and significant upgrades to Sochi's sewer and electricity systems. Competitors from Austria, who also sought to host the games, argued that the use of existing facilities in Salzberg would limit the environmental impact if their site were chosen (International Olympic Committee, 2007, p. 69).

Practice has not lived up to the ideals espoused in the concept of a Green 'Games'. At the Torino 2006 Games, organizers set up the Environmental Consultative Assembly with representatives of 13 environmental organizations and 10 local government institutions. The group was helpful in identifying problems with the Olympics and disseminating information. However, it had little actual impact on the organization of the games beyond reducing the number of snow-making machines to limit their environmental toll (Dansero *et al.*, 2012). An analysis of the 2000 Sydney games found that the bid laid out extensive environmental protections, but the New South Wales government legislation created loopholes and conflicts with the original guidelines, resulting in what watchdog Green Games Watch 2000 described as 'selective compliance' to environmental requirements (Caratti & Ferraguto, 2012). Residents affected by Olympic construction could not file lawsuits against them and the project managers did not have to file the usual environmental impact assessments (Hayes & Karamichas, 2012). Another assessment found that in the cases of Sydney and Athens 2004, the events did not leave an ecological legacy (Karamichas, 2012). In neither place did the Olympics result in a culture change or the adoption of strategies to protect the environment. In preparation for the 2004 Athens Olympics, Greece altered its constitution in order to circumscribe forest protection (article 24.1), ultimately limiting the power of environmental and citizen initiative groups (Hayes & Karamichas, 2012, p. 16). Similarly, the Beijing games failed to stimulate a long-term solution to that city's air pollution problems (Rich, 2012).

Sochi's experience with the games seems to be in line with previous Olympic experience regarding environmental protections: great promises are made up front, but there is little implementation afterwards (Müller, 2013). In its bid for

Political and civil society 47

the games, the Sochi organizers claimed that 'Sochi has developed an integrated and inclusive system for managing natural resources by working closely with public authorities and non-governmental organizations' (Sochi 2014, 2007, p. 31).

Russia's contemporary environmental movement has its roots in the late Soviet period. At that time groups were able to mobilize citizens against nuclear power plants following the Chernobyl accident and water diversion schemes. However, environmental groups have not done a good job engaging with citizens or the state in Russia, as Laura A. Henry argues (Henry, 2006). Citizens have little awareness of the existing environmental organizations and do little to support environmental policies or participate in environmental causes. Similarly, greens have found it diffult to change state policies that generally favour economic development over environmental protection. In May 2001, Putin dissolved Russia's main environmental protection agency (Goskomekologiia) and transferred its functions to the Natural Resource Ministry. Similarly, the government has done a poor job managing its nature parks (Kreindlin, 2014).

However, the small but vocal environmental movement in Russia has criticized the deleterious impact the construction and associated activities will have on the natural surroundings of the city and the nearby ecology, including land allocation, water pollution, waste management, and other consequences of intensified human use. Even before the IOC accepted Sochi's application to host the games, a group of 47 environmental groups from across Russia asked the IOC to reject Sochi's proposal (Kavkazskii uzel, 2007). The activists wrote that they had nothing against hosting the games in Russia, but rejected the high environmental price of bringing the event to Sochi. They noted that seven venues were planned to be created in the Sochi National Park and the buffer zone to the UNESCO World Heritage Site Caucasus State Biosphere Preserve. Violating protected lands, combined with the lack of positive environmental evaluations, the failure to take public opinion into account in making management decisions, and the violation of numerous Russian environmental laws in preparation for the games formed the core of the complaints in an 'anti-bid book' prepared by several environmental groups (Avtonomnoe Deistvie, Druzhina okhrany prirody MGU, Institute 'Kollektivnoe deistvie', & Maikopskoe otdelenie VOOP, 2007).

Once the bid was accepted, Sochi's green movement lodged a number of complaints about the games and the construction associated with them. In evaluating the bid, the commission expressed hope for continued dialogue with environmental NGOs on litigation that they had pending against the government. However, such state-society dialogue seemed unlikely in practice because the bid committee assured the IOC that 'any action by the Supreme Court would have no effect on construction schedules and development of Olympic venues' (International Olympic Committee, 2007).

As noted above, a central dilemma for environmental organizations is whether to work with the event organizers in the hopes that they can reduce the environmental impact or to confront them head on through protests. Observers of mega-event planning have argued that the process is primarily top-down and citizens' participation typically consists of reacting to plans developed elsewhere

48 *Political and civil society*

(Hayes & Karamichas, 2012, p. 22). There was little citizen input in the US games held in Los Angeles, Salt Lake City or Atlanta (Burbank *et al.*, 2001). In the case of Sochi, public opinion polling shows that participation and consultation in planning were marginal and local support for the games shrunk from 86 per cent in October 2006 to 57 per cent by November 2010 (Müller, 2012). In spite of their early promises to cooperate, the authorities ignored the main requests of the environmentalists. Already in 2008 the Ministry of Natural Resources and Ecology changed the zoning of the Sochi National Park to allow construction there (Shevchenko, 2013), a decision that was reinforced on 14 July, 2009, when the Sochi City Council adopted a new general plan for the city's development confirming this change (Perova, Karpova, & Aminov, 2009).

The prominent international environmental groups World Wildlife Fund (WWF) and Greenpeace originally worked with the authorities, but subsequently became disillusioned with the state's failure to follow through on the environmental measures discussed. On 3 July, 2008, Igor Chestin, head of the World Wildlife Fund's Russia chapter, and Ivan Blokhov, a representative of Greenpeace, met with Putin in Sochi and he agreed to move the bobsled run and alpine Olympic Village from their planned location on the Grushev Ridge. After this meeting, Putin seemed to think that the games would now have the environmentalists' stamp of approval and Deputy Prime Minister Aleksandr Zhukov declared that the organizations had no more claims against the Sochi sites (Naumov, 2008).

However, what seemed like a good start quickly fell apart. By 2010 the relationship had turned adversarial because the WWF felt that decisions agreed to at meetings with the authorities simply were not enforced (World Wildlife Fund, 2010a). The group noted, in particular, that the construction of the combined road/railroad from Adler to Krasnaya Polyana, the largest infrastructure project of the Olympic effort, began without a sufficient analysis of the environmental impact. At that time, the United Nations Environmental Programme (UNEP) warned that the organizers were not doing enough to compensate for the environmental damage that the construction was causing (United Nations Environmental Programme, 2010). Russia also moved to exclude the land designated for development from the UNESCO protective designation (Englund, 2013). Subsequent efforts by UNEP to set up a dialogue between the environmental NGOs and the authorities in October 2010 failed, according to WWF, Greenpeace, Ecological Watch on the Northern Caucasus (a group that had consistently opposed the authorities) and other social organizations, because 'as with previous Missions, the bureaucrats either ignored the meetings, created obstacles for the participation of society, or sent people with no power to make decisions to the meetings' (World Wildlife Fund, 2010b). In one case, the bureaucrats started a meeting that had been planned for 2 pm three hours earlier at 11 am without warning the NGOs in advance, thereby making it impossible for them to participate. By January 2011 the NGOs refused to meet with UNEP because they felt that such meetings would not solve environmental problems 'but could be used for the purpose of providing 'green public relations' for the Olympics' (World Wildlife Fund, 2011).

Political and civil society 49

A major problem for the environmental organizations was that Russia had hollowed out the institutions that typically organized Olympic Games, turning them into façades, and shifting power to other organizations that have even less accountability to the public (Robertson, 2011, pp. 194–7). In its January 2011 mission report to Moscow and Sochi, the UNEP itself complained that its main partner, and the institution that was supposed to be implementing the environmental plans, the Sochi 2014 Organizing Committee, in fact had little control over the construction and development of the facilities and that real power lay with organizations like Olympstroy and Russian Railroads, state-controlled corporations with little public oversight (United Nations Environmental Programme, 2011).

Activists working on environmental issues surrounding the Russian Olympics risked their own personal safety. One of the most prominent activists fighting against environmental damage caused by the Olympics was Suren Gazaryan, who represented Ecological Watch on the Northern Caucasus. Along with his colleague Andrei Rudomakha, he was detained by the authorities for several hours when he tried to block the illegal logging of protected trees during the construction of the road/railroad linking Adler and Krasnaya Polyana in August 2009 (World Wildlife Fund, 2009). This was one of many times that the police harassed him, according to OVD-Info, a unit of the Memorial Human Rights Center that monitors the state's use of violence in Russia (OVD-Info, 2013). Gazaryan also spoke out against the use of timber from the Sochi National Park and warned about the dangers of the dumps being created near Sochi. He also participated in efforts to expose the construction of a billion dollar vacation home in Krasnodar Krai, allegedly for Putin, and protests against illegal logging around the governor's dacha. For these activities, Gazaryan and Yevgenii Vitishko were given three-year suspended sentences and, although they were not in prison, restrictions were placed on their movements. Ironically Gazaryan and Vitishko were convicted of damaging a fence that surrounded the governor's illegal house even though the authorities claimed that no such fence or house existed. At the end of 2012, Gazaryan fled Russia for Estonia fearing imminent arrest for his activities.[3]

On 20 December 2013, Vitishko's suspended three-year sentence was converted to real time and he was imprisoned. When Sochi resident David Khakim organized a one-man protest to support Vitishko on 17 February 2014, he was detained and later fined 30,000 rubles. Putin's decree about protests during the Olympics required that all demonstrations have the prior approval of the authorities, a provision that Khakim claimed violated the Russian constitution (Mukhametshina, 2015). Beyond Russia, the international community also spoke out in support of Vitishko and Amnesty International declared him a prisoner of conscience (Kramer, 2014). He finally was released on 22 December, 2015 after two years of incarceration (Digges, 2016). Vitishko claimed that he had no regrets after being released and said he wanted to continue documenting the environmental toll of development in the Sochi region, expanding on the 2014 report that his group had issued and seeking to improve the situation where possible (Gazarian & Shevchenko, 2014).

50 *Political and civil society*

In a situation where the state authorities were both the key decision makers and unwilling to respond to ecological concerns, the environmental movement largely gave up its efforts to protest the games and the infrastructure construction around them. After 2009, WWF declared that 'these Olympic games will never be "green", since they have already caused irreparable damage to unique ecosystems', although they still held out hope in that 'there is still a chance to minimize further negative consequences and carry out territorial compensatory measures (expanding and creating special nature preserves)' (World Wildlife Fund, 2010c). Activities by other groups also petered out. The Institute for Collective Action listed only one Sochi protest in 2013 and that was organized by workers protesting the closing of their sugar factory (www.ikd.ru/taxonomy/term/92). There were two demonstrations in the first days of 2014, one focused on local government and one on the upcoming Olympics. Despite the repressions, Ecological Watch on the Northern Caucasus continued to post news of environmental damage caused by the Olympic construction at its website (http://ewnc.org/) even though the Russian security services searched their office and e-mail on 27 March 2013, and warned them to register as a 'foreign agent' (Human Rights Watch, 2013) under the repressive anti-NGO legislation Russia adopted in 2012.

Despite these overall setbacks, civil society groups did win some victories. In one of the most prominent triumphs, the residents of Kudepsta protested against the construction of a gas-fired power plant from May 2012 to April 2013. In May 2013, when it was clear that construction would not be completed in time for the Olympics, Deputy Prime Minister Dmitry Kozak announced that the project would be removed from the Olympic programme and that all construction would be stopped (Human Rights Watch, 2013). He claimed that the electricity would not be needed after all. Protesters were also able to block the construction of a second port that would only create surplus shipping capacity that could not be utilized (Shevchenko, 2013). Similarly, protests blocked the Evraziiskii company and its French partner Degremont from constructing a 4 billion ruble factory to burn sludge. The firms claimed the factory as part of the Olympic programme and hoped to get state support. However, societal groups opposed the plant and what seemed like a sure thing in 2010 was cancelled in 2011, when the Russian government declared that burning such waste was not ecological (Shevchenko, 2013). While all these cases represent victories for the environmental groups, it is also possible that the organizers decided to curtail the projects for a variety of non-ecology related business reasons because it no longer made sense to proceed with the projects. Even if the groups did not have a direct impact on the Olympic construction, they were able to promote environmental education and raise awareness of specific issues (Henry, 2010, p. 182).

Housing

A common problem for Olympic games is that they can have an adverse impact on the local housing market, such as driving up prices (Rolnik, 2009), making it difficult for local residents to afford home purchases, and moving existing

Political and civil society 51

homeowners from their property in order to build the new facilities necessary for the games. Local residents often feel that outsiders benefit, while they bear the burden of the costs of the games. In other Olympics, the main beneficiaries were construction companies and suppliers, as well as people working in the land development and real estate business who could take advantage of rising land values (Whitson & Horne, 2006). Given these problems, small groups of residents in Sochi demanded changes in the way that the games were organized.

Housing in post-Soviet Russia faces numerous challenges. Most of the existing stock of apartments and houses was privatized when the Soviet Union collapsed. The government has not been able to create an effective market for housing because most prices remain extremely high, blocking young people from purchasing their own home. Russia also has not set up an effective mortgage market, partly due to the high prices, but also because there is little trust in financial institutions (Zavisca, 2012).

Rising property prices turned out to be a temporary problem. Once Sochi won its Olympic bid, the cost of property in the city rose dramatically and became a cause of concern among local citizens, who complained that the influx of outside capital had driven prices up (Müller 2011a). However, while prices went up between 2007 and 2010, they had largely returned to their 2007 level by 2013 due to new construction, especially at the lower end of the market (Zharkov, 2013).

The problems facing those evicted from the homes proved more intractable. In general, well-organized groups that represent economically advantaged residents are more likely to be able to have their voices heard, while Olympic developers are more likely to be able to push aside opposition from poor residents (Case, 2012). The main Olympic sites were located in the Imeriti Lowlands north of Sochi along the Black Sea coast, and the authorities confiscated land in this area from private owners in order to build the Olympic stadium and other facilities. Approximately 2,500 people in Sochi were forced to move, according to official sources (Allenova, 2011a). In contrast to the more than one million people who were required to move ahead of the Beijing Olympics, these numbers were relatively small. As many of the residents forced to sell their property were small-scale farmers or ran small bed-and-breakfast hotels, they also lost their livelihood without gaining comparable jobs in return.

The process was highly contentious, with many of the residents complaining that the compensation or living quarters that they received were not adequate (Allenova, 2011b). According to Russian legislation, Olympstroy, the state corporation in charge of Olympic construction, had the right to pick the company that determined the price of the property and made sure that the prices the state paid were below market value (Karbainov 2013, 126). In December 2009, for example, Krasnodar Krai Governor Tkachev complained that Olympstroy was not living up to assurances that it had made in April 2009, paying only a quarter of what was promised (Perova, 2009). Olympstroy argued that the prices had been increased artificially by speculators. Over the course of the construction process, the residents held a number of protest rallies and met several times with the officials

52 *Political and civil society*

in charge of the Olympic construction, including Deputy Prime Minister Dmity Kozak, Deputy Governor Dzhambulat Khatuov and Sochi Mayor Anatoly Pakhomov (No author, 2009a). At a rally on 6 December 2009, the residents demanded a direct meeting with Putin, though they did not achieve this goal (Fadeev & Kravchenko, 2009).

By October 2012, the government had paid 9.5 billion rubles (approximately $300 million) to resettle 3,000 people, according to Krasnodar Krai Deputy Governor Alexander Saurin (The Moscow Times, 2012). The cost was about $100,000 per person, though the amount of compensation varied depending on the property in question. Two-thirds of the residents accepted money, but the authorities also provided 482 individual homes and 518 apartments. About 20 per cent of the residents did not have the necessary documentation needed to obtain compensation. In these cases, the individuals had been squatting on the land in question, without ever formalizing their ownership. At the end of 2012, the authorities planned to condemn 1,786 land plots and 256 apartments overall.

In this case, the protesters were able to draw some attention to their cause and obtain meetings with important officials, but they were not able to affect the policies of the Olympic developers. Many felt that they had not received a fair price for their holdings. The Olympics were the cause of the problems, but the Olympic spotlight was not sufficient to bring solutions as well.

LGBT issues

On 29 June 2013, Putin signed a law banning 'propaganda of nontraditional sexual relations' and blasphemy (President of Russia, 2013). The lawmakers claimed that they were increasing legal protections for children by banning the distribution to minors of information that makes lesbian, gay, bisexual and transgender (LGBT) sexual minorities attractive. The federal law followed several laws that had been adopted by Russian cities in previous years. The Russian law did not ban nontraditional sexual relations, just their propaganda. By its nature, the law violated the Russian constitution because it did not make sense to ban calling for something that itself was not illegal (Mishina, 2014). Despite this inherent logical problem, on 23 September 2014, the Russian Constitutional Court ruled the law constitutional.

While it is hard to guess Putin's motivation for any particular action, in this case, his purpose in signing the law seems to have been improving his standing with his base of core supporters among less educated and rural voters. It also apparently sought to strengthen his ties with the Orthodox Church, which has long been a key supporter of the Kremlin (Torbakov, 2014). After the protests following the 2011–2012 election cycle, it became clear that the urban intelligentsia and middle class no longer supported Putin and he therefore decided to focus on a more conservative alliance of voters rather than presenting himself as a leader of all the people. The vague wording of the law suggests that the Kremlin planned to use it more as a symbolic gesture than a piece of legislation that it would actually enforce. In making this change, Putin most likely had been focused on his

Political and civil society 53

domestic political situation and had not been thinking about the Olympics and how the West might respond to the new legislation.

The issue of LGBT rights was not important in Russia and did not draw a big reaction domestically. According to Levada Center opinion polling data, 80 per cent of Russians said that they do not know anyone from the LGBT community (Levada Analytical Center, 2013). Fifty per cent said that their opinion would move in a negative direction if someone they knew announced that they were a member of a 'sexual minority'. As with many countries in the West until recently, there was little popular support for LGBT rights in Russia (Lenskyj, 2014).

The reaction to the new law in the West was quick and overwhelmingly negative for Russia and Putin. With the Olympics less than a year away, many LGBT advocacy groups saw an opportunity to connect the legislation and the games, seeking to pressure Russia to repeal the new legislation and raise awareness of LGBT issues in Russia and more generally. In a *New York Times* op-ed, the prominent actor and playright Harvey Fierstein called for the International Olympic Committee to demand a rectraction of the law under threat of boycott (Fierstein, 2013). The American author Dan Savage set up a campaign to 'dump Russian vodka' (vanden Heuvel, 2013). The global LGBT rights organization, All Out, which began working in Russia in June 2011, also sought to use the Olympic platform. It had provided support to local Russian groups, such as Coming Out, one of Russia's largest gay organizations since 2011. In 2013, the Russian authorities filed charges against Coming Out and its director (as well as the Side by Side LGBT Film Festival and its director) under its repressive foreign agent legislation, which requires groups that receive funding from abroad to register as 'foreign agents'. Ultimately, a judge threw the cases out, but despite that legal victory for the defendants, the authorities had achieved their basic goal of intimidating the organizations. In August 2013, All Out turned its focus to the IOC, mobilizing '322,000 people to ask the IOC to speak out against Russia's anti-gay laws'. [4]

Like its counterpart in the US, the movement inside Russia for LGBT rights was divided on which tactics to employ and Nikolai Alekseev, Russia's most prominent LGBT activist and the head of the GayRussia project, rejected calls for the Olympic and vodka boycotts and denounced the leaders of the American LGBT organizations as 'kikes' (using the anti-semitic term) who wanted to 'seize power in Russia – over the LGBT movement' (Shepelin, 2013). He claimed that a small group of American activists were mainly pursuing their own purposes, such as winning grants, and were not really interested in helping the LGBT community in Russia.

The Russian authorities refused to budge on the issue. Kozak, for example, wrote a letter to the IOC stating that all athletes and spectators were welcome to the games regardless of sexual orientation, but that they could not engage in promoting homosexuality (S. Wilson, 2013). This two-part answer raised questions in the West about what would happen if athletes or fans wore rainbow pins or other signs of support for members of the LGBT community. At the beginning of 2014, Putin said that gays were welcome in Sochi, but that they should 'leave children alone',

54 *Political and civil society*

continuing his effort to equate members of the LGBT community with pederasts (Walker, 2014). In his 12 December 2013 state of the nation address to the Russian parliament, Putin made his defence of 'traditional values' the defining feature of Russia's foreign policy and claimed that many people around the world backed Russia's position. In January, Sochi Mayor Pakhomov even claimed that there were no gay people in Sochi, although a BBC reporter had visited a gay club the night before meeting with the mayor.[5]

Although there had been some discussion of an Olympic boycott because of the issue, ultimately, no such action took place. However, key Western leaders, such as President Barack Obama and several European leaders, including French President Francois Hollande, British Prime Minister David Cameron and German President Joachim Gauck, decided that they would not attend the games. In his place, Obama sent a delegation that included three homosexuals, including tennis star Billie Jean King. This snub definitely hurt Putin's effort to show off Russia as hosting the international community for a celebration of youth and sport. The Western media engaged in intense mockery of Putin for this law, with both the *Economist* and *New Yorker* publishing covers depicting him as an ice dancer with feminine characteristics. Others viciously lampooned Putin's efforts at masculine bravado and publicity photos that posed him without a shirt.

In the end, the campaign did not force Russia to change its law and it is not clear if it changed attitudes about sexual minorities in Russia. According to a survey conducted by the website gayrussia.ru of its users (201 individuals participated), 72 per cent said that the calls for boycotts had no effect on changing the situation for the LGBT community in Russia.[6] However, the effort may have raised consciousness about LGBT issues in Russia where there had been none before (Khazov, 2013). Russian politicians had to respond to numerous press inquiries about the status of LGBT people in Russia and the issue was widely discussed in the West. Similarly, the focus on LGBT issues heightened interest in human rights violations in Russia in general (Kasparov, 2015, p. 225).

Conclusion

Overall, the experience of political, environmental, housing, and LGBT groups in the preparations for the Sochi Olympics confirms the expectation that an alliance of state and corporation interests can use a mega-event to propel their pro-development policy while minimizing the extent of public input. Although Russia's overall political climate is hostile to NGO input in public policymaking, the Olympic need to finish all preparations before the opening ceremony and expectations of a global audience provided an excuse for the authorities to further curtail the role of civil society. In this sense, the Olympics did not live up to the expectations of those who saw the games as a platform to promote a variety of progressive causes.

However, while the various groups had little overall impact on the preparations for the games, they were able to achieve some advances. The political groups gained valuable campaign experience that proved beneficial for future election cycles. The greens were able to limit the extent of the environmental impact by blocking

Political and civil society   55

the construction of some facilities that had been included in the Olympic plans. The housing groups forced some concessions from the authorities, while the LGBT groups raised awareness of their issues. In these limited cases, citizen action had consequences. Such experience helps Russian groups to develop skills and knowledge that will accumulate over time. The key question in defining future state-society relations, though, will be whether the regime learns to better deploy its repressive arsenal just as quickly as the civil society groups learn to focus their protests.

Notes

1 http://yashin.livejournal.com/753056.html?page=2 2
2 http://b-nemtsov.livejournal.com/, 22 March 2009.
3 See his blog: http://gazaryan-suren.livejournal.com/, particularly http://gazaryan-suren.livejournal.com/105213.html
4 www.allout.org/en/russia-timeline?locale=en
5 www.bbc.com/news/uk-25675957
6 www.gayrussia.eu/russia/9011/

References

Allenova, O. (2011a). Pik Olimpisma. *Kommersant Vlast.* http://kommersant.ru/doc/1756389 (Accessed 7 October 2016).
Allenova, O. (2011b). Vy protiv Olimpiady, vy protiv Rossii! *Kommersant Vlast.* http://blogsochi.ru/content/kommersant-vy-protiv-olimpiady-vy-protiv-rossii
Avtonomnoe Deistvie, Druzhina okhrany prirody MGU, Institute 'Kollektivnoe deistvie', & Maikopskoe otdelenie VOOP. (2007). Zimnie Olimpiiskie Igry 'Sochi-2014': Antizayavochnaya kniga. www.seu.ru/projects/caucasus/antikniga.htm (Accessed 7 October 2016).
Burbank, M.J., Andranovich, G.D., & Heying, C.H. (2001). *Olympic Dreams: The Impact of Mega-Events on Local Politics.* Boulder: Lynne Rienner.
Caratti, P., & Ferraguto, L. (2012). The Role of Environmental Issues in Mega-Events Planning and Management Processes: Which Factors Count? In G. Hayes & J. Karamichas (Eds), *Olympic Games, Mega-Events and Civil Societies.* London: Palgrave Macmillan.
Case, R. (2012). Event Impacts and Environmental Sustainability. In S.J. Page & J. Connell (Eds), *The Routledge Handbook of Events.* London: Routledge.
Cohen, J.L., & Arato, A. (1994). *Civil Society and Political Theory.* Cambridge, MA: The MIT Press.
Committee for Citizen Oversight. (2008). Za fasadom olimpiada-2014. *Novaya gazeta.*
Dansero, E., Corpo, B.D., Mela, A., & Ropolo, I. (2012). Olympic Games, Conflicts and Social Movements: The Case of Torino 2006. In G. Hayes & J. Karamichas (Eds), *Olympic Games, Mega-Events and Civil Societies: Globalization, Environment, Resistance.* London: Palgrave Macmillian.
Digges, C. (2016). Newly freed from prison, ecologist Vitishko says he wouldn't have changed a thing. *Bellona.org.* Retrieved from http://bellona.org/news/russian-human-rights-issues/2016-01-newly-freed-from-prison-ecologist-vitishko-says-he-wouldnt-have-changed-a-thing (Accessed 7 October 2016).
Englund, W. (2013, June 29). History Imperiled by Rising Prices. *Washington Post.*

56 *Political and civil society*

Fadeev, I. & Kravchenko, S. (2009, December 7). In Sochi, Imereti residents protest against sums for their real estate. *Caucasian Knot*. www.eng.kavkaz-uzel.eu/articles/11925/ (Accessed 9 October 2016).

Fierstein, H. (2013, July 21). Russia's Anti-Gay Crackdown. *New York Times*.

Flyvbjerg, B. (2006). Design by Deception: The Politics of Megaproject Approval. In W.S. Saunders (Ed.), *Urban Planning Today* (pp. 131–51). Minneapolis: University of Minnestoa Press.

Fors, N.M. (2009). *Sochi 2014: Ecology, Sochi-ites 0 – Russian Civil Society 1?* Chapel Hill NC: University of North Carolina at Chapel Hill.

Gazarian, S., & Shevchenko, D. (2014). *Sochi-2014: desat' let bez prava na zakon. Kak stroili 'luchshii mir'*. No location given: Ekologicheskaia Vakhta po Severnomu Kavkazu.

Gel'man, V. (2012). Teshchiny v stene [Cracks in the Wall]. *Pro et Contra*, 94–115.

Gel'man, V.I. (2005). Political Opposition in Russia: Is It Becoming Extinct? *Russian Politics and Law*, *43*(3), 25–50.

Glanin, I. (2009, March 13). Intrigue as prelude to registration: Boris Nemtsov will run for mayor of Sochi. *Vremya Novostei*.

Greene, S.A. (2013). Beyond Bolotnaia: Bridging Old and New in Russia's Election Protest Movement. *Problems of Post-Communism*, *60*(2), 40–52.

Gutterman, S. (2009, March 23). Kremlin critic says he was doused with ammonia. *Toronto Star*. Retrieved from www.thestar.com/news/world/2009/03/23/kremlin_critic_says_he_was_doused_with_ammonia.html (Accessed 7 October 2016).

Hayes, G., & Karamichas, J. (2012). Introduction: Sports Mega-Events, Sustainable Development and Civil Societies. In G. Hayes & J. Karamichas (Eds), *Olympic Games, Mega-Events and Civil Societies: Globalization, Environment, Resistance*. Basingstoke, UK: Palgrave Macmillan.

Henry, L.A. (2006). Russian Environmentalists and Civil Society. In J. Alfred B. Evans, L.A. Henry, & L.M. Sundstrom (Eds), *Russian Civil Society: A Criticl Assessment*. Armonk, NY: M.E. Sharpe.

Henry, L.A. (2010). *Red to Green: Environmental Activism in Post-Soviet Russia*. Ithaca, NY: Cornell University Press.

Howard, M.M. (2002). Postcomunist Civil Society in Comparative Perspective. *Demokratizatsiya: The Journal of Post-Soviet Democratization*, *10*(3), 285–305.

Human Rights Watch. (2013). Russia: Silencing Activists, Journalists Ahead of Sochi Games. www.hrw.org/news/2013/08/07/russia-silencing-activists-journalists-ahead-sochi-games (Accessed 7 October 2016).

International Olympic Committee. (2007). *IOC 2014 Evaluation Commission Report*. Belmont-sur-Lausanne: International Olympic Commission.Retrieved from www.olympic.org/Documents/Reports/EN/en_report_1187.pdf (Accessed 7 October 2016).

Karamichas, J. (2012). Olympic Games as an Opportunity for the Ecological Modernization of the Host Nation: The Cases of Sydney 2000 and Athens 2004. In G. Hayes & J. Karamichas (Eds), *Olympic Games, Mega-Events and Civil Society*. London: Palgrave Macmillian.

Karbainov, N. I. (2013). Kak izymayut sobstvennost' v olimpiiskikh stolitsakh: Olimpiada v Sochi v sravnitel'noi perspektive. *Mir Rossii*(1), 106-29.

Kasparov, G. (2015). *Winter is Coming: Why Vladimir Putin and the Enemies of the Free World Must Be Stopped*. New York: Public Affairs.

Kavkazskii uzel. (2007). Net Olimpiade tsenoi unichtozheniia prirody i narusheniia prav zhitelei Sochi! http://kavkaz-uzel.ru/articles/117869 (Accessed 7 October 2016).

Political and civil society 57

Khazov, S. (2013). Russia's anti-gay own goal. *OpenDemocracy Russia.* Retrieved from www.opendemocracy.net/od-russia/sergey-khazov/russias-anti-gay-own-goal (Accessed 7 October 2016).

Kozlovsky, O. (2013). Seven Challenges of the Russian Protest Movement. *Russian Analytical Digest* (124), 15–18.

Kramer, A.E. (2014, February 12). Russian Environmentalist, and Critic of Olympics, Gets 3-Year Prison Sentence. *The New York Times.*

Kreindlin, M. (2014). Russia's gamekeeper has turned poacher. *OpenDemocracy.* www. opendemocracy.net/od-russia/mikhail-kreindlin/russia%E2%80%99s-gamekeeper-has-turned-poacher (Accessed 7 October 2016).

Kuzmin, V. (2009, March 24). Chtoby ne krasnet' [To avoid blushing]. *Rossiiskaia gazeta.* Retrieved from http://rg.ru/2009/03/24/medvedev.html (Accessed 7 October 2016).

Lenskyj, H.J. (2008). *Olympic Industry Resistance: Challenging Olympic Power and Propaganda.* Albany, NY: State University of New York.

Lenskyj, H.J. (2014). *Sexual Diversity and the Sochi 2014 Olympics: No More Rainbows.* Basingstoke, UK: Palgrave Macmillian.

Levada Analytical Center. (2013). Novyi opros ob LGBT. www.levada.ru/2013/07/03/novyj-opros-ob-lgbt/ (accessed 9 October 2016).

Lussier, D. N. (2002). The Role of Russia's Governors in the 1999–2000 Federal Elections. In C. Ross (Ed.), *Regional Politics in Russia.* Manchester: Manchester University Press.

March, L. (2009). Managing Opposition in a Hybrid Regime: Just Russia and Parastatal Opposition. *Slavic Review, 68*(3), 504–27.

McCarthy, J.D., & Zald, M.N. (1977). Resource Mobilization and Social Movements: A Partial Theory. *American Journal of Sociology, 82*(6), 1212–41.

Mishina, E. (2014). Who Is Troubled by Gay Propaganda? *Institute of Modern Russia.* http://imrussia.org/en/analysis/law/2082-who-is-troubled-by-gay-propaganda (Accessed 7 October 2016).

Mommen, A. (2016). Boris Nemtsov, 1959–2015: The Rise and Fall of a Provincial Democrat. *Demokratizatsiya: The Journal of Post-Soviet Democratization, 24*(1), 5–28.

Mukhametshina, E. (2015). Zhitel' Sochi osparivaet olimpiiskii ukaz prezidenta ob obiazatel'nom soglasovanii odinochnykh piketov. *Vedomosti.* www.vedomosti.ru/politics/news/38363651/olimpijskaya-zhaloba (Accessed 7 October 2016).

Müller, M. (2012). Popular Perception of Urban Transformation through Mega-Events: Understanding Support for the 2014 Winter Olympics in Sochi. *Environment and Planning C: Government and Policy, 30*(4), 693–711.

Müller, M. (2013). *Greening Russia? Mobilising sustainability for the 2014 Olympic Games in Sochi.* Working Paper, April. Retrieved from martin-muller.net (Accessed 7 October 2016).

Naumov, I. (2008, July 4). Ekologi oderzhali pervuyu pobedu na sochinskoi Olimpiade. *Nezavisimaya gazeta.* Retrieved from http://ng.ru/forum/messages/forum3/topic11023/message 11090/#message11090 (posted to forum on March 3, 2013), (accessed 9 October 2016).

Nemtsov, B., & Milov, V. (2009). *Nezavisimyi ekspertnyi doklad Sochi i Olimpiada.* Moscow: Solidarnost – Independent Democratic Movement.

No author. (2009a). Rezolyutsiia mitinga zhitelei Nizhneimeretinskoi doliny g. Sochi. 6 dekabria 2009 g. [Resolutions of the Lower Imeretin Valley Rally on December 6, 2009]. www.kavkaz-uzel.ru/articles/162855/ (Accessed 7 October 2016).

No author. (2009b, August 20). Sud otklonil isk Borisa Nemtsova po vyboram mera Sochi [Court rejected Boris Nemtsov's suit on the mayoral elections]. *Kommersant.* Retrieved from http://kommersant.ru/doc/1223616 (Accessed 7 October 2016).

58   Political and civil society

Orttung, R. (2016). Feeding Russia. *Russian Analytical Digest*, (184), 2–4.

Orttung, R.W. (2013). Navalny's Campaign to be Moscow Mayor *Russian Analytical Digest* (136), 2–5.

OVD-Info. (2013). *Protest na tormozakh: politicheskie zaderzahniia v 2013 godu; Godovoi doklad OVD-Info za 2013 god*. Moscow: OVD-Info.

Pavlovskaya, T. (2009, October 31). V Sochi snova noviy mer. *Rossiiskaya gazeta*.

Perevozchikov, V. (2008, October 31). 114 dnei Afanasenkova. *Expert*. Retrieved from http://expert.ru/2008/10/31/sochi/ (Accessed 7 October 2016).

Perova, A. (2009, December 4). Olympstroi sygral na ponizhenie [Olympstroy played to lower prices]. *Kommersant (Rostov)*. www.kommersant.ru/doc/1285806 (Accessed 9 October 2016).

Perova, A., Karpova, Y., & Aminov, K. (2009, July 15). Sochi narisovali budushchee. *Kommersant*. Retrieved from www.kommersant.ru/doc/1204104/print (Accessed 7 October 2016).

Pound, R. (2008). Olympian Changes: Seoul and Beijing. In M. Worden (Ed.), *China's Great Leap: The Beijing Games and Olympian Human Rights Challenges* (pp. 85–97). New York: Seven Stories Press.

President of Russia. (2013). *Vneseny izmeneniia v zakon o zashchite detei ot informatsii, prichiniaiushchei vred ikh zdorov'iu i razvitiiu [Amendments have been made to the Law on the protection of children from information harmful to their health and development]* (June 30 edn). Moscow: Kremlin.

Price, M.E. (2008). On Seizing the Olympic Platform. In M.E. Price & D. Dayan (Eds), *Owning the Olympics: Narratives of the New China*. Ann Arbor MI: The University of Michigan Press.

Reuter, O.J., & Robertson, G. (2012). Subnational Appointments in Authoritarian Regimes: Evidence from Russian Gubernatorial Appointments. *The Journal of Politics*, *74*(4), 1023–37.

Rich, D.Q. (2012). Association Between Changes in Air Pollution Levels During the Beijing Olympics and Biomarkers of Inflammation and Thrombosis in Healthy Young Adults. *Journal of the American Medical Association*, *307*(19), 2068–78.

Robertson, G.B. (2009). Managing Society: Protest, Civil Society, and Regime in Putin's Russia. *Slavic Review*, *68*(3), 528–47.

Robertson, G.B. (2011). *The Politics of Protest in Hybrid Regimes: Managing Dissent in Post-Communist Russia*. Cambridge: Cambridge University Press.

Robertson, G.B. (2013). Protesting Putinism: The Election Protests of 2011–2012 in Broader Perspective. *Problems of Post-Communism*, *60*(2), 11–23.

Rolnik, R. (2009). Report of the Special Rapporteur on adequate housing as a component of the right to an adequate standard of living, and on the right to non-discrimination in this context. New York: United Nations General Assembly.

Sharafutdinova, G. (2009). Subnational Governance in Russia: How Putin Changed the Contract with His Agents and the Problems It Created for Medvedev. *Publius: The Journal of Federalism*, *40*(4), 672–96.

Shaw, C.A. (2008). *Five Ring Circus*. Gabriola Island, Canada: New Society Publishers.

Shepelin, I. (2013, September 3). Alekseev: Amerikantsy ne pomogaiut LGBT-soobshectvu v Rossii, a prost podryvaiut ego. *Slon.ru*. http://slon.ru/russia/alekseev_menya_na_kazhdom_uglu_obzyvayut_pidorasom_a_ya_ne_mogu_kogo_to_nazvat_zhidami_-985908.xhtml (Accessed 9 October 2016).

Shevchenko, D. (2013). Pechalnyi rekordy Sochinskoi Olympiady. *Ekologiya i prava* (50), 16–21.

Political and civil society 59

Sochi 2014. (2007). Sochi Candidature File 'Sochi 2014 Candidate City: Gateway to the Future'. http://web.archive.org/web/20100103043040/http://sochi2014.com/sch_questionnaire (Accessed 7 October 2016).

Stoner-Weiss, K. (1997). *Local Heroes: The Political Economy of Russian Regional Governance*. Princeton, NJ: Princeton University Press.

Sundstrom, L.M. (2006). *Funding Civil Society: Foreign Assistance and NGO Development in Russia*. Stanford CA: Stanford University Press.

Tarrow, S.G. (2011). *Power in Movement: Social Movements and Contentious Politics, Revised and Updated Third Edition*. Cambridge: Cambridge University Press.

The Moscow Times. (2012, October 31). Evictions for Sochi Olympics Cost $100,000 a Person. *The Moscow Times*. Retrieved from www.themoscowtimes.com/olympic_cover age/article/evictions-for-sochi-olympics-cost-100000-a-person/470665.html (Accessed 7 October 2016).

Titov, Y. (2008, October 31). Sochi. Prichinoi otstavki mera stalo nedovol'stvo vitse-prem'era Dmitriya Kozaka. *Novaya gazeta*.

Titov, Y. (2009, March 19). Glavnyi redaktor 'Delovogo Sochi' byl uvolnen posle togo, kak podderzhal Borisa Nemtsova [The chief editor of 'Business Sochi' was fired after supporting Boris Nemtsov]. *Novaya gazeta*. Retrieved from www.novayagazeta.ru/news/44542.html (Accessed 7 October 2016).

Torbakov, I. (2014). The Russian Orthodox Church and Contestations over History in Contemporary Russia. *Demokratizatsiya: The Journal of Post-Soviet Democratization*, *22*(1), 145–70.

United Nations Environmental Programme. (2010). *Sochi 2014; Report of the UNEP 2nd Expert Mission; 28–30 January 2010*. Retrieved from www.unep.org/sport_env/sochi 2014/Documents/Other/Sochi%202014%20Jan%202010%20Expert%20Mission%20 Report.pdf.

United Nations Environmental Programme. (2011). *Greening Sochi 2014 Olympic Games; Fourth UNEP Expert Mission to Moscow and Sochi; 17 to 25 January 2011; Note from the Mission*. Retrieved from www.unep.org/sport_env/sochi2014/Documents/Other/ Sochi%20Mission%20Report%20Jan%202011.pdf.

vanden Heuvel, K. (2013, August 27). Boycott Sochi? Think again. *Washington Post*.

Walker, S. (2014, January 17). Vladimir Putin: Gay people at Winter Olympics must 'leave children alone'. *The Guardian*. Retrieved from www.theguardian.com/world/2014/jan/ 17/vladimir-putin-gay-winter-olympics-children (Accessed 7 October 2016).

Whitson, D., & Horne, J. (2006). Underestimated Costs and Overestimated Benefits? Comparing the Outcome of Sports Mega-Events in Canada and Japan. In J. Horne & W. Manzenreiter (Eds.), *Sports Mega-Events: Social Scientific Analyses of a Global Phenomenon* (pp. 73–89). Malden, MA: Blackwell.

Wilson, A. (2007). Does Russia Still Have an Opposition? *Russian Analytical Digest* (28), 8–10.

Wilson, S. (2013). Russia defends anti-gay law in letter to IOC. *Associated Press*. http:// bigstory.ap.org/article/russia-defends-anti-gay-law-letter-ioc (Accessed 7 October 2016).

Worden, M. (Ed.). (2008). *China's Great Leap: The Beijing Games and Olympian Human Rights Challenges*. New York: Seven Stories Press.

World Wildlife Fund. (2009). V Sochi zaderzhany predstaviteli 'Ekologicheskoi Vakhty po Severnomu Kavkazu'. www.wwf.ru/resources/news/article/5345 (Accessed 7 October 2016).

World Wildlife Fund. (2010a). Dal'neishee uchastie WWF v ekologicheskom soprovo-zhdenii Olimpiady Sochi 2014 pod voprosom. www.wwf.ru/resources/news/article/6044 (Accessed 7 October 2016).

60   *Political and civil society*

World Wildlife Fund. (2010b). Missiya OON v Sochi ne smogla naladit' dialog mezhdu obshchestvennost'yu i organizatorami Sochi-2014. www.wwf.ru/resources/news/article/7412 (Accessed 7 October 2016).

World Wildlife Fund. (2010c). Olimpiada-2014 v gorode Sochi. wwf.ru/about/positions/sochi2014 (Accessed 7 October 2016).

World Wildlife Fund. (2011). WWF i Grinpis ne budut vstrecht'sya s YuNEP v Sochi. www.wwf.ru/resources/news/article/7728 (Accessed 7 October 2016).

Zavisca, J. R. (2012). *Housing the New Russia*. Ithaca NY: Cornell University Press.

Zharkov, S. (2013). Nedvizhimost' v Sochi posle Olimpiady: perspektivy vyzhivaniya regiona. *Indikatory rynka nedvizhimosti*. www.irn.ru/articles/35084.html (Accessed 9 October 2016).

4 Security

Fighting terrorism and strengthening the military

Olympic hosts have to worry about the problem of terrorism and Russia was certainly no exception. However, the case of the Sochi games was different because, at the same time as preparations for the games were proceeding, President Vladimir Putin was reforming the Russian military and expanding its capabilities. Accordingly, this chapter addresses the overall question of security by first dealing with the terrorism issue and then turning to the military aspects. Finally, it addresses the consequences of the state's enhanced security capabilities for the population.

For the discussion of terrorism, the central question is: how did Russia succeed in preventing a terrorist attack on the Sochi Olympics and at what cost? Equally important is the question of what the legacy of the anti-terrorist efforts was for Russian society.

In the case of the military, under the cover of improving Olympic security, the Kremlin intentionally concentrated in one place its elite military forces, including navy, air forces, and ground troops. If it were not for the Olympics, the international community likely would have protested against this move. During the preparations for the games starting in 2007, the Russian military exercised constantly and intensively. In parallel, Russia conducted a military reform (Gressel, 2015). The 2008 August war against Georgia came at the beginning of this process. The Kremlin managed to conduct a quick and seemingly successful operation, even if it suffered losses against a significantly smaller foe. Already at that stage, the Kremlin had achieved its goal, which was to give the Russian army confidence that it could enter into war, quickly win, and exit with political benefits. Since then, Russian troops were regularly training to improve coordination among the navy, air forces, and ground troops, a set of skills that is certainly useful in the fight against terrorism, but is also required for more conventional war, such as those Russia has prosecuted against Georgia, Ukraine, and the anti-Assad insurgents in Syria (Karagiannis, 2014). By 2014, Russian troops in Sochi joined the ranks of some of the best-trained armies in the world.

In 2013, General Oleg Syromolotov was appointed the head of Olympic security. Observers at the time noted that he was a counterintelligence specialist who had nothing to do with terrorism either before or after the Olympics; after the games, Syromolotov became Foreign Minister Sergey Lavrov's deputy. What

62 *Security*

this strange personnel choice suggests is that Putin used the Olympics as cover for achieving other tasks that were of interest to him: expanding the capacity of the Russian authorities to monitor and control its population and build up a stronger military force. In short, terrorism was a threat to the games and Russia was able to address this threat, though at a great cost to society. At the same time, Putin used the Olympics to facilitate efforts to develop tools that he could use to repress Russian society and expand Russia's borders.

Defeating the terrorist threat to Sochi

Terrorism means violence or the threat of violence, usually for political purposes, often aimed at civilians and designed to have a psychological impact beyond the immediate victims. It communicates a message to various possible audiences: a community of supporters, an adversary, or the international community (Schmid, 2011). With billions of viewers, the Sochi Winter Olympics was a logical place for terrorists to strike.

The 'Munich Syndrome' – fear of terrorist acts similar to those that took place during the 1972 Munich Games in which Palestinian terrorists killed 11 Israeli athletes – has shadowed the Olympic movement for more than four decades. The organizers of the Munich Olympics had paid little attention to security needs before the games, making it easier for the Black September terrorists to carry out their attack (Large, 2012). During the 1996 Atlanta games, Eric Rudolph detonated a nail-filled bomb, killing two people and injuring a hundred by-standers. Whereas the Munich experience demonstrated what an organized group could achieve in attacking the Olympics, the bombing in Atlanta showed the damage that a dedicated individual, in this case focused on the issue of fighting abortion, could perpetrate (Richards, 2011, p. 3). These experiences, combined with the 11 September 2001 terrorist attacks on the United States and the 2013 Boston Marathon bombing, dramatically ratcheted up security concerns in the years before Sochi.

A central part of the Olympics' value to the Kremlin lay in their ability to demonstrate that Russia had returned to the world stage and was a leader among nations. Accordingly, efforts to promote security at the games went beyond an effort to protect athletes, spectators, and facilities. Regardless of the cost, Russia's leaders needed to demonstrate that the Sochi Games could take place in a safe atmosphere to validate Russia's legitimate status among the world's elite nations (Bernhard & Martin, 2014; Boyle & Haggerty, 2012). Moreover, the Sochi Olympics occurred at a time of 'hyper insecurity', characterized as an era of intense risk aversion in which resources were allocated in relation not to the probability of an attack but to the possibility that one might occur (Houlihan & Giulianotti, 2012).

But Russian officials certainly had reason to fear that militants would be targeting the games. According to the US Congressional Research Service, there were 5,472 terrorist incidents in Russia between 2009–2013, averaging about 2–3 per day, with a decline from 1,381 in 2009 to 741 in 2013. Over that period,

1,672 security personnel and civilians were killed, along with 1,921 suspected terrorists. By comparison, 1,826 US troops were killed in Afghanistan during the same period (Nichol, Halchin, Rollins, Tiersky, & Woehrel, 2014). The well-respected Caucasus Knot website claims the total number of deaths was 6,074 from 2010–2015 (see Table 4.1), while Memorial recorded the death of 4,175 law enforcement officers from 2008–2015 (see Table 4.2). All the sources show a relatively high level of terrorist activity in the immediate aftermath of Russia's victory in winning the right to host the Olympics in 2007 and a reduction in the number of deaths as the Olympics approached in 2014.

To protect its $50 billion overall investment in the Sochi games, Russia's usually cautious leadership wanted to ensure that nothing went wrong. Russia spent $2 billion on security for the 2014 Sochi Olympics (Tovkailo, 2011), a sum among the highest paid in Olympic history. Since the Athens 2004 games, security expenditures for Olympic events rose rapidly. Greece spent $1.5 billion on security at the 2004 Olympics shortly after the 11 September 2001 terrorist attacks on New York and Washington, and received considerable aid from the United States and other countries (Bennett & Haggerty, 2011, p. vii). Estimates for Chinese expenditures in 2008 went as high as $6.5 billion, although it is difficult to gauge the actual outlay (Houlihan & Giulianotti, 2012, p. 707). In 2010, Canada spent $852 million for this purpose during the Vancouver games (Dowd, 2010). The United Kingdom spent at least $1.4 billion to provide security during the 2012 London Summer games, with some estimates exceeding $2 billion (Richards, Fussey, & Silke, 2011, p. 236).

Given the expenditures, the official numbers of security personnel for the Sochi Olympics were relatively small, according to Putin's statement on the eve of the games, 'Security is to be ensured by some 40,000 law enforcement and special

Table 4.1 Victims of terrorism and anti-terrorism in the North Caucasus, 2010–2015

	2010	*2011*	*2012*	*2013*	*2014*	*2015*	*Total*
	1705	1375	1225	986	525	258	6074

Source: Caucasus Knot website: Statistika Zhertv Na Severnom Kavkaze Za 2010–2015 Gody Po Dannym Kavkazskogo Uzla. 2016. Kavkazskii Uzel. February 10. www.kavkaz-uzel.ru/articles/277404/

Table 4.2 Number of killed and wounded law enforcement officers before and after the 2014 Sochi Olympics

2008	*2009*	*2010*	*2011*	*2012*	*2013*	*2014*	*2015*	*Total*
747	929	840	475	547	373	182	52	4145

Source: Memorial: 'Kontrterror Na Severnom Kavkaze: Vzgliad Pravozashschitnikov. 2014 G. – Pervaia Polovina 2016 G.' 2016. Moscow, Russian Federation: Memorial. http://zapravakbr.com/images/doklad_severnyy_kavkaz_0.pdf.

64 *Security*

services officers' (Putin, 2014). The number announced by Putin included only regular police and Interior Ministry soldiers, however. According to different sources, the total number of security deployed in Sochi was up to 100,000 – 120,000 military troops, police, and FSB personnel (Nichol *et al.*, 2014). While it is difficult to be sure exactly how many military and law enforcement officers were involved, the number was greater than the 50,000 police and soldiers who guarded the 1980 Moscow Olympics (Sudolskii, 2011). Russia's force was probably comparable to the numbers Greece deployed, 70,000 individuals, in 2004, and China, 100,000, in 2008. The Russian figure was higher, however, than that for the 2012 London Summer Olympics – secured by 40,000 individuals, including 30,000 police officers and members of the armed forces (Coaffee & Johnston, 2007).

Russia's evolving anti-terrorism concept

Anti-terrorism preparations for the Olympics evolved through three distinct phases marked by different security concepts and practical measures. The first concept appeared in 2007, in Russia's candidature file for the Olympics. It reflected Russia's readiness to embrace the International Olympic Committee's (IOC) concept of friendly security for the games, assumed that Russia had achieved stability in the North Caucasus, and implied that the Olympics would be open to everybody, including migrant workers who sought employment building Olympic facilities in the years before the opening ceremonies. The emergence of the Caucasus Emirate (CE), a terrorist organization operating in the North Caucasus region, forced the adoption of a second security concept in 2009. Given the large number of people being killed and the spread of terrorist attacks, securing the entire region became an impossible task. Accordingly, to separate Sochi administratively from the restive North Caucasus region, the Kremlin carved out a new North Caucasus Federal District from the existing Southern Federal District. The third concept, adopted in 2012 after Putin returned to the presidency, enhanced the crackdown on the terrorists by hunting them down and killing them.

2007: The first security concept

From the beginning of the preparations for the games, Russia's security planning for the 2014 Olympics took into account terrorist challenges in the North Caucasus. Planners drew up the first security plan for the games in May 2007, a time when the Chechen insurgency seemed to have been defeated and its leaders were either dead or in hiding. The Kremlin elite considered the Chechen problem solved, did not anticipate other serious threats to stability in the region, and formally ended its 'counterterrorist operation' in Chechnya in April 2009. The stabilization of Chechnya was regarded as a result of President Vladimir Putin's ability to take and centralize power, thus allowing Russia's return to the world stage (Wills & Moore, 2008).

Initially, the Olympic organizers planned security preparations in two stages: 2007–2012 and 2012–2014. Security during each stage required a different set of agencies working within a new hierarchy of institutions. The organizers were so sure that no serious threats faced Sochi that they did not plan to involve any federal agencies in the security preparations during the first period up to 2012. One regional law-enforcement agency, the Sochi Police Department, was responsible for providing all security. Military forces could be added on an ad hoc basis, according to these initial plans.

2010: The second security concept

In October 2007, several months after Russia won its bid to host the Olympics, the leader of the Chechen insurgency, Doku Umarov, proclaimed his intention to establish an Islamic state, the Caucasus Emirate, which would expand beyond Chechnya to include the entire Caucasus region. Umarov set up a group, known as the Caucasus Emirate (CE), which tried to knit together a coalition of insurgents that included 'unholy alliances' of groups representing different ethnicities, regions, and ever-changing mixtures of nationalism, Islam, and separatism (Moore, 2010; Moore & Tumelty, 2009). Although an extreme brand of Salafi Islam was taking hold in the North Caucasus, there was extensive turmoil within the insurgency, leading to 'fragmentation, mutation, and reconstitution' of its ranks (Moore, 2010; Moore & Tumelty, 2009). The grievances were rooted in domestic issues, but foreign jihadists were able to participate in the fighting, although their role was declining since the heyday between 1999 and 2002 (Moore & Tumelty, 2008). Russia's leaders did not try to address the root causes of the problem but sought to suppress the groups they dubbed 'bandits' through a combination of repression and cooption (disbursing large sums of money). Hence terrorism in the area was 'fueled and fostered by corruption that has acquired grotesque forms' (Baev, 2010). While regional leaders worried about the threats raised by these groups, the Kremlin did not employ special measures to secure the Olympic venues from 2007 through 2009, hoping that the combination of repression and cooption would be sufficient.

Such limited measures proved ineffective, and anxiety rose when the CE organized major terrorist attacks on Russian soil. In November 2009, an express train travelling between Moscow and St. Petersburg exploded en route to its destination, killing 25 people and wounding 87.[1] In March 2010, two women detonated suicide belts in the Moscow metro during the morning rush hour; one of the blasts hit the Lubyanka Metro station near the headquarters of the Federal Security Service (FSB). The two blasts killed 38 people and injured 60 (Buribayev, 2010). Other attacks in 2010 caused significant numbers of deaths in Ingushetia and Kabardino-Balkaria. Even though Russian troops and police outnumbered the rebels by more than fifty to one, the authorities' efforts did not eliminate the armed resistance (Kramer, 2005).

In adopting the second Olympic security concept toward the end of 2009, the Kremlin effectively admitted that it could not secure the entire region. It therefore imposed territorial-administrative changes in the North Caucasus and adopted a variety of different military preparations. According to the new

66 *Security*

security concept, the Kremlin separated the greater Sochi area from the centre of destabilization in the North Caucasus republics by dividing the Southern Federal District in January 2010.

In May 2010, Russian President Dmitry Medvedev issued a decree 'On Providing Security During the Twenty-Second Winter Olympic Games and Eleventh Paralympic Games of 2014 in Sochi' (President of Russia, 2010). It created an Operational Staff headed by the FSB director who replaced the minister of internal affairs, who had been given the job in the candidature file's original plan. Representatives of all other security services became subordinate to the head of the Operational Staff in 2010, instead of 2012 as had been planned originally. The practical impact of Medvedev's decree was that Russia launched military and anti-terror preparations for the Olympics much earlier than anticipated – including military drills on the Black Sea, along Russia's borders, and in the Caucasus Mountains.

As early as 2010, regular military regiments from different parts of Russia were sent to the North Caucasus with the official goal of securing the region in preparation for the 2014 Olympics. One such case was reported in the Russian media when the soldiers' parents discovered that a regiment from Leningrad Oblast had been sent to Dagestan.[2] The regular regiments guarded important buildings while the Special Forces conducted anti-terrorist operations, such as efforts to cleanse the nearby mountains of potential terrorists (Ivlent'eva, 2015).

In addition to the anti-terrorist military operations, the local authorities in the North Caucasus tested soft power methods to win over extremists. Starting in 2010–2012, in Dagestan, Ingushetia, and Karachay-Cherkessia, non-violent prominent Salafi leaders made public appeals to the fighters. These soft measures had an immediate positive effect and, for example, Ingushetia became one of the most peaceful republics in the region, with fewer young people joining the insurgency (International Crisis Group, 2016). The number of law enforcement officers killed and wounded by insurgents in 2009–2012 fell by half, from 929 to 475, according to Memorial (see Table 4.2) (Memorial, 2016).

2013: Third security concept

Vladimir Putin's election to a third term in 2012 changed the Olympics security concept again. Having a KGB background, Putin apparently considered the agency to be the most effective tool in any situation and gave the FSB control over the entire security infrastructure. In January 2013, a year before the games, Putin issued a decree establishing the State Committee for Preparing and Conducting the Olympics (President of Russia, 2013b). With the decree, Putin appointed General Oleg Syromolotov, a FSB deputy director, the chairman of the operations staff to provide security at the games. Syromolotov was a specialist in counterintelligence, and his appointment as the head of Olympics' security indicated that the Kremlin included counterintelligence efforts along with the ongoing anti-terrorism actions (Soldatov, Borogan, & Walker, 2013). (We discuss these counterintelligence efforts below in assessing the spectator passes required for the games.)

Russia's anti-terrorism methods changed dramatically after Putin returned to the presidency. According to the Russian human right organization Memorial, the Russian leadership abandoned the soft power methods that it had been using against terrorism under Medvedev and switched to an emphasis on force, often unlawfully: 'Starting in 2012–2013, law enforcement agencies returned to practicing state terror and to provoking antagonism between different trends inside Islam' (Memorial, 2016). Amid this ongoing violence, the CE made verbal threats against the Olympics in Sochi. In July 2013, a video appeared on YouTube in which Caucasus Emirate leader Doku Umarov called on his supporters in Russia not to allow the Sochi Olympics to go forward. With this announcement, Umarov claimed to be ending the moratorium on attacks that he had announced in early 2012 (BBC, 2013; Sokirianskaia, 2013).

According to a 2016 International Crisis Group report, the Russian security services carried out hundreds of anti-terrorism operations, killing both leaders and rank-and-file insurgents. Security service agents followed the insurgents' wives and poisoned food that was sent to the fighters in the forests. This tactic produced results when the FSB managed to fatally poison Umarov six months before the Olympics, on 7 September 2014, killing the greatest terrorist threat to the Olympics. The FSB also cracked down on non-violent Salafi activity, closing prayer houses and charities while also conducting mass arrests of believers in mosques and *halal* cafés (International Crisis Group, 2016). Despite their apparent success, the new heavy-handed methods came at a high cost for the law enforcement agencies and the number of killed and wounded officers increased in 2012 (see Table 4.2).

Despite the death of Umarov, other terrorist groups were able to carry out deadly attacks in Volgograd, a city in Southern Russia, in the months before the games began. An explosion on a bus killed eight people and wounded 37 on 21 October 2013. One of the women killed was from Dagestan and allegedly, a suicide bomber. Later, law enforcement agencies killed her husband, an ethnic Russian, and claimed that he was the organizer of the terrorist act (Evstifeev, 2013). On the eve of the Olympics, two more terrorist acts took place in the same city, leaving no doubt that they were connected to the Sochi games. On 29 December 2013, a suicide bombing rocked the Volgograd train station, killing 18 people and injuring 44. The next day, another suicide attack took place in a trolleybus, killing 16 people and injuring 41. A group named Vilayat Dagestan posted a video taking responsibility for the Volgograd explosions and threatening to conduct terrorist acts during the Sochi Olympics (Heritage, 2014). IOC president Thomas Bach, however, issued a statement the same day expressing confidence that the Russian authorities would deliver 'safe and secure' games in Sochi (Liss, 2013).

The three explosions in Volgograd raised doubts about whether the Russian security system was capable of preventing terrorist attacks. But the deadly crackdown continued. On 8 January, four cars with the bodies of six men were discovered near villages in southern Stavropol Kray, just southeast of Pyatigorsk. Improvised explosive devices had been placed near the cars, apparently to target police and rescue workers, but only one harmlessly detonated (Nichol *et al.*, 2014).

68 *Security*

On the same day, a police officer killed a suspect in Dagestan and on 11 January, secret service officers killed two other suspects, allegedly connected to the insurgents. On 15 January, in a battle in village Karlanyurt, Dagestan, law enforcement forces killed four insurgents. These incidents took place in the non-Russian Republic of Dagestan and, because of that, drew less media attention than the previous three Volgograd terrorist acts. The 2010 separation of Sochi from the more turbulent North Caucasus Federal District, where Dagestan is located, paid off in this way, and the echo of terrorism from the distant Dagestan mountains did not reach Sochi.

The Sochi games proceeded without any terrorist attacks disrupting them. Nevertheless, several incidents raised concerns. On 21 January 2014, the Russian police announced that Sochi had been infiltrated by a 'black widow' – a female suicide bomber who was taking revenge for the killing of her husband. There were even reports of letters threatening athletes if they attended the games, although these were deemed to be a hoax (Nichol *et al.*, 2014). About a year after the Olympics, Russian security services claimed that they had prevented a terrorist attack during the games. According to Olympics security chief Syromolotov, more than one female suicide bomber was supposed to fly from France to Sochi delivering explosive materials hidden inside a hand crème tube with a micro-explosive mechanism provided from Syria (Miranovich, 2015). Russian officials, though, never specified if the security service intercepted the suicide bombers and what happened to those terrorists.

After the death of Umarov, the Caucasus Emirate's terrorist activities dropped significantly. The insurgents' violence decreased due to several causes. First, the newly elected CE leader, Aliaskhab Kebekov, banned suicide bombing, attacks on civilians, and women's participation in the insurgency. In spite of his order, however, a suicide bombing took place in Dagestan after the Olympics and this act of disobedience indicated that the new leader did not have authority over all the insurgents in the region. Second, the emergence of ISIS in Syria made the local North Caucasus radicalism, which was oriented toward Al-Qaeda (Hahn, 2011), less appealing and hundreds of insurgents from the Caucasus went to fight in Syria. Third, some experts believe that the security services opened the borders for the insurgents, making it easy for them to go to Syria (International Crisis Group, 2016). Russian jihadists did not begin to leave for Syria in significant numbers until 2014 when, in the time before the start of the 2014 Olympics in Sochi, the security services in the nearby North Caucasus region made it clear that they would kill any militants they could find. Russia also actively pushed people to leave, according to human right activists, who noted that a few well-known militants held under house arrest suddenly turned up in recruitment videos from Syria (Yeginsu & Callimachi, 2016).

In sum, the Russian authorities killed the leadership of the main terrorist threat to the Sochi Olympics a few months before the opening ceremonies. Other groups were able to carry out terrorist attacks in Russia in the months before the games started, but these attacks were displaced to Volgograd, far enough away from the events so that they did not have a major impact on the games themselves.

Military measures during the games

The Russian military played a crucial role during the Sochi Olympics. During the preparations for the games, the Russian army helped shape the security concept for protecting the Sochi Olympics by winning the 2008 Russian–Georgian war, leading to Russia's recognition of Abkhazia and South Ossetia as territories independent from Georgia. Even though the Georgian conflict was a small local war, it nevertheless became the first real military victory in post-Soviet Russian history. If the main meaning of the Olympic mega-project was to show that Russia was rising up from its knees, one could argue that the army became the first contributor to that concept, bringing a victory to the country before the games started.

Since Georgia was just across the border from Sochi and Abkhazia was the neighbouring area to Sochi inside Georgia, the war became an excuse for Russia to show off militarily during the Olympic preparations, as if the games were a military parade. As part of this strategy, Russia regularly held military manoeuvres on the Black Sea following the 2008 war with Georgia. All these manoeuvres employed a scheme similar to the real military actions during the Georgian conflict.

When Russia submitted its application to host the Olympics, the organizers did not specify what kind of threats they expected the Olympics might encounter. The application did not mention any particular military challenges beyond the possibility of terrorist attacks. The 2007 document used the same framework – no clearly defined threats beyond terrorism – in describing measures to secure the state borders near Sochi.

The Kremlin began to view Georgia as a potential threat to the Sochi Olympics only after the 2008 war. Before fighting broke out, the Sochi Olympics were seen as a positive element in Russian–Georgian relations. President Mikheil Saakashvili of Georgia called President Vladimir Putin the day after Sochi was chosen to host the 2014 Winter Olympics to congratulate his Russian counterpart on Sochi's win; he described it as a great victory for Russia. 'Both [presidents] expressed confidence that an event of such a global scale in Russia's South will bring positive changes to the region, helping ensure peace and understanding in the Caucasus', the Russian presidential press service said (No author, 2007). On 22 February 2008, Putin and Saakashvili met during a Commonwealth of Independent States summit. In July 2008, during US Secretary of State Condoleezza Rice's visit to Tbilisi, Saakashvili announced that Georgia would officially approach Russia with a proposal to create a joint committee for security at the 2014 Olympics.[3]

The Russian–Georgian 2008 war shredded these proposals. After the cease fire went into effect, Georgia changed its attitude toward the 2014 Olympics and actively opposed holding them in Sochi. In September 2008, Georgia appealed to the IOC to move the Olympics from Sochi to another location because of security issues. The letter declared, 'Sochi is a very dangerous place.'[4] The IOC rejected Georgia's proposal. In May 2010, the Georgian parliament recognized the fighting that took place in nineteenth-century Sochi as a genocide carried out by imperial Russia against the Circassian people, hoping that it would violate Olympic

70 *Security*

principles to hold the games in a place where genocide had been committed. This declaration also had no impact on the IOC.

The Kremlin particularly feared NATO support for Georgia. In February 2011, President Dmitry Medvedev stated that Russia has 'certain problems with its neighbour Georgia' concerning the Sochi Olympics and ordered the security forces to prevent any pre-Olympic provocation.[5] In January 2012, Putin said that if NATO put a missile defence complex in Georgia, Russia would have no choice but to point its missiles 'toward Georgian territory'.[6]

After the 2012 Georgian elections removed Saakashvili from office, the new Georgian government adopted a more favourable attitude toward Russia. Russia, however, continued to demonstrate its military might just off the Georgian coast. Although the Kremlin showed no intention of instigating another conflict in the region prior to the 2014 Winter Olympics, it felt free to demonstrate its power.

After Putin's return to power in 2012, he took the military preparations for Sochi Olympics to a new level and, under the pretext of security measures, gathered and trained significant military forces in and around Sochi. In March 2013, Putin personally issued an order to hold 'snap' manoeuvres from his presidential airplane on his return to Sochi after a visit to South Africa. The drills included approximately 30 ships, more than 20 airplanes and helicopters, and 7,000 personnel on the Black Sea. Despite the scale of the manoeuvres and the Russian leader's direct participation, observers claimed that the operation had no military goal and merely sought to demonstrate Russia's power in the region. The absence of any military goal was so self-evident that the official news agency, RIA Novosti, tried to justify the exercises by suggesting that the manoeuvres might be motivated by a 'shakeup at the top of a military establishment demoralized by persistent evidence of rampant corruption' (Ryzhkov, 2013). Later events demonstrated, however, that during these Olympic drills Putin became ready to extensively use his army outside the country, including in Ukraine in 2014, and in Syria, in 2015.

The Russian air force, navy, and army all made important contributions to Russia's Olympic preparations. The Russian air force provided 'aviation support, airspace control, and interdiction' for the Olympics (Sochi 2014, 2007, p. 39). The air force was prepared to resolve a number of hypothetical threats during the games, including terrorists crashing a civilian plane into the Olympic site, drones, and other intruders. The 1721st Missile Rocket Regiment was stationed in Sochi and provided SA-11 Gadfly rockets for defeating cruise missiles and aviation.[7] The Seventh Russian Military Base was situated in Abkhazia, with 3,800 Russian personnel and an S-300 missile complex (Mukhin, 2011a). Air defence missile batteries, including Pantsyr-S1 surface-to-air missiles, to protect against airplanes, helicopters, drones, and cruise missiles, were deployed in the region; space satellites, unmanned aerial vehicles, and dirigibles monitored the area from the air (Nichol *et al.*, 2014).

Russia's air force security measures for the Olympics were not unprecedented, but they were unique in size. When NATO provided the security defence for the 2004 Olympics in Greece, it deployed a couple dozen Patriot missile systems around the Olympic Village. Three police helicopters and a Zeppelin blimp were in the sky (Ivanov, 2004). Two military ships, The Ocean and The Bulwark, together with air-to-ground missiles, Typhoon jet fighters and helicopters, secured the 2012 London Olympics.[8]

Russian naval bases on the Black Sea – Sevastopol (Ukraine), Novorossiisk (Russia), and Ochamchira (Abkhazia) – provided maritime security. During the years of Olympic preparations, the ships of the Red Flag Water Region Security Brigade of the Black Sea Fleet patrolled the Caucasus coast from Sevastopol. Neustrashimyi and Iaroslav Mudryi, two ships from the Baltic Fleet, were relocated to the Black Sea Fleet. According to the State Military Program for 2011–2012, the Black Sea Fleet also received 18 new ships, including six diesel submarines (Mukhin, 2011a).

The navy had the most continuous presence in the dramatic events before, during, and after the games. The distinguishing feature of the Black Sea Fleet was that it had recent battle experience from the 2008 war, providing security for the games, and later, would participate in the annexation of Crimea. A local Crimean newspaper, *The Flag of the Motherland*, reported later that the marines from Novorossisk navy military base, for example, provided security for the Olympics, Paralympics, and the Crimean referendum (Pasiakin, 2015b). Captain-Lieutenant Vadim Kolesnik, the commander of the ship Vitse-Admiral Zakhar'in, said, 'From the beginning, Zakhar'in, with diverse military forces, actively provided security for the Winter Sochi Olympics . . . Our ship received an assignment to politely (*vezhlivo*) provide security for the Crimean referendum from the sea.'[9] The term 'polite men' was what the Kremlin called the Russian Special Forces who wore no identifying markings that occupied Crimea after the games. In his statement, Kolesnik provides one of few cases when this term was applied to Russian soldiers, other than the FSB. After the games, Putin awarded Dmitry Dronov, the captain of the Black Sea missile carriers, with a medal for helping to organize the Sochi Olympics (Pasiakin, 2015a).

The Fifty-Eighth Army was the main military force in southern Russia. Its greatest military campaign came during the 2008 war, which it called 'Forcing Georgia to Peace'. It traced its history to the Fifty-Eighth Army of the Soviet Union, which had participated in the liberation of the Caucasus in 1942 during World War II. In January 2012, Major General Andrei Gurulev was appointed commander of the Fifty-Eighth Army. He said that he understood his task as obtaining new equipment for the army, which had only 60 per cent of what it needed at the time.[10]

The Thirty-Fourth Zelenchuk Brigade was particularly important to the Sochi security system. It directly secured Sochi from the north and east in coordination with PSB border troops, the Seventh Russian Military Base in Abkhazia, and paratroopers (Mukhin, 2011b). The brigade was strengthened with two battalions, one formed from contract (paid) solders from the Moscow military district and the other from the Volga-Urals military district – four thousand soldiers in all.

Some of these army forces assigned to the Sochi games later participated in the annexation of Crimea. One of them was the mountain brigade of the South Military District that, according to the army newspaper *Red Star*, provided both

72 *Security*

security during the Sochi Olympics and the Crimean referendum for joining Russia (Borodin, 2016).

Before Putin's return to the presidency in 2012, the Russian Defense Ministry had only one large special forces regiment. Later, especially after the appointment of Sergei Shoigu as defence minister, several other regiments were established to provide Olympic security (Mikhailov, 2015). According to the research of the Moscow-based Center for Analysis of Strategies and Technologies (CAST), 'Using the pretext of providing security for the Winter Olympics in Sochi, in 2011 and 2012 the MoD [Ministry of Defense] created the new 346th Spetsnaz Brigade and the new, elite 25th Spetsnaz Regiment (Stavropol)' (Barabanov, 2014, pp. 107–8). An April 2016 issue of the Russian military newspaper *Military-Production Courier* pointed out that two special Defense Ministry centres, in Senezh and Zazabor'e, performed the most difficult tasks' because they had 'defended the Olympics in Sochi, and conducted a brilliant operation in Crimea, and now, work in Syria' (Mikhailov, 2016).

Alongside the regular army, 40,000 police officers provided security for Sochi, including 10,000 soldiers from the Ministry of Internal Affairs (MVD) troops, 3,000 Sochi police officers, and 24,500 police officers from other regions. In Sochi, 26 buildings were provided to house them (Sudolskii, 2011). Special new barracks were built for a new military headquarters for 12,000 soldiers (Portnov, 2015).

The military played a large role in the Sochi Olympics. The inclusion of these troops in the games helped concentrate Russian forces for their deployment to Crimea. The numerous drills surrounding the games gave the Russian leaders the confidence they needed to invade Ukraine.

Security measures during the Olympics

Though the law enforcement agencies did not face an actual terrorist attack during the games, they were extremely busy with other issues. Using the terrorist threat, the FSB employed unprecedented measures of control over the Sochi area. A Russian government decree (8 November 2013) ordered that all phone calls in Sochi during the games be recorded and stored for three years, giving the FSB '24 hour access to the data'. A special attachment to the decree provided a list of people to be monitored, including the organizers, athletes, spectators, IOC and World Anti-Doping Agency (WADA) members, referees, foreign delegations, journalists, physicians, and everybody else (Government of the Russian Federation, 2013). The implications of this effort are enormous. As we discuss in the legacy chapter, while the FSB was monitoring all the phone communications in the area, including WADA members in charge of testing athletes for illegal doping, an FSB officer was tampering with the Russian athletes' urine samples, covering up their use of illegal drugs. The FSB could thus use its position in charge of Olympic security overall to ensure that Russian cheating went undetected.

Of course, Russia was not the first country to listen in on Olympic participants' communications. In 2013, Rocky Anderson, the former mayor of Salt Lake City, told the *Washington Post* that

Security 73

We just discovered a week ago that the NSA [National Security Administration], completely in violation of statutory and constitutional law, subjected every person in the Salt Lake City area [during the 2002 Olympics] to surveillance of the contents of their e-mails and texts messages. . . . It was a tremendous betrayal. (Moyer, 2013)

While the state actions were the same, the difference between the Russian and American cases was that the Russian agencies conducted the surveillance openly on the basis of a presidential decree, while the American actions were hidden and only revealed later.

Additionally, the Russian authorities required that all spectators acquire special passes to attend the events.[11] The rules for the passes noted that the 'Spectator Pass is issued free of charge for the purpose of providing security for all ticket holders.'[12] To attend the events and enter the Olympic Park, any visitor, aged three and above, needed to obtain a spectator pass. The organizers reserved the right to deny entry to anyone, guaranteeing ticket refunds to rejected applicants. The newspaper *Kommersant* described the spectator pass as an 'Olympic visa'.[13] To obtain one, the applicant needed to upload personal data to the web site https://pass.sochi2014.com. The organizers defined 'personal data' as 'any information related to an individual identified or identifiable by such information, including citizenship, family name (surname), first and middle name(s), date and place of birth, gender, ID information, address, photograph, e-mail address, telephone number, and so on'.[14] The organizers of the games and Russian law-enforcement agencies thus constructed a database of all visitors attending the 2014 Olympics in advance.

The use of such a spectator pass was unprecedented for the Olympics, though in 2008 the Italian authorities forced fans to obtain a document called the Tessera del Tifoso to attend domestic and international soccer games in Italy. The Italian experiment cut ticket sales by 20 per cent and experts stated that it did not improve the security situation (Furmaniuk, 2010). In 2010, an Italian court ruled that it was illegal to make spectators submit their personal data to watch a sports event and prohibited any further use of the Tessera del Tifoso (Furmaniuk, 2011).

On August 19, 2013, President Putin issued a decree restricting movement and assembly in Sochi during the games (President of Russia, 2013a). Critics said that the decree violated human rights by creating a prohibited zone encompassing much of the sprawling city, barring travel into Sochi by road without special permission and banning public gatherings not connected with the Olympics in high security areas on land and sea (Gutterman, 2013).

Putin had reason to worry about political protests during the games. Moscow and other cities saw street rallies after the December 2011 parliamentary elections and again in May 2012 after the presidential elections. Subsequently, the Kremlin issued a number of orders cracking down on civil society. The Russian authorities required NGOs that accepted donations from abroad to register as 'foreign agents', an ominous term suggesting that they were spies. The authorities also dramatically increased the penalties for organizing and participating in unsanctioned street rallies, holding show trials for select participants in the Bolotnaya Square rallies, tightening the

74 *Security*

definition of treason, and making it easier for the Kremlin to censor Internet sites it did not like (Gorenburg, 2013). The severe restrictions on assembly and protest at the Olympics were clearly an extension of Kremlin efforts to limit political unrest in the country; they fit well with the Olympic Charter's ban on political activity during the games. While the Olympics were relatively protest free, the performance group Pussy Riot, whose two most prominent members had been released from jail in a public relations amnesty just before the games, staged a few street performances in Sochi. In one prominent case, they were attacked by Cossack fighters who had been hired by the Russian authorities to monitor the situation outside of the games.

The deployment of the newest military technologies during the games also aimed to promote the export of Russian weaponry. Russia is perennially one of the biggest exporters of weapons in the world, holding 27 per cent of the market (President of Russia, 2014). During the games, Russian media advertised that the security package deployed in Sochi, including the Pantsyr-S1, would be sold to Brazil after the games for $1 billion, and would become a key element of the air defences during the 2014 FIFA World Cup and 2016 Summer Olympics there.[15] The negotiations between the Brazilian and Russian governments proceeded for several years and finally stopped after the West put sanctions on Russia. Instead, the Pantsyr-S1 and S-300 missile complexes were deployed in Crimea on the eve of the Russian annexation (Papchenkova, Tovkailo, & Vinogradova, 2014). According to Russian media, several of the same Pantsyr-S1 deployed in Sochi were later sold to the Syrian government and Syrian soldiers used them on June 22, 2015, to down a Turkish F-4 Phantom (Tuchkov, 2016). Part of the Olympics defence system remained in Sochi after the games.[16]

Two months after the games, Putin met with the Russian Commission for Military Technology Cooperation with Foreign States and announced that foreign orders for Russian weapons grew to $49 billion from $35 billion earlier in the year. He did not specify if the Sochi security arrangements helped increase the export of weapons. However, he specifically mentioned the S-300 and Pantsyr-S1 defence systems, which were deployed during Sochi, as 'undisputed leaders on the global market in terms of their technical and military characteristics, reliability and simplicity of use. We should build up capacity to manufacture the most in-demand air defense systems,' he said (President of Russia, 2014). A year after the games, Sergei Goreslavsky, the deputy CEO of Rosoboronexport, the Russian company that deals with the export of Russian weapons, announced that Russia was prepared to export the security package that proved effective during the Sochi games. The package included air defence, secure city, and radio systems.[17]

Conclusion

The security aspects of the Sochi games included four components. First, Russia successfully prevented a terrorist attack on the games. Second, it used the games to expand its military activities and exercises, facilitating a more aggressive posture as revolution began to brew in Ukraine. Third, it used the security measures to crack down on civil society and increase its overall ability to monitor Russian

Security   75

society. Finally, Russia used the Olympic security arrangements to advertise its newest military technology for export after the games.

In the counter-terrorism sphere, Russia successfully prevented a terrorist attack on the Sochi Olympics. The key to this success seems to have been a campaign aimed at killing terrorist leaders and cracking down on groups in society that supported the terrorist goals. The short-term result was that there was no violence at the games themselves, though some of the attacks were likely displaced to Volgograd, which suffered three deadly terrorist bombings in the months leading up to the games. While the emphasis on repressive measures secured the Olympics, the longer term consequences are less clear. Attacking the terrorists without addressing the underlying causes of the problems, Russia's traditional strategy for dealing with the North Caucasus, was likely to simply inflame the situation over time. Russia will continue to face terrorist attacks until conditions improve in its restive south. The use of soft power solutions has proven effective in some cases and could profitably be expanded over time.

On the military front, the games provided Putin an opportunity to concentrate forces in Sochi and to conduct ostentatious exercises in the Black Sea. The quick military victory in Georgia in 2008 and then the efforts protecting the Olympics, combined with Russia's ongoing military reforms, provided the Russian leadership with a feeling of confidence that likely helped make it possible for Putin to authorize the invasion of Ukraine. We discuss the details of that decision in the context of the Sochi Olympics in the next chapter.

The games provided the Russian authorities with the chance to dramatically increase their abilities to monitor civil society groups and other members of Russian society. While these new capabilities were developed to meet the specific needs of holding the Olympics in the volatile North Caucasus, they will remain as a part of the security forces' repertoire. While all Olympics seem to increase the ability of the state to monitor the activities of its own citizens, in Russian conditions the new tools simply added to an already heavily laden tool box of repression.

Finally, the Russian export of weapons increased after the Olympics, particularly the air defence system used during the games. Russia actively promoted the Sochi games' weaponry following the closing ceremonies, including an unsuccessful attempt to sell systems to Brazil for the 2014 World Cup and 2016 Rio de Janeiro games. Parts of the weapon systems deployed during the Sochi games were later used during the annexation of Crimea and the Syrian conflict.

Notes

1 Derailed Nevsky Express Train Was Blown Up – Law Enforcement Source, RIA Novosti (28 November 2009), at http://en.rian.ru/russia/20091128/157015151.html.
2 Srochnikov perebrosiat v Dagestan dlia okhrany Olimpiiskikh obektov (Conscripts Sent to Dagestan to Guard Olympic Venues), Lenta.ru (21 September 2010), at http://lenta.ru/news/2010/09/21/enemy.
3 Saakashvili: Gruziia khochet uchastvovat v podgotovke Olimpiady v Sochi (Saakashvili: Georgia Hopes to Participate in the Preparations for the Olympics in Sochi), Kavkazskii uzel (10 July 2008), at www.kavkaz-uzel.ru/articles/139019.

76 *Security*

4 Gruziia prosit MOK perenesti olimpiadu-2014 iz Sochi (Georgia Asks the IOC to Move the Olympics from Sochi), Kavkazskii uzel (20 November 2008), at www.kavkaz-uzel.ru/articles/144320.
5 Medvedev trebuet ne dopustit provokatsii pered olimpiadoi-2014 (Medvedev Demands that There Be No Provocations Before the 2014 Olympiad), RIA Novosti (18 February 2011) at http://ria.ru/society/20110218/335730959.html.
6 Putin: Rossiia obespokoena vozmozhnostiu razmesheniia PRO SShA v Gruzii (Putin: Russia Is Concerned About the Possibility that the United States Will Place Missile Defense Systems in Georgia), RIA Novosti (18 January 2012), at http://ria.ru/defense_safety/20120118/542707064.html.
7 Analiz vooruzhennykh sil Rossii (Analysis of the Armed Forces of Russia), Warfare.ru, at http://warfare.be/db/lang/rus/catid/264/linkid/1690/base/750/title/1721-zrp.
8 K okhrane Olimpiiskikh igr v Londone privlekut armiiu. Chas pik (16 December 2011), www.chaspik.spb.ru/world/k-oxrane-olimpijskix-igr-v-londone-privlekut-armiyu/.
9 Borodin, Iurii, Timur Gainutdinov, Kristina Ukolova, Iurii Belousov, Vladimir Sosnitsky, Oleg Pochiniuk, and Anna Potekhina. Medal' Za Vezhlivost'. http://dlib.eastview.com/browse/doc/43313889
10 58-ia Armiia poluchila novogo komanduiushego (The 58th Army Received a New Commander), Voennoe obozrenie (January 29, 2012), at http://topwar.ru/10617-naz nachili-novogo-komanduyuschego-58-oy-armieykotoraya-deystvuet-na-kavkaze.html.
11 Dlia posesheniia Sochi-2014 ponadobitsia Pasport Bolelshika (To Visit Sochi-2014, You Will Need a Spectator Pass), Newsland (14 December 2012), at http://newsland.com/news/detail/id/1091439/.
12 General Rules for Obtaining and Using the Spectator Pass, U 18 Worlds, at http://u18worlds2013.iihf.com/media/144265/Spectator-pass-ENG_RUS.pdf.
13 Nelishnie bilety. Kak popast na olimpiadu i pomoch Rossii v Sochi (Necessary Tickets: How to Get to the Olympics and Help Russia in Sochi), Kommersant-online (April 23, 2013), at www.kommersant.ru/doc/2172117.
14 General Rules for Obtaining and Using the Spectator Pass.
15 Brazil Hopes to Ink Pantsir-S1 Air Defense Deal With Russia by Mid-2015. 2015. *Sputnik*. January 28. http://sputniknews.com/military/20150128/1017436526.html; Russia and Brazil in the Final Stages of Talks for the Delivery of Russian Pantsir-S1 Air Defense System. 2013. *Army Recognition*. October 20. www.armyrecognition.com/october_2013_defense_industry_military_news_uk/russia_and_brazil_in_final_stages_of_talks_for_delivery_russian_pantsir-s1_air_defense_system_201013.html
16 DTP S Uchastiem Raketnogo Kompleksa Pantsyr-S1 Proizoshlo Pod Sochi. 2015. *Interfax Russia*. October 19. www.interfax-russia.ru/South/main.asp?id=663670
17 Rossia Predlagaet Na Export Ispytannuyi v Sochi Sistemu Bezopasnosti. 2015. RIA Novosti, March 3. http://ria.ru/defense_safety/20150302/1050538925.html

References

Baev, P.K. (2010). The Terrorism-Corruption Nexus in the North Caucasus. *PONARS Eurasia Policy Memo, 114*.
Barabanov, M. (2014). Changing the Force and Moving Forward after Georgia. In C. Howard & R. Pukhov (Eds), *Brothers Armed: Military Aspects of the Crisis in Ukraine*. Minneapolis MI: East View Press.
BBC. (2013, July 3). Umarov prizval ne dopustit provedeniia Olimiady v Sochi" (Umarov Called for Stopping the Olympics in Sochi). *BBC Russian Service*. Retrieved from www.bbc.co.uk/russian/russia/2013/07/130703_sochi_olympics_umarov.shtml (Accessed 7 October 2016).

Security 77

Bennett, C.J., & Haggerty, K.D. (Eds). (2011). *Security Games: Surveillance and Control at Mega-Events*. London: Routledge.

Bernhard, D., & Martin, A.K. (2014). Rethinking Security at the Olympics. In C.J. Bennett & K.D. Haggerty (Eds.), *Security Games: Surveillance and Control at Mega-Events* (pp. 21–35). New York: Routledge.

Borodin, I. (2016, June 8). Lichnyi' Protezhe Komandarma. *Krasnaia Zvezda*. Retrieved from www.redstar.ru/index.php/advice/item/29180-lichnyj-protezhe-komandarma (Accessed 7 October 2016).

Boyle, P., & Haggerty, K.D. (2012). Planning for the Worst: Risk, Uncertainty and the Olympic Games. *The British Journal of Sociology, 63*(2), 241–59.

Buribayev, A. (2010, March 29). Suicide Bombers Kill At Least Thirty-Eight in Moscow Subway. *Reuters*. Retrieved from www.reuters.com/article/2010/03/29/us-russia-metro-blast-idUSTRE62S0FM 20100329

Coaffee, J., & Johnston, L. (2007). Accommodating the Spectacle. In J.R. Gold & M.M. Gold (Eds), *Olympic Cities: City Agendas, Planning, and the World's Games, 1896–2016* (pp. 145–148). London: Routledge.

Dowd, A. (2010, 12 March). Vancouver Games Will See Balanced Budget: Organizers. *Reuters*. Retrieved from www.reuters.com/article/us-olympics-vancouver-idUSSGE62 L01T20100322 (Accessed 7 October 2016).

Evstifeev, D. (2013, October 21). Teraktom v Volgograge Bandity Otvetili Na Operatsii Spetssluzhb. *Izvestiia*. Retrieved from http://izvestia.ru/news/559227 (Accessed 7 October 2016).

Furmaniuk, A. (2010, September 19). Tessera del Tifoso: Pervye vpechatleniia (Tessera del Tifoso: First Impressions). *Calcio News*. Retrieved from http://calcionews.net/? p=8397 (Accessed 7 October 2016).

Furmaniuk, A. (2011, December 16). Vvedenie v Italii 'Pasporta Bolelshika' priznano nezakonnym ('Spectator Pass' Introduction to Italy Declared Illegal). *Calcio News*. Retrieved from http://calcionews.net/?p=16132 (Accessed 7 October 2016).

Gorenburg, D. (2013, August 5). Sochi Olympic Security Measures. *Russian Military Reform Blog*. Retrieved from http://russiamil.wordpress.com/2013/08/05/sochi-olympics-security-measures (Accessed 7 October 2016).

Government of the Russian Federation. (2013). Postanovlenie ot 08.11.2013 'Ob Osobennostiakh Okazaniia Uslug Sviazi i o Poriadke Vzaimodeistviia Operatorov Sviazi s Upolnomochennymi Gosudarstvennymi Organami, Osushshchestvliayushschimi Operanivno-Rozysknuiu Deatel'nost', Na Territorii g.Sochi v Period Provedeniia XXII Olimpiiskikh Zimnikh Igr i XI Paralimpiiskikh Zimnikh Igr 2014 Goda v g. Sochi.'. http://pravo.gov.ru:8080/page.aspx?67396

Gressel, G. (2015). *Russia's Quiet Military Revolution and What It Means for Europe*. London: European Council of Goreign Relations.

Gutterman, S. (2013, August 24). Critics Say Putin's Olympic Security Decree Violates Rights. *Reuters*. Retrieved from www.reuters.com/article/2013/08/24/olympics-russia-decree-idUSL6N0GP02520130824 (Accessed 7 October 2016).

Hahn, G.M. (2011). *Getting the Caucasus Emirate Right*. Washington: Center for Strategic & International Studies.

Heritage, T. (2014, January 20). Militant Islamist Video Threatens Winter Olympics. *Reuters*.

Houlihan, B., & Giulianotti, R. (2012). Politics and the London 2012 Olympics: The (in)security Games. *International Affairs, 88*(4), 701–17.

International Crisis Group. (2016). *The North Caucasus Insurgency and Syria: An Exported Jihad? No. 238*. Brussels: International Crisis Group.

78 *Security*

Ivanov, V. (2004, August 6). NATO okruzhilo Afiny 'Patriotami' (NATO Surrounded Athens with Patriots). *Nezavisimoe voennoe obozrenie*. Retrieved from http://nvo.ng.ru/notes/2004-08-06/8_athenes.html

Ivlent'eva, T. (2015, December 18). Kontrakty Temirkhana Saitova. *Kaspiets*. Retrieved from http://dlib.eastview.com/browse/doc/45941581 (Accessed 7 October 2016).

Karagiannis, E. (2014). The Russian Interventions in South Ossetia and Crimea Compared: Military Performance, Legitimacy and Goals. *Contemporary Security Policy*, *35*(3), 400–20.

Kramer, M. (2005). Guerrilla Warfare, Counterinsurgency, and Terrorism in the North Caucasus: The Military Dimension of the Russian-Chechen Conflict. *Europe-Asia Studies*, *57*(2), 209–90.

Large, D.C. (2012). *Munich 1972: Tragedy, Terror, and Triumph at the Olympic Games*. Lanham: Rowman & Littlefield.

Liss, A. (2013, December 20). Volgograd Blasts: IOC 'Confident' Games Will Be Safe. *BBC News*. Retrieved from www.bbc.com/news/world-europe-25551835 (Accessed 7 October 2016).

Memorial. (2016). *Kontrterror Na Severnom Kavkaze: Vsglyad Pravozaschitnikov. 2014 g. – Pervaya Polovina 2016 g*. Moscow: Memorial.

Mikhailov, A. (2015, May 13). Komu Streliat' iz Manlikhera. *Voenno-Promyshlenny Kur'er*. Retrieved from http://vpk-news.ru/articles/25170 (Accessed 7 October 2016).

Mikhailov, A. (2016, April 20). Boitsy Chetvertogo Izmereniia. *Voenno-Promyshlennyi' Kur'er*. Retrieved from http://vpk-news.ru/articles/30319 (Accessed 7 October 2016).

Miranovich, G. (2015). Bditel'nost' – Poniatie Konkretnoe. *Krasnaia Zvezda*. Retrieved from www.redstar.ru/index.php/2011-07-25-15-57-07/item/26606-bditelnost-ponyatie-konkretnoe

Moore, C. (2010). *Contemporary Violence: Postmodern War in Kosovo and Chechnya*. Manchester: Manchester University Press.

Moore, C., & Tumelty, P. (2008). Foreign Fighters and the Case of Chechnya: A Critical Assessment. *Studies in Conflict and Terrorism*, *31*(5), 412–33.

Moore, C., & Tumelty, P. (2009). Assessing Unholy Alliances in Chechnya: From Communism and Nationalism to Islamism and Salafism. *Journal of Communist Studies and Transition Politics*, *25*(1), 73–94.

Moyer, J. (2013, September 1). Should Washington Go for the Games? *The Washington Post*, p. B5.

Mukhin, V. (2011a, April 11). Abkhazskii front sochinskoi Olimpiady (The Abkhaz Front of the Sochi Olympiad). *Nezavisimaia gazeta*. Retrieved from www.ng.ru/nvo/2011-04-11/1_abhazia.html

Mukhin, V. (2011b, February 7). Voenno-Olimpiiskaia gruppirovka (The Military-Olympic Group). *Nezavisimaia gazeta*. Retrieved from www.ng.ru/regions/2011-02-07/1_group.html

Nichol, J., Halchin, E., Rollins, J. W., Tiersky, A., & Woehrel, S. (2014). *The 2014 Sochi Winter Olympics: Security and Human Rights Issues. R43383. Congressional Research Service Report*. Washington, DC: US Congressional Research Service.

No author. (2007, July 6). Russia, Georgia Praise Sochi Olympics as Peace Deal for the Caucasus. *RIA Novosti*. Retrieved from https://sputniknews.com/russia/20070706/68509015.html (Accessed 7 October 2016).

Papchenkova, M., Tovkailo, M., & Vinogradova, E. (2014, March 17). Skol'ko Stoit Krym. *Vedomosti*. Retrieved from www.vedomosti.ru/newspaper/articles/2014/03/17/skolko-stoit-krym (Accessed 7 October 2016).

Pasiakin, V. (2015a, July 28). Bol'she, Chem Prazdnik. *Flag Rodiny.* Retrieved from http://sc.mil.ru/files/morf/military/archive/%5B«FR»%5D%5B2015–07–21%5D.pdf

Pasiakin, V. (2015b, September 18). Na Strazhe Yuzhnykh Rubezhei. *Flag Rodiny.* Retrieved from http://sc.mil.ru/files/morf/military/archive/FR_2015_09_18.pdf (Accessed 7 October 2016).

Portnov, S. (2015, August 6). Krasnet' Za Podopechnykh Ne Pridetsia. *Shchit i Mech.*

President of Russia. (2010, May 15). Ukaz Prezidenta RF ot 14.05.2010 No. 594 'Ob obespechenii bezopasnosti pri provedenii XXII Olimpiiskikh zimnikh igr i XI Paralimpiiskikh zimnikh igr 2014 goda v Sochi' (Decree of the RF President of May 14, 2010, no. 594, On Supplying Security During the Conduct of the Twenty-Second Olympic Winter Games and the Eleventh Paralympic Winter Games in 2014 in Sochi). *Russian president's Web site.* Retrieved from http://graph.document.kremlin.ru/page.aspx?1;1263337

President of Russia. (2013a, August 23). Ukaz Prezidenta RF ot 19 avgusta 2013 g. No. 686 (Decree of the RF President from August 19, 2013, no. 686). *Rossiiskaia gazeta.* Retrieved from www.rg.ru/2013/08/23/bezopasnost-dok.html (Accessed 7 October 2016).

President of Russia. (2013b). Ukaz Prezudenta Possiiskoi Federatsii Ot 15.01.2013 g. No. 29 "O Gosudarstvennoi Komissii Po Podgotovke i Provedeniyu XXII Olimpiiskikh Zimnikh Igr i XI Paralimpiiskikh Zimnikh Igr 2014 Goda v g. Sochi.

President of Russia. (2014). Meeting of the Commission for Military Technology Cooperation with Foreign States. http://en.kremlin.ru/events/president/news/20865 (Accessed 7 October 2016).

Putin, V. (2014, January 19). Interview to Russian and Foreign Media. *Kremlin.ru.* Retrieved from http://en.kremlin.ru/events/president/news/20080(Accessed 7 October 2016).

Richards, A. (2011). Terrorism, the Olympics and Sport: Recent Events and Concerns for the Future. In P.F. Anthony Richards, and Andrew Silke (Ed.), *Terrorism and the Olympics: Major Event Security and Lessons for the Future.* London: Routledge.

Richards, A., Fussey, P., & Silke, A. (2011). Towards an Understanding of Terrorism and the Olympics. In P.F. Anthony Richards, and Andrew Silke (Eds), *Terrorism and the Olympics: Major Event Security and Lessons for the Future.* London: Routledge.

Ryzhkov, S. (2013, April 1). Russia Not Obliged to Notify West of War Games-Ministry. *RIA Novosti.* Retrieved from https://sputniknews.com/military/20130401/180382997/Russia-Not-Obliged-to-Notify-West-of-War-Games---Ministry.html (Accessed 7 October 2016).

Schmid, A.P. (Ed.). (2011). *The Routledge Handbook of Terrorism Research.* London: Routledge.

Sochi 2014. (2007). Sochi Candidature File 'Sochi 2014 Candidate City: Gateway to the Future'. web.archive.org/web/20100103043040/http://sochi2014.com/sch_questionnaire

Sokirianskaia, E. (2013, December 5). Winter Games, Caucasian Misery. *The New York Times.* Retrieved from http://nytimes.com/2013/12/06/opinion/winter-games-caucasian-misery.html (Accessed 7 October 2016).

Soldatov, A., Borogan, I., & Walker, S. (2013, October 6). As Sochi Olympic Venues Are Built, So Are Kremlin's Surveillance Networks. *The Guardian.* Retrieved from www.theguardian.com/world/2013/oct/06/sochi-olympicvenues-kremlin-surveillance (Accessed 7 October 2016).

Sudolskii, M. (2011, May 28). Bezopasnost Olimpiiskikh Igr v Sochi Budut Obespechivat Bolee 40 Tysiach Sotrudnikov MVD i Voennosluzhashikh Vnutrennikh Voisk" (Security at the Olympic Games in Sochi Will Be Provided by Forty Thousand Employees of the Ministry of Internal Affairs and the Soldiers of the Interior Forces). *IA Oruzhie Rossii.*

80 *Security*

Retrieved from www.arms-expo.ru/news/archive/mihail-suhodol-skiy-bezopasnost-olimpiyskih-igr-v-sochi-budut-obespechivat-bolee-40-tysyach-sotrudnikov-mvd-i-voennosluzhaschih-vnutrennih-voysk31-05-2008-13-13-00/ (Accessed 7 October 2016).

Tovkailo, M. (2011). Tsena Spokoistviia (The Price of Peace). *Vedomosti*. Retrieved from www.vedomosti.ru/lifestyle/articles/2011/01/31/cena_spokojstviya (Accessed 7 October 2016).

Tuchkov, V. (2016, March 14). Pantsyr-S1 vs M6 Bradley Linebacker. *Svobodnaya Pressa*. Retrieved from http://svpressa.ru/war21/article/144260/ (Accessed 7 October 2016).

Wills, D., & Moore, C. (2008). Securitising the Caucasus: From Political Violence to Place Branding in Chechnya. *Place Branding and Public Diplomacy, 4*(3), 252–62.

Yeginsu, C., & Callimachi, R. (2016, June 30). Turkey Says Airport Bombers Were From Kyrgyzstan, Russia and Uzbekistan. *The New York Times*. Retrieved from www.nytimes.com/2016/07/01/world/europe/istanbul-airport-attack-turkey.html (Accessed 7 October 2016).

5 International issues
Circassians, the former Soviet countries, and the West

Even as he delivered the speech that clinched Russia's bid to host the 2014 Winter Olympics, Putin made a political mistake provoking the Sochi games' first international problem, one that became known as the Circassian question (Goble, 2014). While reflecting on Sochi's history in his speech to the IOC (Putin, 2007), Putin failed to mention the Circassians, the indigenous people of the region, in spite of the fact that Sochi was once the capital of Circassia and the Russian conquest of the Black Sea coast, in 1864, resulted in the mass killing and exodus of Circassians from the region (King, 2008b; Richmond, 2013). Putin's omission was a mistake characteristic of an authoritarian leader, similar to China's decision to ignore the Tibet problem during the 2008 Beijing Olympics. By contrast, the Australian and Canadian leaders avoided such mistakes as they honoured their 'First Nations' during the 2000 Sydney and 2012 Vancouver games.

As Russia planned to showcase its world-class athletes, culture, and economic development at the games in Sochi, signifying the country's increasingly high international profile, it also exposed its domestic political system and an array of unresolved issues with its fellow post-Soviet neighbours to international scrutiny. The honour of presenting the Olympics is a challenge and opportunity for the host country, which must be ready for a number of unexpected, if inevitable, domestic and foreign trials. Criticism and controversy have accompanied the run-up to every Olympic games. No doubt, some foreign countries and NGOs were trying to capitalize on the globalized nature of the Olympics to urge the Kremlin to come to terms with troublesome topics, from the Russian occupation of Georgian territories to LGBT rights and the scandal surrounding asylum-seeker Edward Snowden. What patterns emerged in the Kremlin's responses to major issues and challenges? How did the Kremlin handle increasing global scrutiny as the games came closer?

This chapter examines three different approaches that the Kremlin exercised toward the international challenges during the run-up to the Sochi games. First, the Kremlin tried to deal with domestic issues by ignoring them even though some of them attracted international attention. As a case study, we will look into the well-researched history of Sochi (King, 2008b; Richmond, 2013), so unwisely ignored by Putin, and then follow the development of the Circassian question in connection with the Olympics. Instead of recognizing Putin's mistake and repairing

82 International issues

the damage, the Kremlin tried to deal with it by working to silence the problem. Linked to the Olympics, however, the Circassian question developed from a domestic problem into an international issue. The games had a mobilizing and politicizing effect on the Circassian movement within Russia and among the diaspora (Hansen, 2013).

Second, while working to quash domestic issues, the Kremlin aggressively positioned itself as the dominant political, economic, and military actor among the former Soviet countries (Freire & Kanet, 2012). In August 2008, Russia invaded Georgia, a neighbouring state that bordered Sochi. In the conflict, Russian troops occupied two breakaway Georgian territories, Abkhazia and South Ossetia, and the Kremlin recognized their independence (Asmus, 2010; Cornell & Starr, 2009; King, 2008a; Mankoff, 2011). After the August war, Moscow refused to compromise with Tbilisi and firmly withstood all challenges, including termination of diplomatic relations between the two states, the Georgian parliament's recognition of the nineteenth-century Circassian Genocide, and Georgia's threat to boycott the games and appeal to IOC for cancelling them. No matter how aggressive Russia was toward Georgia, the Kremlin managed to localize the conflict by letting the European leaders take the initiative to mediate between Moscow and Tbilisi and all post-conflict resolution meetings between the Russians and Georgians took place in Brussels. Later, when the situation in Ukraine began to spin out of control, Putin and his closest inner circle, all former KGB agents, gathered on the morning of the Olympic closing ceremony and made the decision to invade Crimea (Myers, 2014a). Following its victory in its bid to host the Sochi games, Russian foreign policy, including wars with both Georgia and Ukraine, indicated a major shift in Moscow's relations with the former Soviet republics, confirming the formation of a new and more assertive Russian policy in the region and aiming to prevent further NATO enlargement eastwards and regain geo-political influence regionally (Biersack & O'Lear, 2014; Karagiannis, 2014).

Third, the Kremlin exercised self-restraint in its policy toward the West, a sharp contrast to Russia's aggressive behaviour in Eurasia. Rather, Moscow's policy toward the West was responsive but never preemptive. Exercising a 'symmetric response' policy, Moscow aimed to mirror Western countries' diplomacy, however in reality, the Russian response was always more restrained and openly demonstrated that the Kremlin would be happy to overcome its differences with the West. At the same time, the Kremlin constantly engaged in challenging the West through human right violations of the rights of its own citizens and through regional military aggression (Lucas, 2014). Moscow seemed to be constantly seeking to find the 'red line' in relations with the West, and always stopped short from crossing the point of no return with the European countries and the US.

The Kremlin successfully kept those three approaches apart for almost seven years in the run-up to the Sochi Olympics. It seemed as if nothing could affect the glory of the Olympics, including the decision by many Western leaders not to attend the games, international and domestic protests against holding the games in Sochi, and even a war with neighbouring Georgia. Yet, Moscow's political

International issues   83

mistakes began piling up as soon as it won its bid in 2007. During the games, all
the tension that had accumulated for years exploded in the most unattractive way.
First, Moscow could not pretend to ignore the Circassian movement anymore, and
in the middle of the Olympics, Putin issued a statement blaming the US for using
the Circassian issue against Russia, going as far as calling it a new form of containment theory similar to Cold War era policies (Anishchuk, 2014). Second, Putin
suddenly disappeared in the middle of the games, and plotted, with a group of ex-
KGB generals, the invasion of Crimea on the morning of the closing ceremony.
Russia, however, failed to finish the war against Ukraine as fast and effectively
as the Russian-Georgian war six years earlier. Also, the Kremlin could not keep
the war against Ukraine localized inside the post-Soviet agenda and it became an
international problem. Third, and most important, the Kremlin lost its political
balance, crossed the red line with the West in the case of Ukraine, and reached
the point of no return, after which the European Union and the US imposed
sanctions on Russia (Black & Johns, 2016). Thus, the Kremlin's elaborate seven-
year policy of keeping separate domestic issues, post-Soviet ambitions, and good
relations with the West came to an end on the very last day of the games. Instead
of benefiting from the Olympics, Russia found itself in the worst international crisis
since the end of the Cold War.

Battles over Sochi: From a Circassian capital to a Russian resort

Circassians are the major ethnic group of Russia's Caucasus, with a population
of approximately 800,000 in Russia and between five to seven million living in
the diaspora. Despite having played a critical role in the history of Russia's
expansion into the Caucasus in the nineteenth century, Circassians were largely
unfamiliar to the public before the Sochi games. The Sochi Olympics touched a
nerve among Circassians for several reasons. By an irony of history, the 2014 games
marked the 150th anniversary of the Circassian defeat at the hands of Russia
in 1864. In that final battle, after more than a century of fighting, hundreds of
thousands of Circassians were killed by the czar's imperial forces. The memory
of this defeat was kept keenly alive in the Circassian community across the decades.
Every year on May 21, Circassians around the world light 101 candles and
observe a minute of silence in memory of the 101-year war. Sochi itself was the
site of the war's last clashes and its port was the place from which the Circassians were deported to the Ottoman Empire. Krasnaya Polyana, the centre of the
Olympic skiing events, marked the spot on 21 May 1864 where a parade of Russian
troops celebrated the end of the war. Sochi was named after the Circassian ethnic
group Shache, which had lived there until 1864. It was also the last capital of
independent Circassia.

From its founding, Sochi was the capital of Ubykh Principality, part of the Circassian Confederation on the lands of today's Krasnodar Krai and Adygea. The Ubykh
Principality was traditionally under the political influence of the Ottoman Empire;
almost every Ubykh family had Turkish relatives. Early in the nineteenth century,

84 *International issues*

Russian sources stated that the Ubykhs 'had a democratic society and practiced Islam' (Caucasus Archeographic Commission, p. V10:2331).

The first contacts between Sochi and Russia took place after the 1829 Adrianople Treaty, according to which the Ottoman Empire recognized Circassia as part of the Russian Empire's sphere of influence. To gather information about the new territory, Russia sent intelligence officer Fyodor Tornau to Circassia on a reconnaissance mission. While in Circassia, he met with the prince of Sochi, Ali Oblagu, who governed over 10,000 citizens (Tornau, 1864, p. 134). Tornau, however, failed to arrange a meeting with the leader of the Ubykh Principality, Dogomuko Berzek, whose headquarters sat higher up the Sochi River. Berzek was one of the most influential figures in the Circassian Confederation at the time. His two British advisers, James S. Bell and John A. Longworth, called him 'a Circassian George Washington' for his anti-colonial resistance (Bell, 1840, pp. 344–346; Longworth, 1840).

In September 1837, the Russian Emperor Nicolas I sailed to Circassia to personally inspect the shores of the Black Sea. After the trip, the czar commanded: 'We need to control Sochi and Tuapse. Accordingly, the neighbouring villages should be destroyed.'[1] Following his order, on 24 April 1838, an 8,000-man Russian regiment disembarked at Sochi. Prince Oblagu organized the defence of the city. The Russians occupied a hill next to Sochi and erected a fortress, named Alexandriia, after the Russian czarina Alexandra Fyodorovna, and later, renamed Navaginsky, after the regiment that occupied it.

The establishment of the fortress caused a controversy between Circassian and Russian historians about when to celebrate the founding of Sochi. The city administration annually organized its celebration of the 'Sochi birthday', including the 174th birthday in 2012, counting since the establishment of the Russian fortress. Those celebrations provoked protests by Circassian NGOs, and the leaders of the Shapsug Circassian Council appealed for clarification from the Russian Academy of Sciences' Institute of History, receiving an answer that the year of 1838 was not the year Sochi was founded, but the date of the Russian invasion into the Circassian capital. Nevertheless, the Sochi administration continued celebrating the day in spite of Circassians' protests. However, in 2013, on the eve of the Sochi games, the city administration avoided specifying any historical dates and acknowledged the day just as 'City Day', for the first time not stressing 1838 as the year when the city was founded and not calling it the 175th anniversary.[2]

The Russian fortress at Sochi was guarded and supplied by the Russian fleet, anchored in the Black Sea by the mouth of the Sochi River, until it was destroyed by a storm on 30 May 1838. The news of this catastrophe found its way even into the American newspapers of the time, with Rhode Island's *Newport Mercury* reporting on September 8:

> It was believed that no less than 30 Russian ships had been put hors du combat by the hurricane. The garrison of the fort Sotcha, having made two sorties to protect the wrecks of the two corvettes, was attacked by the natives, and

International issues   85

compelled to retreat with the loss of 1,000 men out of 1,100 of which the party had consisted.

The Circassian forces under the command of Berzek constantly kept the Russian fortress under siege. Nicolas I did not take kindly to the 'Circassian George Washington's' activities and offered a reward 'to anyone who would assassinate him, and carry his head into any of the forts'. Bell, who had the utmost respect for Berzek, witnessed and described how a letter with

> the promise of reward for murder was handed, open as it had been received, to the Hadji [Berzek], in the midst of the congress. Immediately after it had been read, Kerantuk – a young and near relative of the Hadji and every way worthy of the relationship – got hold of it, tore it into three fragments, and threw it in wordless but bitter indignation upon the ground. I interposed for its preservation, explaining to them its value as a proof, in other countries, of the extreme wickedness of the Russian character. (Bell, 1840, p. 347)

In October 1841, another Russian regiment reached Sochi – the first travelling by land – and reported, 'We are in the heart of Ubykh land' (Caucasus Archeographic Commission, Vol. 9, p. 5132). The advance, however, turned into a military disaster; the *Newport Mercury* reported on 26 February 1842,

> of the autumn campaign of the Russians against the Circassians and of [the Russians'] defeat at Sotcha, where some 500 were slain. It is believed that the Russians have lost some 8,000 men, mostly by disease. The Crimean hospitals are filled with the sick.

Losses on the Ubykh side were significant as well. Of the Berzek family 11 members were killed, and his son was wounded. After the bloody battle for Sochi, the London *Times* on 18 January 1842 demanded, 'The European Powers ought by all means to interfere to stop the useless and demoralizing effusion of blood.' Dogomukho Berzek died on 2 July 1846, on his way home from his last pilgrimage to Mecca, and his nephew, Kerantuk Berzek, took over the Ubykh Principality. The new ruler organized the 1848 Adagum Assembly, at which the Ubykh Principality became the leading member of the Circassian Confederation. Thus, Sochi became the new capital of the Confederation, replacing Tuapse.

In the meantime, the Russian fortress next to Sochi remained a constant threat to the new capital. In February 1852, the Russian troops pulled off a successful military manoeuvre and managed to burn down the city of Sochi. However, the success was short-lived and, during the 1853–6 Crimean War, the European powers forced Russia to destroy all its fortresses on the Circassian coast, including the one in Sochi. After the Crimean War, as the London *Times* reported on 28 February 1856, Circassian ambassadors travelled from Sochi to Constantinople to request the recognition and guarantee of the independence of their country by England and France. The Europeans, however, did not satisfy the request.

86 *International issues*

Eventually, the 1856 Paris Treaty allowed Russia to concentrate significant military forces near Sochi. As a result, 300,000 Russian soldiers began a campaign against Circassia. Each year, the Russians lost 30,000 soldiers and one-sixth of the state's budget was spent on the war (Milyutin, 2004, p. 198). By contrast, the Circassian Confederation had up to 80,000 well-equipped soldiers and 50,000 reservists (Caucasus Archeographic Commission, Vol. 12, p. 8493).

As the Russian military forces exceeded the Circassian forces by many times, the Confederation faced the necessity of creating a more efficient state (Manning, 2009). On 13 June 1861, Circassia became a federative republic, with three federal districts: Ubykh, Shapsug, and Natukhai. Fifteen members were elected to the parliament, which was established in Sochi. The *New York Times*, on 4 September 1861 announced that the 'Circassians proclaimed a Republic.'

Circassian political leaders were aware that the republic could not long struggle against the Russian Empire without international military support. The first decree of the Sochi parliament was to accept Russia's patronage while maintaining Circassia's status as an independent state. The speaker of the parliament and leader of the Confederation, Kerantuk Berzek, requested a meeting with the Russian czar, Alexander II. While preparing for the negotiations, Russian military minister, Dmitri Milyutin, directed the Russian czar's attention to the difference in the two sides' understanding of the subject of the negotiations. The Circassian side was 'asking for *peace*, despite our demand for *submission*' (Milyutin, 2004, p. 198) (italics in the original). The minister presumed that the Circassians had a 'secret intention to draw out the struggle until a new European war, which is eagerly anticipated by our enemies, domestic and foreign' (Caucasus Archeographic Commission, Vol. 12, p. 9335). Alexander II and Berzek met in a Russian military camp on the Fars River on 16 September 1861. As a representative of the Circassian people, Berzek 'asked His Majesty to accept them as Russian citizens'. Alexander II replied that he 'was very glad to see them as his citizens' but demanded that the Circassians clear their country and migrate either within Russia or to Turkey (Caucasus Archeographic Commission, Vol. 12, p. 934). Given the conflicting demands, the Russian-Circassian negotiations proved to be fruitless.

A year later, the Circassian parliament sent an ambassador, Ismail Dziash, to London with a petition requesting military assistance from Britain to aid in Circassia's war against Russia. One of the British MPs, David Urquhart, voiced his support for the Circassians, comparing their war to the recent Polish insurrection in Russia, 'Circassia offers [to Great Britain] a second Poland which English ships can reach' (Urquhart, 1863, p. 65). Urquhart became the supreme international supporter of the Circassians (King, 2007). However, international complications prevented the British Parliament from offering real support to Circassia.

Fearing interference from European powers, the Russian government made a final push to resolve the Circassian question. War Minister Dmitri Milyutin openly stated in 1863, 'if the mountaineers cannot be civilized, they have to be exterminated.' Recent research has revealed documents showing evidence that high-ranking Russian decision makers were prepared to commit mass murder. Scholar

International issues 87

Walter Richmond quotes general field marshal Aleksandr Bariatinskii, an active participant in the Russian–Caucasus Wars, as saying, 'We must assume that we will need to exterminate the mountaineers before they agree to our demands' (Kreiten, 2009; Richmond, 2013, p. 71).

The Russian army moved toward Sochi burning every settlement to ashes on its way. The Russians and the Circassians clashed in their final battles, the last of which took place next to a destroyed ancient Christian monastery. Ivan Drozdov, a Russian officer who participated in the fighting, wrote in his memoirs, 'A disaster of such a scale has rarely befallen mankind. . . . The entire north-east shore of the Black Sea was covered with corpses and dying people' (Drozdov, 1877, pp. 257, 248). On May 21, Prince Mikhail Nikolaevich held a parade in Krasnaya Polyana to celebrate Russia's victory over Circassia. *The New York Times* called the Circassians 'a Murdered Nation' (23 August 1879). Only 10 per cent of the Circassians remained in the Caucasus. About half of a million were deported to Turkey. The rest were killed or starved to death during the war. According to Russian registration records, 74,567 citizens of Sochi fled to Turkey together with their leader, Kerantuk Berzek (Berzhe, 1882).

The tragedy for the Circassian people did not end in 1864. Richmond's book, *Circassian Genocide* (Richmond, 2013, pp. 98, 114, 126, 141, 169), describes how most survivors had to leave their homeland and become 'a homeless nation' scattered around the world, including in Syria, 'the Siberia of Turkey', and in Turkey under a regime with the ideology, 'Speaking Circassian is Forbidden'. Those who stayed behind eventually were doomed to 'slow death under the Soviets'. In the last chapter of his book, Richmond analyses the Putin regime's projects to conceal the Circassians' tragic history, leading up to the 2014 Winter Olympics and states, 'Today, the battle over Sochi continues.'

After the Russian conquest, Sochi remained abandoned for decades, and later, gradually turned into a resort. The first small sanatorium, Kavkazskaya Riviera, opened in 1909 and Sochi became an official Russian settlement in 1917. The independent Democratic Republic of Georgia annexed Sochi in 1918 (Welt, 2014), but later, the Bolsheviks re-captured Georgia, and Sochi became a Russian town. A few thousand Shapsugs, a Circassian ethic group, resettled next to Sochi and established the Shapsug National District in 1924. Stalin, however, abolished the District in 1945 and renamed its main town Lazarevskoe, after Russian admiral Mikhail Lazarev, a commander of the Russian Black Sea Fleet in the 1830s, notorious for destroying coastal Circassian villages. At the time of the 2014 Olympics, about 15,000 Circassian Shapsugs lived in Lazarevskoe. The Circassians demanded the restoration of the Shapsug National District (1924–45), changing the name of the town to Psyshu, the historical Circassian name, and removing Mikhail Lazarev's statue from the central square of the town.

In Soviet times, Joseph Stalin made it his family tradition to spend most of his holidays in Sochi (Alliluyeva, 1967). Stalin also dispersed the remaining Circassians among six regions of the Russian Soviet Federative Socialist Republic – the republics of Adygea, Kabardino-Balkaria, Karachay-Cherkessia, and North Ossetia as well as the ethnic Russian-dominated Stavropol Krai and Krasnodar Krai of

88 *International issues*

the North Caucasus. Though all Circassians identified themselves as one people, Soviet official terminology divided them among different ethnic terms, mostly depending on a territorial definition and enforced two different alphabets, causing a dialectal split in the language (Tsutsiev, 2014).

Sochi slowly developed into a resort during the Soviet era as planners erected massive neoclassical buildings to house state sanatoria along the coast. Post-Stalin Soviet leaders, however, favoured Crimea for their vacations, and Sochi remained neglected until the Soviet Union fell apart and Russia lost Crimea to Ukraine. In the post-Soviet era, Putin favoured Sochi, and made it his second most frequented city after Moscow. Between 2000 and 2014, Putin spent more than 300 days in Sochi,[3] which unofficially gained the title of Russia's summer capital, thanks to the many official domestic and international meetings and events held there by the Russian president. During his time in the city, Putin stayed in the presidential residence, Bocharov Ruchei, built for Stalin in 1934.

The Circassian dimension of the Sochi Olympics

After Russia had applied for holding the Winter Olympics and before it won the bid, Circassian activists supported the idea of convening the games in Sochi with the hope that the organizers would acknowledge the fact that Sochi used to be Circassian territory a century and half earlier. Their hopes, however, were crushed by Putin's speech to the IOC, when the Russian leader eliminated the Circassians from Sochi's history (Putin, 2007). Putin's speech launched the Circassian anti-Sochi movement (Goble, 2014). According to the non-governmental organization (NGO) Adyge Khase of the Adygea Republic, during the night after Putin's speech, they received phone calls from Circassians in Russia and among the diaspora who were upset by what they had heard.[4] The next morning, Arambi Khapai, a three time world champion in martial arts (sambo), made a statement that the organizers of the Sochi Olympics 'deleted the Circassians from history' and announced, 'I am against holding the Olympics in Sochi.'[5] Other Circassian NGOs in Russia and all over the world made similar statements and started the first international campaign against holding the 2014 Winter Olympics in Sochi. Circassian activists in the homeland, however, had to restrict their demands and their activities, being under pressure from the Russian special services. Circassians in Russia became isolated from the international movement and regarded the Circassian issue as an internal Russian problem, focusing on further developing Circassian culture, language, and political rights inside the regions where they lived, without entering into the dangerous sphere of Russian federal or international politics.

Circassian politicians and businessmen initially hoped that investments in Sochi would have a positive effect on the neighbouring Circassian republics of Kabardino-Balkaria, Adygea, and Karachay-Cherkessia.[6] The presidents of Kabardino-Balkaria and Adygea argued that the republics should have a chance to participate in the Olympics through three important projects: hosting part of the games in the Elbrus (Kabardino-Balkaria) and Lago-Naki (Adygea) mountains and participating in other economic projects in Sochi to develop the overall economy of the North Caucasus; building a road that would transform the region into one large mountain-and-sea resort, where tourists could swim in the Black Sea and then drive half a day to ski on the slopes of Mount Elbrus; and including Circassian elements in the Sochi Olympic symbols to spread information about the Circassians throughout the world. But the Kremlin did not follow up on any of these initiatives.

The Circassian diaspora was more active in protesting against the games. Nearly 90 per cent of the global Circassian population lives outside Russia, mostly in the states of the former Ottoman Empire – mainly Turkey, Syria, and Jordan – to which they were deported in the nineteenth century. As a share of the total Circassian population, the Circassian diaspora is the largest in the world. It is also the second largest diaspora from Russia, after the 25-million strong ethnic Russian diaspora itself (Besleney, 2014).

Circassian activists in the diaspora strongly opposed holding the games in Sochi on the grounds that mass killings had taken place at the sites where the Olympic venues were planned to be built. On 23 July 2007, 12 organizations in Turkey established the Organization Committee of Sochi – the Land of Genocide, and signed an appeal to the International Olympic Committee to cancel the Sochi Olympics. While officially ignoring the Circassian issue, the Kremlin, however, responded in KGB style. A prominent Circassian Turkish activist, Cihan Candemir, was arrested by the customs service in Sochi and kept in custody for five days, without any explanation, though he did not sign the letter. His release coincided with the International Olympic Committee's answer to the Circassian NGO's letter, promising to look into the ecological and social implications of the Sochi Olympics, but avoiding a direct answer to the request to cancel them (Zhemukhov, 2012).

Circassian American activists in New Jersey played a special role in the anti-Sochi movement (Persson, 2013). They established a broad international campaign, No Sochi 2014, including the Sochi–Land of Genocide movement, uniting 30 Circassian organizations, and developing '14 Reasons to Oppose the Sochi Olympics'. On 4 October 2007, Circassian Americans appealed to Putin to cancel the games in Sochi and recognize the Circassian Genocide, but did not get an answer. On the same day, Circassians in the United States and Turkey organized demonstrations in front of the Russian consulates in New York and Istanbul with the slogan 'Free Circassia Now.' While Circassians in the homeland regarded the anti-Sochi movement as an internal Russian issue, Circassians in the diaspora claimed that the Circassian issue was an international one. This conceptual problem was addressed at a conference, 'Russia and the Circassians: Internal Problem or International Matter?' organized at the Harvard Kennedy School (Tlis, 2007).

The 2010 Winter Olympics in Vancouver fully revealed the Kremlin's policy of ignoring the Circassian element in connection with Sochi. As part of the indigenous element of the Vancouver games, Russia sent a Cossack folk dance group to Canada, even though numerous Circassian groups had expressed their

90 *International issues*

readiness to participate. It became clear that the organizers of the Sochi games would block the Circassian element of the upcoming Olympics. In response, the New Jersey-based Circassian Cultural Institute organized a meeting in Vancouver with a message to the world: 'If you let the 2014 games go on as planned in Russia, you'll be skiing on the graves of our oppressed ancestors.'

The activity of the campaign was based on the idea that the Sochi Olympics represented the Circassians' last chance to reclaim their past and if the Olympics went forward,

> it erases our people, it erases the crime that has been done because the whole world is saying 'okay' to Russia, the whole world is saying 'nothing happened here and we are going to come here and celebrate peace between the nations.'
> (Alexander, 2010)

The Vancouver demonstration gave a new impulse to the Circassian movement in Russia in their demands to include Circassian elements in the 2014 Olympics. The demonstration brought to Circassians' attention the way the Canadian organizers of the Vancouver games connected to the ideological foundation of the Olympics showing respect for the indigenous peoples of Canada who were called the 'First Nations' (Goble, 2010). The Circassians in Russia addressed the Olympic organizing committee on various occasions, offering to include elements of Circassian culture in the opening ceremony of the games. They cited the examples of the 2000 Sydney Olympics and the 2010 Vancouver Olympics, at which references to the aboriginals were included in the opening ceremonies. But these attempts were ignored. On 24 March 2010, the Parliament of Adygea spoke with unusual criticism of Russian federal policy, expressing that to our

> great sorrow the state and civil structures absolutely ignore the history and culture of the Circassians, the indigenous people of Black Sea shore. The Circassian element has been fully ignored during the solemn transition of the Olympic Fire from Vancouver to Sochi.[7]

In response, the Russian Olympic Committee (ROC) agreed that Circassian elements should be included at Sochi, however, the ROC never fulfilled its promise.

Instead, the Kremlin pursued its policy of silencing the Circassian issue (Markedonov, 2014). In the same way, the Kremlin ignored the Parliament of Israel when, on 6 April 2008, it fulfilled the request of the Circassian community in Israel and established May 21 as an official Day of Memory and Sorrow for the Circassian People.

On the eve of the 147th anniversary of the Circassian Genocide, two Circassian American NGOs appealed separately to the Russian and Georgian parliaments. The Circassian Association of California appealed to the Russian State Duma with a 'Program to Save and Rehabilitate the Circassian Culture and Nation' (Cicek, 2011). The Russian parliament, however, did not respond. Meanwhile, the

International issues 91

Circassian Cultural Institute appealed to the Georgian parliament to recognize the Circassian genocide. On 20 May 2011, the Georgian parliament voted to recognize the nineteenth-century killings and deportations of ethnic Circassians by tsarist Russia as genocide (Barry, 2011).

The Kremlin-controlled Russian media ignored the Circassian anti-Sochi protests. Annually on May 21, Circassian activists held demonstrations in front of the Russian consulates in the United States, Germany, Turkey, and Israel with the slogan, 'Stop the Sochi Olympics of 2014.' One of the authors of this book (Sufian Zhemukhov) witnessed three Circassian demonstrations in Istanbul on 21 May 2012, including two in front of the Russian consulate. Two more demonstrations took place the same day in different parts of Turkey. The Russian consulate in Turkey and the Russian media ignored all five demonstrations. At the same time, Zhemukhov participated in a conference on the 'Future of the Caucasus', sponsored by the Istanbul administration. Strangely enough, the Russian Ministry of Foreign Affairs officially protested the conference, but never mentioned the five demonstrations. Accordingly, the Kremlin-controlled Russian media mentioned the academic conference in a negative light, but completely ignored the demonstrations.

During the opening ceremony, Russian police arrested 37 Circassian activists who gathered in Nalchik, the capital of Kabardino-Balkaria. The demonstrators were not so much protesting against the games, as seeking to draw attention to the historic grievances of their nation (Myers, 2014b). To protest the Nalchik arrests, the Circassian diaspora took to the streets in New York and Istanbul.

In Sochi, the Kremlin allowed Circassians to present a folklore exhibition in a Sochi park, though it prohibited all other Circassian elements from the games. A world-class Circassian athlete, Murat Kardanov, Olympic wrestling champion in the 2000 Sydney games, participated in the exhibition, and that was as close he could get to the opening ceremony. The organizers never invited Kardanov to join other Russian Olympic champions who carried Olympic torches during the opening ceremony, nor did they invite other Circassian Olympic gold medal athletes, including Aslanbek Khushtov (2008 Beijing wrestling champion), Elena Akhaminova (1980 Moscow volleyball champion), Mukharbi Kirzhinov (1972 Munich heavy lifting champion) and Boris Shukhov (1972 Munich bicycling champion). It remains an unanswered question why the organizers did not invite even one of the six Circassian Olympic champions to participate in the opening ceremony, a measure that would have softened the Circassian discourse surrounding the games (Akopov & Volkov, 2013). It is true that all Circassian Olympic champions won their gold medals in summer games. The organizers, however, explained that they did not restrict themselves to choosing only winter athletes. As Konstantin Ernst, the creative producer and scenarist of the opening ceremony stated:

> We chose first of all the greatest athletes known to the whole world. That was our main motive. People who watch the opening ceremony on TV want to see celebrities . . . And it didn't matter if the athletes represented Winter or Summer kinds of sports. (Gal'kevich, 2014)

92   International issues

The Kremlin's policy of ignoring and blocking the Circassian question did not reduce the pressure brought to bear by the domestic and international protests of the Circassian activists. During the games, Putin finally broke his silence and engaged in an emotional discussion of the Circassian issue at a meeting with the Public Council for the Preparation of the 2014 Winter Olympics on February 10. A Circassian activist from Sochi, Mejid Chechukh, was invited to the meeting, though he was not a member of the Public Council. Chechukh was provided with an opportunity to thank Putin personally for allowing local Circassian activists to set up a folklore exhibition in a Sochi park during the games. In response, Putin announced that the West used the Circassian issue as an instrument in a new strategy of 'containment' (*sderzhivanie*), referring to the Cold War era policy. (The Kremlin's official English translation incorrectly used the term 'deterrence'.)

> A theory took shape in 'cold war' times– it was called the deterrence theory. This theory and practical actions were aimed at hindering the development of the Soviet Union. Unfortunately, now we are seeing the same thing – the remains of this deterrence theory tend to come out into the open here and there. Whenever Russia demonstrates any positive development, the appearance of a new strong player, of competition is bound to cause concern in the economy, in politics and in the security sphere. We see attempts to deter Russia here and there. Unfortunately, this had to do with the Olympic project and the Circassian factor was used as an instrument. However, frankly speaking, as soon as I realised that such attempts are being made I did not have any doubt that this was a futile attempt. I know what the mood is among the Circassians, I know the leaders of the Circassian organisations personally, and I know what their attitude is to both their native land and to their home country – Russia. It was obvious for me that this had no prospect. (Putin, 2014)

Some experts saw in Putin's speech a demonstration of divide-and-rule politics and a tendency to dismiss the Circassian complaints by claiming that moderate and mainstream elements of the Circassians did not subscribe to the anti-Olympics activism (Petersson & Vamling, 2015). Indeed, Putin's belief in the 'mood' among the Circassians did not prevent an increase in anti-Circassian repressions during and after the Olympics. If before the games the Kremlin ignored the activities on the annual Circassian Mourning Day of May 21, after the games, the law enforcement agencies openly harassed Circassian activists in 2014. Beslan Teuvazhev, a member of the Circassian NGO Circassian World, was detained in Moscow for giving away anniversary badges, as he did every year. The irony of his arrest was in the fact that that particular NGO was designed in the most pro-Kremlin fashion. The NGO's title, Circassian World, copied the Kremlin's favourite expression 'Russian World' (*Russkii Mir*) and the confiscated badges were designed in the way of badges that pro-Kremlin patriotic activists gave away two weeks before, on May 9 at the WWII Victory Day. The prosecution could not find any extremist meaning in the Circassian badge inscriptions and

International issues 93

released the activist (Tvardovskaya, 2014). More alarmingly, on the eve of the 150th anniversary of the Circassian Genocide, unidentified sources spread rumours that a group of young Circassian Muslims had prepared a provocation against the Circassian activists. Timur Kuashev, a 26-year-old journalist and human rights activist connected with the Russian opposition party Yabloko, was named as the organizer of the provocation. Kuashev denied the accusations (Arslanova, 2014). Later, Kuashev's dead body was found in the suburbs of Nalchik though the cause of death was never explained (Tuayev, 2015).

After the games, Circassian activists continued appealing to different countries for recognition of their genocide, including to Poland, Romania, Lithuania, Estonia, and Ukraine. The Russian media never covered those appeals. Trying to silence the Circassian independent media, Russian authorities interrogated Aslan Shazzo, the editor-in-chief of NatPress, three times for publishing information about those appeals (Shazzo, 2014). Overall, however, the Russian authorities tried to continue their 'low-key containment strategy' toward the Circassian movement, apparently regarding the Circassians as a serious force that could not easily be suppressed without repercussions (Dzutsati, 2015).

What was the outcome for the Circassian community in Russia and the diaspora connected with the Sochi Olympics? The most evident result was that, for the first time since the Russian colonization, Circassians reached out to a global audience that was ready to listen while they communicated the case for their cause (Hansen, 2014). Paul Goble, one of the Circassians' most attentive international experts, highly evaluated such an outcome,

> No nation more skillfully used an international event than did the Circassians during the Sochi Olympiad to call attention to the Russian-orchestrated genocide of their people 150 years earlier. Despite Moscow's best efforts, few independent reporters talked about Sochi without talking about the continuing crimes against the Circassians. (Goble, 2015)

Most importantly, the Circassian community in Russia and the diaspora united around the protests against holding the games in their former capital.

Russia's aggressive policy in post-Soviet Eurasia

Moscow enjoys a reputation for pursuing an aggressive foreign policy in the post-Soviet space that mirrors its repressive policies at home. There have been many cases over the past two and a half decades when post-Soviet Russia played on the weaknesses of its neighbours, using all kinds of instruments, from trade sanctions to actual military invasion. But how did Moscow itself react to a neighbour's attempts at coercion? The case of the 2014 Olympics demonstrated that the Kremlin stood firm against such threats.

Russia faced many unresolved issues in the post-Soviet space, any of which could have escalated rapidly during the short timeframe leading up to the Olympics. These included Russian diaspora problems in the Baltic states; political

94 *International issues*

pressures in Moldova and breakaway Transnistria; Russian-Georgian relations in light of Russia's recognition of Abkhazia and South Ossetia; relations with Baku and Yerevan, who themselves were at war; the US military transit centre in Kyrgyzstan; tension in Russian-Ukrainian relations; and new Eurasian customs union regulations, which led to some friction with Kazakhstan and Belarus. In fact, most post-Soviet states had issues with Russia and could have used the threat of a boycott of the games as an instrument with which to pressure Moscow.

Political tensions between Russia and its neighbours remained, however, disconnected from the Olympic spirit. Perhaps one of the most eloquent examples of this was when Georgian President Mikheil Saakashvili was the first to congratulate Vladimir Putin when Russia won its Olympic bid in 2007. Tbilisi's initial enthusiasm did not soften Moscow's position over Russian-Georgian relations, however. In spite of the fact that Sochi was close to the Georgian border, Russia did not hesitate to declare war against Georgia in August 2008. The deterioration of Russian-Georgian relations culminated in the five-day conflict between Russia and Georgia and, subsequently, Russian recognition of Abkhazia and South Ossetia as independent states. The Kremlin recognition of Georgia's breakaway territories led Tbilisi to use the Olympics as a platform to garner international attention in condemnation of Moscow's actions.

In response to Russian interference in its affairs, Georgia also turned its attention to the North Caucasus. In particular, it took an interest in the international Circassian movement, which was seeking recognition of the genocide committed against Circassians by tsarist Russia. The Georgian government established a satellite television channel, First Caucasus, to reach out to audiences in the North Caucasus. It was announced that the main purpose of the channel was, as the Russian daily *Kommersant* reported it, 'to supply the Russians, and especially the North Caucasians, with true information about what is going on in Georgia and in the North Caucasus'. In February 2010, the Georgian parliament established a Group of Friendship and Cooperation with the parliaments of the North Caucasian republics. The Georgian parliament called on the North Caucasian parliaments to work jointly 'to develop the Caucasian civilization' and 'to save historical and friendly ties between the nations of the Caucasus in spite of the worsening of political relations between Georgia and the Russian Federation'.

With the support of some US politicians, Georgia applied in vain to the International Olympic Committee in September 2008 requesting that the games not be held in Sochi. Then, Tbilisi declared it would not send Georgian athletes to Sochi. Proving its determination, Tbilisi also boycotted the Women's World Chess Championship in Nalchik in 2008 (despite projections that the Georgians were the favourites to win). In another move, the Georgian parliament recognized the nineteenth-century killings and deportations of ethnic Circassians by tsarist Russia as genocide (Barry, 2011). The Russian parliament quickly responded to the Georgian initiative, branding it as 'support for separatism' in the North Caucasus.

Initially, during a September 2008 press conference, one month after the August war, Putin formulated the Kremlin's uncompromising policy toward the challenge

International issues   95

of an Olympic boycott, saying: 'If they do it once, it will destroy the entire structure of the Olympic movement . . . . However, on the other hand, if they want to take [the Sochi Games away], let them take on this burden.'[8] Indeed, the August 2008 war, the occupation of Georgian territory next to Sochi, the UN resolutions against Russia, and the recognition of Sochi as a territory where genocide was committed did not convince the IOC to change its decision to hold the Olympics in Sochi. This was not surprising. In the past, the IOC had tolerated much larger controversies: it did not move the 1980 Moscow Games in spite of the USSR's invasion of Afghanistan and the ensuing mass boycotts, nor the 1984 Los Angeles games, which were boycotted by the USSR and its allies.

The firmness with which the Kremlin addressed the Georgian challenge prevented similar challenges from other post-Soviet states that might have been tempted to exert the same kind of pressure in their complicated relations with Russia. Ultimately, in 2013, Tbilisi changed its position and announced that Georgia would not boycott the Sochi Olympics. On the eve of the games, the Georgian prime minister, Irakli Garibashvili, made a statement, 'No delegation of our government will be present in Sochi,' he stated. 'Our athletes and senior officials of the Georgian National Olympic Committee will surely be there, though' (Zaccardi, 2013). Four Georgian athletes participated in Sochi games, without winning any medals.

One could argue that the shift in Tbilisi's policy was the result of a change in government following the 2012 Georgian elections rather than the result of the Kremlin's firm policy. In any case, Georgia was a remarkable example of how the same country tried to play the Olympic card three times, first supporting the event in 2007, then deciding to boycott in 2008, and finally deciding to participate in 2013. Tbilisi's political inconstancy strikingly contrasted with Moscow's permanent line not to let its post-Soviet neighbours exert pressure through the games.

Kremlin policies with the West: Stopping short of the point of no return

Russian policy toward the Western states incorporated a much higher level of restraint and flexibility than Russia exhibited in its relations with post-Soviet states and in domestic issues. Russian-British relations before the Olympics were an example of this kind of discontinuous rapport. In 2006 there was high bilateral tension due to the assassination in London of Alexander Litvinenko, the former KGB operative who had defected, but in 2013, relations were stable even though the UK supported the Magnitsky list, the US policy that punished Russian officials who were responsible for the death in prison of Sergei Magnitsky, who had exposed corruption among Russian officials (Quinn & Aldrick, 2013). Generally, Moscow rarely applied to the West the same wide range of consistently tough policy tools it used with the post-Soviet states, namely economic sanctions and military threats. Nonetheless, when it came to threats from Western states, Moscow enjoyed the reputation of challenging them by applying policies of 'symmetric

96   *International issues*

response'. That said, when it came to such a sensitive issue like a possible boycott of the 2014 Olympics, the Kremlin restrained itself even from 'symmetric response', choosing not to cross certain 'red lines' or 'points of no return' in the escalation of crises.

Russia's policy toward the United States was less risk adverse than its approach to Europe, with the Kremlin edging very close to a point of no return. A series of confrontations brought the US threat of Olympic boycott to the fore. The first US boycott threat emerged in September 2008 as a reaction to the Russian–Georgian war, when US Representatives Allyson Schwartz (D-PA) and Bill Shuster (R-PA), co-chairs of the House Georgia Caucus, introduced Congressional Resolution No. 412 ('No Russian Olympics in 2014') calling on the IOC to strip Russia of the 2014 Winter Olympics and to find a more suitable alternative location.[9] At the time, however, the White House's 'reset' policy, seeking to improve relations with Russia and emphasizing areas of mutual interest, made the idea of a boycott politically irrelevant.

Between 2008 and 2013, there were no discussions in the US of boycotting the Sochi Olympics. In 2013, however, the threat of a US boycott again emerged during the scandal connected with Edward Snowden. On July 16 Senator Lindsey Graham (R-SC) suggested that the United States should boycott the Olympics if Russia granted Snowden asylum, but Graham found little support among his colleagues in Washington or more broadly within the American public (Goyette, 2013). The senator's position did not alarm the Kremlin because even the more popular 2008 initiative in the US Congress to boycott the Olympics had no consequences. Public opinion, however, shifted as the Snowden controversy dragged on and even more so as Russia's restrictive laws regarding sexual minorities attracted greater attention. The Kremlin miscalculated the White House's outlook when instead of relieving Russia-US tensions from converging controversies, it escalated them by granting Snowden asylum. President Barack Obama responded by cancelling his planned meeting with Putin and for the first time referenced an Olympic boycott. The US President went as far as negatively describing Putin as 'like a bored kid' (Holland & Chadbourn, 2013). Even though Obama announced his personal position as against the boycott, the very fact that he referenced it demonstrated that the Kremlin had pushed the White House to the limit.

Feeling this, the Kremlin went silent and did not further escalate bilateral tensions. According to the Kremlin's 'symmetric response' policy, one would expect Putin to do something in response to the cancellation of the presidents' meeting and 'cancel' something in response. However, Moscow preferred not to escalate tensions with the United States. At its red line, the Kremlin did not cancel the 2013 meeting between the US Secretaries of State and Defense, John Kerry and Chuck Hagel, and the Russian Ministers of Foreign Affairs and Defense, Sergey Lavrov and Sergey Shoigu, which the US Department of State then framed as generally productive (Shanker & Gordon, 2013).

On the social level, after the Russian parliament adopted laws against sexual minorities in Russia, the LGBT community and social activists in the United States, Europe, and elsewhere made anti-Olympic statements to which the Kremlin quickly responded with a statement assuring that there would be no persecution of LGBT athletes during the 2014 Olympics. European politicians distanced themselves from any anti-Olympic activists. The Russian parliament that had been active in adopting anti-gay laws abruptly became quiet. Though they did not go so far as to undo the laws, Russian officials explained that these laws were not against the LGBT community, but against propaganda of so-called 'untraditional sex', trying to show that there was some fine line there that had not been crossed. In their statements and interviews, many Russian officials, including Putin, were quick to assure the international community that there would be no danger to gay athletes during the games (Radia, 2014). In an interview with the Associated Press in September 2013, Putin, for the first time, expressed his readiness to meet with representatives of LGBT community, which many experts interpreted as caused by the pressure of LGBT athletes and community in the West.[10]

Before the 2014 Sochi Olympics, the games were treated as diplomatic capital in relations with the West. The Kremlin, for its part, became hostage to the Olympics, as it dealt with challenges of negative publicity and possible boycotts. With lasting tensions and new unexpected challenges, Russia several times came close to provoking different countries to boycott the games. In the end, the Kremlin navigated this uphill course, with a firm hand toward neighbours like Georgia and more flexibility with the West. While Western athletes participated in the games and a boycott was avoided, ultimately leaders like Obama and German Chancellor Angela Merkel decided not to attend the opening and closing ceremonies, delivering a blow to the prestige of the games.

Conclusion: The annexation of Crimea as the legacy of the Sochi Olympics

The international status that Russia might have gained from holding the Sochi games evaporated almost immediately after the closing ceremony. Russia's annexation of Crimea and launch of an ongoing war against Ukraine overshadowed any international benefits Russia could have achieved from pulling off the Olympics without any major problems. With the two events so closely connected in time, the question remains what role, if any, did the 2014 Sochi Olympics play in the annexation of Crimea? And, what ultimately, were the international consequences of the games?

Putin recalled in the 2015 documentary *Crimea. The Way Home* that he made the decision to annex Crimea in the Kremlin on February 23, in the morning just before departing for the closing ceremony and after the operation to save Ukrainian President Viktor Yanukovych had safely brought the disgraced Ukrainian leader to Russia. Putin said in the film,

> I will not deny that as we were leaving [around 7:00 am on February 23], I told the four colleagues who were with me, 'The latest developments in Ukraine force us to begin working on returning Crimea to Russia ... I gave them some instructions about what needed to be done.'[11]

98 *International issues*

According to the *New York Times*, the small circle of people who were then with Putin included Sergei Ivanov, Putin's chief of staff; Nikolai Patrushev, the secretary of the security council; Aleksandr Bortnikov, the director of the Federal Security Service; and Sergei Shoigu, the minister of defence (Myers, 2014a), Putin's statement shows that the Russian leaders made the decision to invade Crimea before the 2014 Olympics were over. The connection between these two events, however, remains unexplained. On one hand, the Kremlin spent more than $50 billion on the Olympics, in part, aiming to improve Russia's international profile; on the other hand, Russia's reputation was dramatically damaged by the invasion of Crimea.

Though contradictory from an outsider's perspective, the Sochi Olympics and annexation of Crimea were logically connected from the Russian perspective. Both events were part of the Kremlin's narrative of Russia standing up from its knees after the fall of the USSR – the 2014 Sochi Games matched the 1980 Moscow games, and the annexation of Crimea brought back the 'glory' of Stalin's annexations of new territories to the USSR before WWII.

In practical terms, the Kremlin regarded the annexation of Crimea as another mega-project. From the military perspective, the Kremlin's use of the unprecedented security forces accumulated during the Sochi Olympics partly explains why the Russian invasion into the nearby Crimean Peninsula was so effective. From the economic perspective, through a presidential decree issued on April 20, 2014, the organizers of the Sochi Olympics transferred their post-games resources to Crimea, with Olympstroy, the state corporation that Putin had set up to oversee the preparations for the Olympics, becoming Krymstroy, a new entity designed to manage the incorporation of occupied Crimea into Russia (Russia, 2014). Of 37 board members working on Olympstroy, 16 were transferred into the Crimean organization,[12] including Dmitry Kozak who served as the head of both committees, thus marking the continuity between organizing the Olympic mega-project and the annexation of Crimea. Additionally, much of the property associated with Olympstroy (office equipment and automobiles) was transferred to the Ministry for the Development of Crimea and regional authorities in the occupied territory (Tovkailo, 2014). As of April 2014, Olympstroy had 1,206 employees, while the ministry only employed 230 (Tovkailo, 2014). In terms of media, after mobilizing all its propaganda efforts around the Sochi Olympics, the Kremlin switched its efforts over to effectively conducting what it called the 'information war' after the Crimean invasion.

Ultimately, Putin's decision to use military force against Ukraine marked the collapse of the Russian president's efforts to keep his domestic and post-Soviet area policies separate from his approach to the West. The invasion of Ukraine, followed by the annexation of part of its territory, crossed a red line by upending the international security system that had been in place in Europe since the end of WWII and led the West to impose sanctions on Russia. Western countries also began building up their defence forces and the NATO alliance in order to counter an increased threat from Russia. The Olympics that had been sponsored in part to restore Russia's status as a world power and build a world-class resort on the Russian banks of the Black Sea instead marked the high point of Russia's openness

International issues 99

to the rest of the world. The invasion of Crimea, which the games had to some extent facilitated, ultimately led Russia into a policy of isolation and autarky in relation to the West, one that could no longer be kept separate from its repressive domestic policies and aggression against its immediate neighbours.

Notes

1 Abkhazia and Abkhazians in Russian Periodicals. Volume 1: The 19th – Beginning of the 20th Centuries. Sukhum, Abkhazian Academy of Science. 2005 (In Russian), p. 92.
2 22 Noiabrya 2012: V Sochi Prodolzhayut Otmechat' Den' Goroda. 2013. *Administratsiia goroda Sochi.* November 22. www.sochiadm.ru/press-sluzhba/23178/; 24 Noiabrya 2012: Sochi Prasdnuet Den' Goroda. 2012. *Administratsiia goroda Sochi.* November 24. www.sochiadm.ru/press-sluzhba/2476/
3 Kak Sil'no Vladimir Putin Lyubit Sochi. *SCAPP.* (16 May 2015). Retrieved from: http://sochi.scapp.ru/scapp-gorod/kak-vladimir-putin-lyubit-sochi/
4 Cherkesskii kongress vystupil protiv Olimpiady v Sochi. Kavkasskii uzel (5 July 2007). Retrieved from: www.kavkaz-uzel.ru/articles/117988/?print=true
5 Arambii Khapai: adygi vycherknuty iz istorii Sochi. (5 July 2007). Retrieved from: www.kavkaz-uzel.ru/articles/117986/?print=true
6 Tkhakushinov: Adygeia reshaet problem bezrabotitsy. Kavkazskii uzel (1July 2007). Retrieved from: www.kavkaz-uzel.ru/articles/117619/?print=true
7 Parlament Adygei Prinial Obrashschenie Po Uchastiyu Cherkesov V Sochi-2014. *NatPress.* (25 March 2010). www.natpress.net/index.php?newsid=4439.
8 Putin: Khotiat utashit' u nas Olimpiadu – pust' tashat, Rosbalt. (9 February 2008). Retrieved from: www.rosbalt.ru/main/2008/09/02/519818.html.
9 Rep. Allyson Schwartz, 'Members of Congress Announce 'No Russian Olympics in 2014'; Resolution,' Legistorm, (19 September 2008). Retrieved from: www.legistorm. com/stormfeed/view_rss/273815/member/465.html.
10 Putin Ready To Meet Gay Community Representatives, RFE/RL, (4 September 2013). www.rferl.org/content/russia-putin-ready-to-meet-gay-representatives/25095927.html
11 Krym. Put' na Rodinu. A Documentary by Andrey Kondrashov. Russia 24. (15 March 2015). www.youtube.com/watch?v=t42–71RpRgI
12 Those 16 people who served in both the Sochi and Crimea Committees included – Kozak D.N., Gromov A.A., Bel'ianinov A.Iu., Donskoi S.E, Konavolov A.V., Livanov D.V., Medinskii V.R., Mutkov V.L., Nikiforov N.A., Novak A.V., Puchkov V.A., Romodanovskii K.O., Siluanov A.G., Skvortsova V.I., Sliuniaev I.N., and Sokolov. M.Iu.

References

Akopov, S., & Volkov, V. (2013). Olympism and Empire: The Olympic Myth in the Contestation of the Caucasus. In B. Petersson & K. Vamling (Eds), *The Sochi Predicament: Contexts, Characteristics and Challenges of the Olympic Winter Games in 2014* (pp. 124–41). Newcastle upon Tyne, UK: Cambridge Scholars.

Alexander, A. (2010, February 8). North Jersey Circassians 'in Exile' Launch Olympic Protest. *NorthJersey.com.* Retrieved from www.northjersey.com/cm/2.1593/story-archives/north-jersey-circassians-(in-exile-launch-olympic-protest-1.1239552) (Accessed 8 October 2016).

Alliluyeva, S. (1967). *Twenty Letters To A Friend.* London: HarperCollins.

Anishchuk, A. (2014, February 10). Putin Courts Georgia, Accuses West of Cold War-Style 'Containment'. *Reuters.* Retrieved from www.reuters.com/article/us-olympics-putin-idUSBREA191NV20140210 (Accessed 8 October 2016).

100 *International issues*

Arslanova, Z. (2014, May 20). Den' Skorbi Kak Povod Dlya Provokatsii. *Kavpolit.* Retrieved from http://kavpolit.com/articles/den_skorbi_kak_povod_dlja_provokatsii-4771/ (Accessed 8 October 2016).

Asmus, R. (2010). *A Little War That Shook the World: Georgia, Russia, and the Future of the West.* Basingstoke, UK: Macmillan.

Barry, E. (2011, May 20). Georgia Says Russian Slaughter of Circassians Was Genocide. *The New York Times.* Retrieved from www.nytimes.com/2011/05/21/world/europe/21georgia.html (Accessed 8 October 2016).

Bell, J.S. (1840). *Journal of a Residence in Circassia during the Years 1837, 1838, and 1839.* London: E. Moxon.

Berzhe, A.P. (1882). Vyselenie Gortsev S Kavkaza (Deportation of the Mountaineers from the Caucasus). *Russkaia Starina, 33,* 161–76.

Besleney, Z.A. (2014). *The Circassian Diaspora in Turkey: A Political History.* London: Routledge.

Biersack, J., & O'Lear, S. (2014). The Geopolitics of Russia's Annexation of Crimea: Narratives, Identity, Silences, and Energy. *Eurasian Geography and Economics, 55*(3), 247–69.

Black, J.L., & Johns, M. (Eds). (2016). *The Return of the Cold War: Ukraine, The West and Russia.* Abingdon: Routledge.

Caucasus Archeographic Commission. *Acts of Caucasus Archeographic Commission, 1866–1908 (12 vols.) Vol. 10.* Tiflis: Caucasus Archeographic Commission.

Cicek, C. (2011, May 17). Circassian Association of California: Address to the Members of the Russian Duma. *Aheku.* Retrieved from https://aheku.net/news/policy/2429 (Accessed 8 October 2016).

Cornell, S.E., & Starr, S.F. (2009). *The Guns of August 2008.* New York and London: M.E. Sharpe.

Drozdov, I. (1877). Poslednyaya Bor'ba S Gortsami Na Zapadnom Kavkaze (The Last Fight with the Mountaineers in the Western Caucasus) *Kavkazskii Sbornik, Vol. 2.* Tiflis Tipographiia Okruzhnogo Shtaba Kavkazskogo Voennogo Okruga.

Dzutsati, V. (2015, June 1). Circassian Activists in Russia Become a Serious Force. *The Jamestown Foundation.* Retrieved from www.jamestown.org/single/?tx_ttnews%5Btt_news%5D=43982&no_cache=1 (8 October 2016).

Freire, M.R., & Kanet, R.E. (Eds). (2012). *Russia and Its Near Neighbours.* London: Palgrave Macmillan.

Gal'kevich, S. (2014). Fakel Na Tseremonii Otkrytiia OI Nesli Velikie Sportsmeny – Ernst. *RIA Novosti.* Retrieved from http://ria.ru/sochi2014_around_games/20140208/993820961.html (Accessed 8 October 2016).

Goble, P. (2010, October 7). Circassians Increase Efforts to Secure Recognition of 1864 Genocide. *Window on Eurasia.* Retrieved from http://windowoneurasia.blogspot.com/2010/10/window-on-eurasia-circassians-increase.html (Accessed 8 October 2016).

Goble, P. (2014, May 21). How Putin Launched the Circassian National Movement. *The Interpreter.* Retrieved from www.interpretermag.com/how-putin-launched-the-circassian-national-movement/ (Accessed 8 October 2016).

Goble, P. (2015, May 23). 151 Years After the Genocide and One Year After Sochi, the Circassian Issue Isn't Going Away. *The Interpreter.* Retrieved from www.interpretermag.com/151-years-after-the-genocideand-one-year-after-sochi-the-circassian-issue-isnt-going-away/(Accessed 8 October 2016).

Goyette, B. (2013, July 16). Lindsey Graham: Boycott 2014 Olympics If Russia Gives Snowden Asylum. *The Huffington Post.* Retrieved from www.huffingtonpost.com/2013/

07/16/lindsey-graham-boycott-olympics-snowden_n_3607528.html (Accessed 8 October 2016).

Hansen, L.F. (2013). Sochi as a Site of Circassian Long-Distance Memorialisation. In B. Petersson & K. Vamling (Eds), *he Sochi Predicament: Contexts, Characteristics and Challenges of the Olympic Winter Games in 2014* (pp. 95–123). Newcastle upon Tyne, UK: Cambridge Scholars.

Hansen, L.F. (2014). *The Circassian Revival: A Quest for Recognition, Mediated Transnational Mobilisation and Memorialization among a Geographically Dispersed People from the Caucasus.* PhD diss., University of Copenhagen.

Holland, S., & Chadbourn, M. (2013, August 9). Obama describes Putin as 'like a bored kid'. *Reuters.* Retrieved from www.reuters.com/article/2013/08/09/us-usa-russia-obama-idUSBRE9780XS20130809 (Accessed 8 October 2016).

Karagiannis, E. (2014). The Russian Interventions in South Ossetia and Crimea Compared: Military Performance, Legitimacy and Goals. *Contemporary Security Policy, 35*(3), 400–20.

King, C. (2007). Imagining Circassia: David Urquhart and the Making of North Caucasus Nationalism. *The Russian Review, 66*(6), 238–55.

King, C. (2008a). The Five-Day War: Managing Moscow After the Georgia Crisis. *Foreign Affairs.*

King, C. (2008b). *The Ghost of Freedom: A History of the Caucasus.* Oxford: Oxford University Press.

Kreiten, I. (2009). A Colonial Experiment in Cleansing: The Russian Conquest of Western Caucasus, 1856–65. *Journal of Genocide Research, 11*(2–3), 213–241.

Longworth, J.A. (1840). *A Year among the Circassians.* London: H. Colburn.

Lucas, E. (2014). *The New Cold War: Putin's Russia and the Threat to the West.* New York: Palgrave Macmillan.

Mankoff, J. (2011). *Russian Foreign Policy: The Return of Great Power Politics.* 2nd Edn, Lanham, MD: Rowman & Littlefield Publishers.

Manning, P. (2009). Just like England: On the Liberal Institutions of the Circassians. *Comparative Studies in Society and History, 51*(3), 590–618. doi: 10.1017/S00104175 09000243

Markedonov, S. (2014). *The 2014 Sochi Olympics: A Patchwork of Challenges.* Washington DC and Lanham, MD: Center for Strategic & International Studies and Rowman & Littlefield.

Milyutin, D.A. (2004). *Memoirs: 1856–1860.* Moscow: Rosspen.

Myers, S.L. (2014a, March 7). Russia's Move Into Ukraine Said to Be Born in Shadows. *The New York Times.* Retrieved from www.nytimes.com/2014/03/08/world/europe/russias-move-into-ukraine-said-to-be-born-in-shadows.html (Accessed 8 October 2016).

Myers, S.L. (2014b, February 7). Scores Detained in Russia Before Olympic Ceremony. *The New York Times.*

Persson, E. (2013). Olympism and Empire: The Olympic Myth in the Contestation of the Caucasus. In B. Petersson & K. Vamling (Eds), *The Sochi Predicament: Contexts, Characteristics and Challenges of the Olympic Winter Games in 2014* (pp. 72–94). Newcastle upon Tyne: Cambridge Scholars.

Petersson, B., & Vamling, K. (2015). Fifteen Minutes of Fame Long Gone: Circassian Activism before and after the Sochi Olympics. *Sport in Society.* doi: 10.1080/17430437.2015.1100887

102 *International issues*

Putin, V. (2007, July 4). Speech at the 119th International Olympic Committee Session. *Kremlin.ru*. Retrieved from http://en.kremlin.ru/events/president/transcripts/24402 (Accessed 8 October 2016).

Putin, V. (2014, February 10). Meeting with the Public Council for the Preparation of the 2014 Winter Olympics. *Kremlin.ru*. Retrieved from http://en.kremlin.ru/events/president/news/20203 (Accessed 8 October 2016).

Quinn, J., & Aldrick, P. (2013, July 8). Russians linked to Sergei Magnitsky case banned from entering UK. *The Telegraph*. Retrieved from www.telegraph.co.uk/finance/finan cial-crime/10167401/Russians-linked-to-Sergei-Magnitsky-case-banned-from-entering-UK.html (Accessed 8 October 2016).

Radia, K. (2014, January 19). Vladimir Putin Defends Anti-Gay Law, but Vows No 'Problems' for Olympic Visitors. *ABC News*. Retrieved from http://abcnews.go.com/Inter national/vladimir-putin-defends-anti-gay-law-vows-problems/story?id=21588617 (Accessed 8 October 2016).

Richmond, W. (2013). *The Circassian Genocide*. New Brunswick: Rutgers University Press.

Russia, P.O. (2014). Ukaz Prezidenta RF Ot 20 Aprelia 2014 G. N 263. O Gosudarctvennoi Komissii Po Voprosam Sotsial'no-Ekonomicheskogo Razvitiia Respubliki Krym i g. Sevastopolia i Ob Uprazdnenii Gosudarstvennoi Komissii Po Podgotovke i Provedeniyu XXII Olimpiiskikh Zimnikh Igr i XI Paralimpiiskikh Zimnikh Igr 2014 Goda v g. Sochi. *Garant.ru*. Retrieved from www.garant.ru/products/ipo/prime/doc/70540582/ (Accessed 8 October 2016).

Shanker, T., & Gordon, M.R. (2013, August 9). Kerry and Hagel Meet With Their Russian Counterparts. *New York Times*. Retrieved from www.nytimes.com/2013/08/10/world/europe/kerry-and-hagel-meet-with-their-russian-counterparts.html (Accessed 8 October 2016).

Shazzo, A. (2014, November 21). Glavu 'Natpress' Snova Vyzyvali V Tsentr 'E' Po Pros'bam Priznat' Genotsid Cherkesov. *NatPress*. Retrieved from www.natpressru.info/index.php?newsid=9266 (Accessed 8 October 2016).

Tlis, F. (2007, August 16). The Challenges of the Sochi Olympics and Russia's Circassian Problem. *North Caucasus Analysis – Jamestown Foundation*. Retrieved from www.jamestown.org/programs/nc/single/?tx_ttnews%5Btt_news%5D=4382&tx_ttnews%5 BbackPid%5D=189&no_cache=1 (Accessed 8 October 2016).

Tornau, F. F. (1864). *Vospominaniia Kavkazskogo Ofitsera*. Moscow: Katkov i Ko.

Tovkailo, M. (2014). Kryma Poluchit Nasledstvo ot Sochi. *Vedomosti*. www.vedomosti.ru/newspaper/articles/2014/06/10/krym-poluchit-nasledstvo-ot-sochi (Accessed 8 October 2016).

Tsutsiev, A. (2014). *Atlas of the Ethno-Political History of the Caucasus* (N.S. Favorov, Trans.). New Haven, CT: Yale University Press.

Tuayev, M. (2015, March 30). Experts Note Similarities In Deaths of Kuashev and Magomedragimov. *Caucasian Knot*. Retrieved from www.eng.kavkaz-uzel.ru/articles/31269/ (Accessed 8 October 2016).

Tvardovskaya, M. (2014, May 16). Pamiatny Den' Cherkesov: Traur Kak Ekstremizm. *Kavpolit*. Retrieved from http://kavpolit.com/articles/pamjatnyj_den_cherkesov_traur_kak_ekstremizm-4653/ (Accessed 8 October 2016).

Urquhart, D. (1863). *The Circassian War as Bearing on the Polish Insurrection*. London: Robert Hardwicke.

Welt, C. (2014). A Fateful Moment: Ethnic Autonomy and Revolutionary Violence in the Democratic Republic of Georgia (1918–1921). In S.F. Jones (Ed.), *The Making of Modern Georgia, 1918–2012: The First Georgian Republic and Its Successors* (pp. 205–31). London: Routledge.

Zaccardi, N. (2013, December 2). Georgia Will Send Athletes to Olympics but Not Government Officials. *NBC Sports*. Retrieved from http://vplayer.nbcsports.com/p/BxmELC/nbcsports_embed/select/media/Fymjc30DQefO (Accessed 8 October 3026).

Zhemukhov, S. (2012). The Birth of Modern Circassian Nationalism. *Nationalities Papers*, *40*(4), 503–24.

6 The legacy of the Sochi Olympics

After the closing ceremonies, it is reasonable to ask: Were the games a success? Will they leave a positive, sustainable legacy? More than two years after Russia welcomed the world to Sochi, the legacy of the games continues to evolve.

Addressing the question of legacy immediately raises the question of criteria for judging – how do you define success and how do you measure it? There is an extensive literature examining the legacies of mega-events like the Olympics and FIFA World Cup (Baumann & Matheson, 2013; Dansero & Puttilli, 2010; Edds, 2012; H. Lenskyj, 2016; Mangan, 2008; Terret, 2008) and the methodologies have been improving over time (Li & Jago, 2012). While fully summarizing this literature is beyond the scope of this chapter, a crucial issue is how long one must wait before analyzing the legacy of an event the size of the Olympics. Some have suggested that 15 years is an appropriate time frame (Mangan, 2008). Accordingly, this analysis, conducted two years after the Sochi closing ceremonies, is necessarily only a preliminary discussion for a process that will take decades to fully unfold. In an earlier era, the Soviet leaders faced a rude surprise when their entire country disintegrated a decade after the 1980 Moscow games, with some seeing the Olympiad as the beginning of the process because it highlighted the difference between the elites and the masses and the profligacy of pouring money into sporting spectacle when the country was essentially bankrupt (Riordan, 2007).

One possible approach to examining a legacy would be to ask if the organizers achieved what they said that wanted to do. Since 2003, four years before the IOC selected Sochi for the 2014 games, considerations of Olympic legacy have been an official part of the Olympic Charter and must be described in each city's bid to host the games (Cashman & Horne, 2013, p. 51). Many of the reports on previous games are scathing in pointing out that the organizers of the events made numerous promises about the how the Olympics would transform local communities when in reality these promises were rarely fulfilled (Zimbalist, 2015). These promises included such benefits as promoting greater public involvement in sports activities, spurring economic growth, creating new jobs, generating additional tax revenue, building affordable housing, and redeveloping depressed parts of the host city. In reality, the consequences were often increased debt for cities and the construction of sport facilities that subsequently sat empty.

The Sochi bid book promised that the games would leave Russia in possession of 'critically-needed alpine, sliding and skijumping facilities', which would

The legacy   105

stimulate interest among young Russians in these sports; create a year-round tourism industry for Sochi, including the development of 'modern entertainment, exhibition, retail and accommodation facilities along the coast', which would make Sochi a 'world-class resort destination'; and improve 'environmental standards conditions and the increase of protected areas in the Sochi region' combined with the 'heightening of environmental awareness in Sochi and the rest of the world's largest country' (Sochi 2014, 2007).

Certainly, the organizers delivered on some of these promises. In summing up the results of the games, the IOC noted 'strong urban legacies from the games' (International Olympic Committee, 2015) including the transformation of Sochi into a year-round destination, 367 km of new roads and more than 200 km of new rail links with 54 bridges and 22 tunnels, three new sewage treatment facilities, three electric power plants with 1200 MW capacity, 480 km of gas pipelines, airport facilities, a new seaport for passengers, 25,000 additional hotel rooms with 56 hotels now rated four-star and above, a new theme park, Russia's first waste re-cycling treatment plant, green building standards, and a model for other Russian cities in improving accessibility for disabled citizens. In other areas, the organizers obviously fell short. As our chapter on civil society demonstrated, constructing the Olympic facilities cut into the protected national park in the Caucasus Mountains and, given the Russian government's ongoing crackdown on civil society groups, there is no evidence that the games changed popular Russian attitudes toward the environment.

Of course, the authors of the Sochi bid could not have predicted that Russia would invade Ukraine immediately after the games closed and that the country's relationship with the West would deteriorate to levels not seen since the Cold War. Two years after Sochi, this situation has not changed and it is hard to predict whether Russia will continue its occupation of Ukrainian territory and efforts to reduce its interactions with the West. On the one hand, certainly the military action had an impact on Sochi's ability to attract international tourists, but, on the other, Russia's isolationist politics helped to increase the number of domestic tourists in Sochi (Bulanov, 2016).

The following discussion focuses on topics that were particularly relevant to the Sochi games at the city, national, and international levels. A final section looks at the implications of Sochi for the Olympic movement itself. At the city level, we examine the effectiveness of the outlays seeking to turn Sochi into a year-round tourist destination, examining the impact on local infrastructure, the local business community, and environmental sustainability. Many questions remain unanswered. At the national level, the games did not promote any positive political change. Rather, they helped the president spread assets among his cronies, use the centralized system to favour one city over others, and continue to expand the divide between the state and society. At the international level, Putin's invasion of Ukraine threw away any legacy from the Sochi games that Russia could have used to promote the city as a tourist destination. Finally, many of the negative experiences with Sochi caused the IOC to adopt a number of reforms in efforts to prevent discrimination, curtail excess spending, and limit doping in the future.

106   *The legacy*

Moreover, the Sochi experience raised many questions about the integrity of the IOC and particularly the World Anti-Doping Agency.

The legacy of the Olympic Games for the city of Sochi

In the case of Barcelona, which is frequently cited as a model of success for using the Olympics to stimulate positive urban outcomes, the Olympics spurred a major process of urban renewal, creating an improved city for residents and an attractive tourist destination. Barcelona famously devoted 83 per cent of its budget to urban improvement rather than sport (Gold & Gold, 2008). The 1976 Montreal and 2004 Athens games frequently appear as counter-examples: Montreal took 30 years to pay off $1.5 billion in debts incurred by the games, while Athens ran up a 7 billion euro debt and spent massively on a new airport and metro, helping to fuel Greece's ongoing economic problems.

Many questions remain about whether Sochi will live up to the example of its illustrious Catalan predecessor. As noted in the introduction, one of Putin's purposes in hosting the games was to make Sochi a premier city, both internationally and within Russia (Golubchikov, 2016). Before the Olympics, Sochi was a deteriorating Soviet-era beach resort with poor infrastructure. All of the sporting facilities were built from scratch and much of the city infrastructure was remade. The scale of construction was enormous, enabled by the authoritarian nature of the regime (Koch & Valiyev, 2015; Wurster, 2013).

Long before the sport competitions began, critics wondered whether the billions in investment would produce viable businesses that could thrive after the Olympic competitors left town. Some researchers have found evidence of venues with little post-Olympic use, which create ongoing financial problems, dating back as far as the 1908 London games (Darcy & Taylor, 2013, p. 101). Simply dumping huge amounts of money into the city did not necessarily provide the basis for balanced development. If the state has to provide support for workers who will be employed in loss-making enterprises, it will take away resources that could otherwise have been used for development investment. Building up one sector of the economy with extensive state support, such as tourism, would make it difficult to develop other sectors of the Sochi economy because there would be higher expectations for wages and the costs of working there would be too expensive for other industries to thrive.

Developing Sochi as a year-round resort destination

Research on the impact of mega-events suggests that the event itself it usually not enough to increase tourism and other flows of visitors, meaning that city officials have to make additional efforts (Müller, 2016). Following the Olympics, Russia hoped to turn Sochi into a major destination. Putin's decision to annex Crimea and launch hostilities in the eastern part of Ukraine led the West to impose sanctions on Russia. The result was the cancellation of high profile events planned for post-Olympic Sochi. After the G8 suspended Russia's membership, Sochi had to scrap plans to host a major summit with the Western leaders that had been planned for June 2014. However, Sochi did manage to host a Formula One automobile race in October that year and the world chess championship in November. But, while such big events attract international headlines, Sochi will likely need a series of smaller festivals to bring in a steady stream of tourists throughout the year (Wynn, 2016). Moreover, even the high profile events that took place caused problems. The Formula One race was supposed to feature racers driving through city streets with the construction of temporary bleachers. Instead, the track encircled four of the Olympic arenas and remained in place after the event instead of being removed. At the beginning of 2015, a giant fence surrounded much of the Olympic park, making access difficult (Dobrynin, 2014). The krai authorities want to continue using the track, arguing that taking it down would be expensive and that the facility could turn a profit (Fedorova, 2014).

Despite the authorities' promise to turn Sochi into a major tourist attraction, two years after the games ended, Sochi had not entered any of the lists of the world's major holidaymaker destinations. For example, Sochi did not figure in the Top 100 City Destination Rankings for 2014 prepared by Euromonitor International. Sochi also did not appear in the 132 cities listed by Mastercard's 2015 Global Destination Cities Index.

Additionally, the Olympics did not really make Sochi a much more attractive tourist destination in the immediate aftermath of the games. In 2013, before the Olympics, 4 million tourists visited Sochi, during the 2014 Olympic year, there were 5.2 million tourists, and in 2015, the figure was 4.7 million (Committee for Russian Economic Freedom, 2016). The number of people working in tourist agencies in Krasnodar Krai in 2014 rose by 120 employees over the previous year, from 2,259 to 2,379 (Federal'noe Agenstvo Po Turizmu, 2015). The growth in tourists after the Olympics was about 17.5 per cent and this influx was most likely due to the fact that following the Olympics the value of the ruble declined to less than half of its previous level, limiting the ability of Russians to travel abroad and redirecting them to domestic destinations. In 2015, the number of Russian tourists travelling abroad dropped by 31.3 per cent (Meduza, 2016).

The tourist situation in Sochi differed from other Russian regions, where the number of jobs in the tourist business fell dramatically in 2014 (due to the Olympics in Sochi and the beginning of the war with Ukraine). In Moscow, the number of tourist jobs fell from 7,658 to 6,760 and in St. Petersburg, it plummeted from 5, 869 to 1,763 (Federal'noe Agenstvo Po Turizmu, 2015). Russia's economy is closely tied to the price of oil and the commodity's price dip in 2014 severely cut the spending power of Russian consumers. One bright spot was the New Year and Orthodox Christmas holiday in early 2015, when Sochi was full to capacity (Demirijian, 2015). According to Prime Minister Dmitry Medvedev, 160,000 tourists stayed in the Sochi's hotels and 183,000 visited the resort during that time (Kriviakina, 2015). This success even boosted Krasnodar Krai Governor Aleksandr Tkachev's rating among Russia's 83 governors to 11th place (Regnum, 2015).

During the summer following the Olympics, however, many of the new hotels sat vacant. After the Olympics, no one really made an effort to advertise hotels in

108   *The legacy*

the Olympic development area or tried to fill the new arenas with events. The official data from the Russian Federal Tourist Agency indicated that hotel room space in Krasnodar Krai significantly increased in 2014, from 1,819,100 to 2,574,800 square metres (Federal'noe Agenstvo Po Turizmu, 2015) thanks to the many hotels that started working in Sochi (see Table 6. 1). The new hotels, however, were not fully occupied and the number of employees in the hotel business increased by only 1,500 workers.[1] That number was only a small fraction of the overly-optimistic promises made by officials at the beginning of the construction; in 2007, the organizers had promised 150,000 new jobs (Olimprus, 2007).

Potential small business leaders did not see any benefit to opening a café in the area because there were few people nearby. Although the games brought a huge amount of money and development to Sochi, future investors will not initiate new projects until there is evidence that there is demand for their services. Aleksandr Valov, editor-in-chief of Blogsochi.ru, noted that by February 2015, there were few visitors to the Olympic Park and those who came mainly were interested in seeing a 'Museum of Corruption', much like visitors to former Ukrainian President Viktor Yanukovych's ostentatious palace Mezhyhirya, built with Ukrainian public funds before the Euromaidan revolution chased the leader from his country (Valov, 2015). Valov's pictures of the Olympic facilities posted on-line show vacant stadiums surrounded by empty parking lots. Sochi shares a problem with other Olympic cities, where the facilities are often far from the city centre and difficult to access (Andranovich & Burbank, 2011). There are also few users for the expensive road and train tracks linking the coastal and mountain Olympic clusters, which were built at a final cost of $10.3 billion, with a capacity of 20,000 passengers an hour. Passenger flows have been low ever since the games concluded (Golubchikov, 2016).

Kozak oversaw the implementation of the initial phases of the legacy programme that was adopted in February 2013 and that outlines how each of the 419 newly-built facilities should be used in the post-Olympic period. The state corporation Olympstroy, which built the facilities, distributed them to state owners at the municipal, regional and federal levels as well as some private entities. However, most of the new owners did not have the resources required to support the new infrastructure that they took over. While the legacy planning foresaw the distribution of property, it did not lay out how the newly created infrastructure

Table 6.1 Tourism indicators in Krasnodar Krai

Indicator	2009	2010	2011	2012	2013	2014
Employees at hotels	62,700	57,800	54,200	52,600	50,100	56,600
Employees at tourist agencies	1,801	1,959	2,369	2,183	2,259	2,379
Hotels room space (square meters)	2,549,000	2,191,100	2,407,700	1,906,500	1,819,100	2,574,800

Source: Russian Federal Tourist Agency

would be able to generate profits on its own (Fedorova, 2014). Several innovative plans were developed during the years before the games began, but they were never implemented. The idea of dismantling some of the facilities and moving them to other parts of Russia, for example, simply turned out to be too expensive and was shelved.

In February 2014, Oleg Deripaska said that it was necessary to spend 10–15 per cent of what had already been spent on the Olympic infrastructure to make it suitable for future use as a resort. However, Putin made clear at that time that the state would no longer invest in Sochi projects and that the various oligarchs and state companies who had supported the Olympics would have to find other sources to develop the area further. Similarly, Kozak claimed that it would cost 4 billion rubles a year to maintain the roads and stadiums built for the Olympics (Fedorova, 2014). Maintenance costs also shaved the regional budget: On 16 April 2014, Governor Tkachev claimed that upkeep for the new sports facilities would cost the region 12 billion rubles a year (about $350 million) (V. Volkov, 2014).

Another problem was that ownership of the various facilities had been dispersed among a variety of groups who do not work together to develop the area. The media centre was only used twice in the year following the games and the krai-controlled company that owned it was on the brink of bankruptcy. The Fisht Stadium had found no other purpose after the opening and closing ceremonies, however it is being rebuilt for the 2018 World Cup and then will host a local soccer club. The hockey club Sochi Leopards, a new team in Russia's Continental Hockey League, is now based in the Bolshoi Ice Arena; the Adler Arena is now a tennis academy because it was too expensive to maintain the ice rink; and the Shaiba Arena now hosts the All-Russia Children's Center.

The authorities have developed a variety of schemes to support business in the area. For example, they have announced plans to build a casino in Sberbank's Gorky Gorod in Krasnaya Polyana at the initiative of Sberbank head German Gref as a way for the facilities to make money and pay back the credits they received from state lenders. Building the new casinos required the closing of another casino area that had already been constructed in Krasnodar. In 2009, Russia outlawed gambling except in four designated areas: Azov-City gambling complex on the border of the Krasnodar and Rostov regions, Primorskii Krai, Kaliningrad, and Altai Republic. Only Azov-City was functioning by the end of 2014 and it would have to shut down in favour of Sochi (Gribtsova & Tovkailo, 2014). Despite these hopes, however, gambling may not provide much income for the area. Azov-City began operations in 2010 and did not turn a profit in its first five years of operations, in part because it is located far from populated areas. Russian legislation also allowed gambling in Crimea as a way to generate money for the budget of this vacation destination now under Russian occupation (Moscow Times, 2014). Putin had earlier opposed opening casinos in Sochi because doing so would lead to rising prices for low and medium income tourists who wanted to vacation there with their kids (Titov, 2014).

Looking forward, and given the souring ties to the West, Sochi is hoping to attract Chinese tourists with new flights connecting Sochi and Beijing and Sochi

110 *The legacy*

hotels announcing plans to serve Asian food in their restaurants (NESru.com, 2015). Whether Sochi will be able to attract a large foreign customer base from non-Western countries remains one of the keys to its future development.

The Olympics' impact on Sochi's local business community

In typical Western cities that host the Olympics, local real estate developers are the main drivers bringing in the games. While they see many benefits coming from hosting the mega-event, they are particularly interested in attracting additional subsidies from the federal government that might otherwise go to other cities.

In the case of Sochi, it was the federal government that initiated the games and its extensive role in their organization and facility construction process had negative consequences for the local business community. During the preparations for the games, large federal companies with close ties to the Kremlin were able to get the most important contracts for facility construction. At best, local business could only win small subcontracts. After the games, the federal subsidies dried up and many of the national businesses withdrew from the city. Following their departure, the remaining local businessmen and bureaucrats launched a permanent fight among themselves over property rights and other issues that created a disorganized economic environment (Fedorova, 2014). Since there are no legal ways to resolve their contradictions, the local businessmen and bureaucrats have to keep appealing for mediation help to the federal authorities who had been prominent in the buildup to the games, but subsequently left Sochi.

One anecdote related in *Kommersant* shows the extent of the problem (Fedorova, 2014). In late 2014, the administration of Ledovy Stadium was organizing an event. The stadium did not have enough parking space and the administration approached colleagues at the nearby Shaiba Stadium asking to use that facility's parking lot, but could not secure their permission. The conflict was resolved just five hours before the event, after Deputy Minister of Construction Yury Reilian, who coordinated Olympic construction, made a personal call and asked the Shaiba administration to allow the Ledovy spectators to use their parking lot during the event.

Another sign that the development of Sochi favoured mainly big business in the early years was that many of the new tourists began to stay in hotels in the city; the rate went from 2,463,200 in 2013 to 3,649,000 in 2014, but the number fell again in 2015 (Federal'noe Agenstvo Po Turizmu, 2015). Similarly, the

Table 6.2 Distribution of tourists at hotels in Krasnodar Krai, (by thousands)

	2009	2010	2011	2012	2013	2014
Domestic tourists	2,431,200	2,382,500	2,369,900	2,404,100	2,463,200	3,649,000
International tourists	58,200	53,700	60,700	66,000	77,300	288,600

Source: Russian Federal Tourist Agency

The legacy   111

number of international tourists increased in Sochi for the games from 77,300 in 2013 to 288,600 in 2014. It was mainly the federally connected hotels that could benefit from this new business (see Table 6.2).

The overall effectiveness of spectacle-driven development

Were the billions Russia spent on Sochi's infrastructure development a good investment? Does it make other cities want to do something similar?

Even though 'sustainable development has come to join peaceful coexistence in the syncretism that is modern Olympism' (Chappelet, 2008, p. 1898), a common criticism of the games is that they lead to spectacle-driven development which places the needs of a two-week sporting event over those of the city at large. In this light, mega-events are not the best way to promote sustainable urban and economic development (Müller, 2016). For example, as Müller & Pickles point out 'the focus of the event itself on the spectacular poses real challenges for the long-term needs of cities, regions and the broader population' (Müller & Pickles, 2015). Observers frequently consider the emphasis on massive new construction required for many Olympic host cities as a form of development that is environmentally reckless. As Müller concluded in a study of Sochi,

> Although some sustainability policies were mobilized to come to Russia, the subsequent transformation through ineffective governance, an absence of institutional controls, both at the domestic and at the international level, and high time pressure led to irreversible environmental damage, oversized infrastructure and limited public engagement and benefits. (Müller, 2015)

Of course, the situation is not completely bleak for the citizens of Sochi, who have benefitted from many of the infrastructure investments. Locals point out that traffic jams along the coast are a thing of the past thanks to new roads paid for by Moscow. Similarly gone are the blackouts that used to affect the city thanks to the Kremlin investments in new power generating capabilities (Weir, 2016). Without the Olympics, it is unlikely that the federal government or other investors would have paid for such costly infrastructure upgrades.

Questions about the sustainability of Olympic infrastructure development drive away potential hosts in democratic countries, but they remain an object prized by authoritarian leaders who seek international attention and legitimacy. The high price tag for the Sochi Olympics (more than $50 billion) continued a trend from the Beijing summer games ($40 billion) that had the impact of scaring off Western cities from bidding for the games because they fear the great expense. However, authoritarian leaders inspired by the 'Sochi Syndrome' in countries like Azerbaijan, Kazakhstan, and Turkmenistan have sought to build similar showcases as a way of redistributing money among top elites and boosting the image of key cities (Koch & Valiyev, 2015).

The competition for the 2022 winter games ultimately came down to a contest between two authoritarian countries: Kazakhstan and China. Other cities, Krakow,

112   *The legacy*

Poland; Lviv, Ukraine; Stockholm, Sweden; and Oslo, Norway, which had considered competing for the right to host the competition pulled out. Switzerland's St. Moritz and Germany's Munich also considered competing for the 2022 Games, but financial concerns and local opposition forced them to leave the competition as well. In Oslo, Conservative Prime Minister Erna Solberg said. 'A big project like this, which is so expensive, requires broad popular support and there isn't enough support for it' (Solsvik, 2014). Even though the proposed Oslo games were only expected to cost $5 billion, many feared that the costs would balloon once the bid was accepted.

For the 2024 summer games, Boston won the right to compete on behalf of the US with a bid estimating the cost of the games at $4.5 billion (Longman, 2015), but this effort, chronically short of public transparency, proved unpopular with local residents. A key to keeping the price tag down for bid cities is to stress that, in contrast to Sochi, they have much of the infrastructure in place already, including sports facilities and hotel rooms. And where the infrastructure does not exist, cities can emphasize the use of temporary facilities – Boston, for example, was planning a temporary Olympic stadium for the opening and closing ceremonies that would hold 60,000 people. However, even these measures proved insufficient to please Boston residents, who failed to support the idea of holding the Olympics in their city and were discussing the possibility of a ballot measure to prevent any state aid. Unlike President Putin, Boston Mayor Marty Walsh refused to guarantee that the city's taxpayers would cover any cost overruns or fundraising shortfalls (Diaz, 2015). On 27 July 2015, the US Olympic Committee and the city agreed to withdraw Boston's bid to host the games and seek a different city to carry the flag for the US. The problem with host cities has even led to proposals that future games be held in a single site in Greece for the summer games and Switzerland for the winter games.

Dubious domestic political legacy

While most Olympic legacies are focused on the city level, the case of the 2014 games was different in the sense that they had been organized personally by the president and that he had taken a keen interest in every aspect of their implementation. In rare cases, Olympic games have had lasting consequences for a country's political system. The 1988 Olympics in South Korea helped to consolidate a recent transition from military to civilian democratic rule by drawing international attention to the new regime shortly before the opening ceremonies and helping it to consolidate power (Jeong, Jafari, & Gartner, 1990). The Sochi games did little more than bolster the status quo authoritarian regime in Russia, temporarily shoring up Putin's popularity and helping him distribute resources to powerful supporters.

Putin's popularity and ability to maintain his political system

The Olympics did not do much to reverse the long-term secular decline in Putin's popularity that he had experienced in recent years (D. Volkov, 2014). Putin won no more than a 3–4 per cent popularity bump from the Olympics. In fact, with

The legacy 113

that modest gain, the Levada Center's Lev Gudkov thought that Putin's long-term slide in the ratings was inevitably going to continue (Sokolov & Bigg, 2014). Ultimately, it was only Russian moves in Ukraine, an expanding media crackdown, and the surrounding propaganda campaign that brought Putin's apparent popularity rating above 80 per cent. While the Olympics may have been a precursor to the Kremlin's ability to manipulate an ostensible outpouring of support for Putin's actions in Ukraine, it was the military adventures that gave Putin the means to boost his standing with his own people, not his ability to pull off a complex mega-event. Despite their contrasting character, the Olympics and war united Russians in 2014 (Sinitsyn, 2015).

Ultimately, though, the high cost of the Sochi Olympics may ultimately become a liability for Putin. The figure of $50 billion has become a measure of comparison in the Russian press. For example, it is the same amount that The Hague Arbitration Court ordered Russia to pay to Yukos' creditors to compensate them for removing the company assets from their control and transferring them to the aegis of the state-owned Rosneft. It is also equal to the amount Rosneft President Igor Sechin requested from the government to help his company cope with sanctions placed on it following the annexation of Crimea (Polukhin, 2014). The Sochi Olympics were unique for Russia and could only be conducted during a time when the Kremlin leadership had full control over the country and could inject massive amounts of money into the project. Immediately after the games, it was obvious that such a feat could not be repeated soon given the slow grinding down of Russia's economic model and the low price of oil (Blant, 2014).

The main audience for the Sochi Olympics was always Russia's population. Existing evidence suggests that Russians were generally impressed by Putin's handling of the games even if they did not dramatically boost his popularity. According to the Levada Center, Russia's most respected polling agency, 77 per cent of Russians considered the games successful and claimed that they evoked feelings of pride and joy among the hosts (Levada Center, 2014). Two-thirds said that it made sense for Russia to host the games, though 20 per cent claimed that it did not. Eighty-one per cent said that the games encouraged feelings of greater patriotism in the country, while 56 per cent said the games were the personal achievement of Putin, and 73 per cent said that they raised Putin's authority. Despite these successes, the audience remained sceptical to some degree: 57 per cent complained that the 'billions spent on the Olympics, should have been spent on the development of Russian cities: the construction of new housing to replace the old, and the modernization of healthcare' (Levada Center, 2014). Additionally, 71 per cent said that the country's leadership used the games to boost the prestige of the authorities.

Below the elite level, the Kremlin obviously hoped to use the obvious 'bread and circus' elements of the Olympics to keep the domestic audience distracted. As the satiric political observer Viktor Shenderovich pointed out,

> We go from Eurovision to world hockey championship, from the Olympics to the World Cup . . . We are going from holiday to holiday, entertainment

114　*The legacy*

everywhere. Entertainment and pathos. Because if people begin to move beyond this fervor, and cool off a bit, clean themselves, then, you see, they will begin to see some things that the regime does not want them to see. Therefore, we will continue to go from victory to victory, from holiday to holiday, it will be impossible to escape from all these holidays. Holidays and war. Anything that will serve as a distraction. Fight for fellow Slavs, anywhere needed, we will step in for someone else and so on. (Felgengauer, 2014)

The Sochi Olympics served as useful fodder for Russia's relentless propaganda machine.

Putin and his cronies

Putin also apparently used the games to solidify support for his continued rule among Russia's ruling elite. Not only did the Olympics not force the Russian economy to become more efficient, it seems to have further stimulated the corrupt distribution of state assets to key cronies. That was one of the main findings of the Navalny report detailed in Chapter 2 (Anti-Corruption Foundation, 2014).

After the games, Putin awarded medals to the key Sochi supporters in a secret ceremony that took place in the Kremlin at the end of March 2014, according to a report in the newspaper *Vedomosti*, one of the few remaining newspapers independent of Kremlin control (Terent'eva, Nikol'sky, & Tovkailo, 2014). Among the recipients of the prizes were Interros owner Vladimir Potanin, Sberbank President German Gref, Gazprom Management Committee Chairman Alexei Miller, Russian Railroads Chairman Vladimir Yakunin, Renova Chairman of the Board Viktor Vekselberg, and Basic Elements Board Chairman Oleg Deripaska. These companies were in charge of constructing key elements of the Olympic infrastructure, though most of the funding ultimately came from the state budget.

As many as 500 additional individuals who played a role in the Olympic construction are expected to receive awards in the future. Conspicuously missing from the first list, for example, was Arkady Rotenberg, whose companies were among the largest recipients of construction contracts. Neither the presidential administration, nor *Vedomosti* explained why the ceremony was not held in public. However, the newspaper did remind readers that before the games took place, many observers had assumed that afterwards prosecutors would file criminal cases because of the numerous cost overruns and missed deadlines. However, there has been no such process. In fact, Arkady Rotenberg accepted the offer to build a bridge linking Russia to occupied Crimea, stepping in after Gennady Timchenko, another Putin friend, rejected the offer because he feared further retaliation from the West (Popov & Kiseleva, 2015).

However, not all of the contractors who worked on the Olympic sites are doing well in the games' aftermath. In fact, two have entered bankruptcy – Mostovik and Tunnel Brigade 44, whose chief has been arrested – and Inzhtransstroy announced its liquidation (Liauv & Tovkailo, 2014). Reasons for the contractors'

The legacy   115

problems included rapidly rising costs, poor project planning leading to unexpected expenses once construction began, and complicated government regulations that were often outdated and inconsistent from region to region. In some cases, the customer delayed approval of the plans until the last minute, forcing the contractors to complete all construction in an extreme hurry and therefore raised costs.

One interesting and unusual case is that of Russian Railroads Chairman Vladimir Yakunin, a key member of the Putin elite who lost his position and access to an enormous state budget shortly after the games. Yakunin had been a member of Putin's Ozero dacha group in the early 1990s, making him a key member of the inner circle. Nevertheless, he stepped down as head of Russian Railways in 2015, after serving in the that position for 10 years and apparently being pushed out, rejected an offer to serve in the Federation Council, the upper chamber of the Russian parliament, and announced plans to set up his own think tank. The reasons for Yakunin's fall from the inner circle have never been made clear, but it is possible that given Russia's difficult financial circumstances in 2015, his management of the railroads may have been too inefficient, leading the Kremlin to seek a more effective manager of its economic assets and one who would not place such a strain on public finances.

Russian regions

Just as there were winners and losers in Sochi, so too did the spectacle-driven economic development model provide winners and losers among the various Russian regions. On one hand, Putin's effort to develop Sochi partially rebalanced growth away from Moscow and helped to more evenly distribute resources across Russia. On the other, though, the concentration of resources in a favoured region meant that other regions did not have nearly as much access to the federal purse. As Trubina points out, the intersection between Russia's particular form of capitalism and the over-centralization of the political system meant that some places benefitted from 'systematic privileges' such as serving as sites of capital accumulation (Trubina, 2015). Such uneven development may not serve Russia's overall interests in the long term because some regions may resent having to pay more to the federal government than they receive back at the same time that it is obvious that favoured regions benefit from federal subsidies. While Sochi residents might consider the beneficial infrastructure investments as an 'Olympic windfall', residents of other regions would see the money spent as an opportunity cost that could have developed their area. Seeing what happened in Sochi, though, some other regions sought to get in on the act. Perm Governor Oleg Chirkunov sought to attract federal infrastructure investment in his region by promoting it as a European Capital of Culture, where residents and newcomers could make artistic careers and take advantage of local museums, theatres and arts festivals (Rogers, 2015, p. 305).

The Kremlin was satisfied with the way the regional authorities addressed the challenges of hosting the games and promoted Krasnodar Krai governor Alexander Tkachev to the position of Minister of Agriculture of the Russian Federation shortly

116 *The legacy*

after the Olympics. The situation in the region, however, did not improve after the games, but on the contrary, deteriorated in many ways. In 2016, the Committee for Civil Initiatives issued a report evaluating the socio-economic, political, and protest tensions in Russian regions, including Krasnodar Krai (Kynev, Petrov, & Titkov, 2016). The authors of the report stated that the Olympic investments provided a strong start for the krai, but that the crisis caught up with the region after the Crimean annexation and economic slowdown. Owing to the specifics of the Russian authoritarian system, the promotion of the ex-governor to a high level position had a negative impact on the local political machine. The new governor of Krasnodar, Veniamin Kondratyev, was not immediately able to re-structure the local elites or replace the pool of bureaucrats appointed by the ex-governor. Recent studies of patronal regime cycles indicate that elites in post-Soviet countries usually form a single 'pyramid' of power every time a regime change takes place (Hale, 2014). In the case of Krasnodar Krai, however, instead of demonstrating loyalty to the new authoritarian governor, part of the local elite has remained loyal to the ex-governor, whose political influence increased after his promotion to a high federal position, and such a situation destabilizes the regional political machine. The tensions inside the elite, together with the economic crisis and the growing number of civil protests, put Krasnodar Krai among the seven most unstable Russian regions in 2016 (Kryuchkov & Vinokuriv, 2016).

Russian state and society

The Sochi Olympics continued the ongoing process in Russia of increasing the power of the state, while simultaneously decreasing the power of society. Russia's police forces and military used the opportunity of the games to increase their capacities to monitor and control Russian society. At the same time, the authorities used their extensive powers to quash groups, like environmentalists, who opposed their policies. The result in Russia was typical of outcomes in other countries – the games served to concentrate power in the hands of elites while blocking much public participation in the urban development process. Likewise, the games did not help stimulate a process of healthy civic oversight in Russia.

Before the Olympics, the North Caucasus republics, including Dagestan and Ingushetia, were developing a soft power approach toward radical Islamist movements and achieved positive results in establishing dialogue among human right activists, law enforcements agencies, and other groups in society. The Kremlin, however, forced the local authorities in the Caucasus regions to abandon this soft approach before the Sochi Olympics. According to Memorial, the leading Russian human right organization,

> siloviki [the military and law enforcement agencies] succeeded in persuading the Russian leadership that only force (often un-lawful) would guarantee [stability in the region]. Later, since Spring 2013, with the increase of hysteria about events in Ukraine, the return to the methods of state terror in the North Caucasus became the main course. (Memorial, 2016)

The legacy 117

No positive international legacy

To some extent, Putin threw away any positive legacy that he might have earned from the games with the decision to annex Crimea and invade the eastern part of Ukraine (Orekh, 2015). The decision to host the Sochi Olympics was part of an effort to integrate into the broader world, though Russia wanted to do so on its own terms. On the eve of the games, Russia made a few concessions to what it perceived as international opinion, including the release of oligarch Mikhail Khodorkovsky after 10 years in prison, the slightly early release of two members of the punk group Pussy Riot (who had been jailed for singing an anti-Putin song in a Russian church), and the decision not to prosecute the members of Greenpeace who had been arrested in the fall of 2013 as they protested against Russia's off-shore oil drilling in the Arctic waters.

Putin's relationship with Western leaders was already confrontational before the games began. US President Obama and German Chancellor Angela Merkel refused to attend the opening ceremonies, seriously snubbing Putin in a move that may have had deep consequences as Putin took the games so seriously. The US-Russia relationship, in particular, had been flagging for some time, particularly after the US imposed smart sanctions on Russians deemed responsible for the death of lawyer Sergei Magnitsky in a Russian prison and Russia banned Americans from adopting Russian orphans (Gilligan, 2016). Russia's adoption of a law targeting the LGBT community in 2013 gave the Western leaders reason not to participate in the games, though their athletes all competed. Even with this downward trajectory, the decision to invade Ukraine changed the situation dramatically and led the West to impose broader sanctions on Russia, bringing the entire relationship to a new low.

Potentially, if Obama and Merkel had attended the Sochi opening ceremony, they would have had an opportunity to speak directly with Putin and perhaps could have prevented the subsequent invasion of Ukraine. Bush and Putin talked face-to-face in Beijing during the 2008 Summer Olympics in China and then had a chance to discuss the conflict in Georgia just as the five-day war was getting under way. However, such an outcome seems unlikely given Putin's willingness to risk so much in taking control of Crimea and destabilizing eastern Ukraine.

In his public statements, Putin blamed the deterioration of relations on the West. For example, at his press conference on December 18, 2014, he said,

> Let me remind you about the preparations for the 2014 Olympics, our inspiration and enthusiasm to organize a festive event not only for Russian sports fans, but for sports fans all over the world. However, and this is an evident truth, unprecedented and clearly orchestrated attempts were made to discredit our efforts to organize and host the Olympics. This is an undeniable fact! Who needs to do so and for what reason? And so on and so forth. (Putin, 2014)

In the same press conference, Putin blamed the events in Ukraine on the West as well, building on suspicions that had been growing since the time of the revolution itself (Myers, 2015, p. 459). However, he also seeks to continue relations

118   *The legacy*

in such a way that visitors will continue to come to Russia for an ongoing stream of mega-events:

> I think we achieved everything we wanted in the preparation of and the hosting of the Olympic Games. We achieved even more than we dreamt of. We won the Olympics . . . Regarding Ukraine, it's true, the games were just coming to a close when these tragic events began to unfold. But it was not our fault. We did not start the coup. It had nothing to do with us. I wish it had never happened, but it did. Speaking about whether we are pleased with the Olympics, of course we are pleased. By the way, we can see this from what is happening with the facilities. As you probably know, in many countries the Olympic facilities are just left empty after the games. Completely empty. Between the seasons our facilities are more or less empty too. But we planned some efforts in advance and built the Formula 1 track there. Then the Olympic Park hosted the World Chess Championship and some other events. Let me see. I think you know that the facilities are all booked up starting in December and until the end of February. (Putin, 2014)

Despite Putin's efforts to put a brave face on the Western sanctions, his foreign policy toward Ukraine began to hinder the further evolution of the mega-projects that he had staked Russia's development on in the years leading up to the games (Aptekar', 2014). In fact commentators like journalist Yury Saprykin warned that the decision to cut ties with the West would lead to further consequences at home:

> I fear that the Olympics will be the final and incontrovertible reason for cutting ties with the outside world – and that the leadership will stop being afraid to do anything in domestic politics: if you don't have to worry about the international community, then everything is permitted. (Rozhdenstvensky, 2015)

Indeed, Russia imposed counter-sanctions on the West, banning the import of food produced in countries that had imposed sanctions on Russia. Rather than opening up to the world, Russia turned to a policy of autarky in the years after the Olympics. The main goal of government policy was to replace imported goods with those produced at home.

Crimea

The Olympics closing ceremony took place on the night of February 23, but already in the early hours of that morning, the Russian president had put in place his plan to invade Crimea (Myers, 2015, p. 460). Putin took the decision relying only on the advice of his closest allies. The Kremlin executed the invasion and subsequent annexation with precision, reflecting the military reform that Russia had been carrying out since its 2008 war with Georgia and the impressive propaganda machine Putin had built to prosecute what he saw as a necessary information warfare (Cottiero, Kucharski, Olimpieva, & Orttung, 2015).

The legacy   119

Regardless of Putin's motivation in annexing Crimea, there is a strong organizational link between Sochi and Crimea since many of the resources used to prepare the Olympics were repurposed to facilitate the incorporation of Crimea into the Russian Federation. Most likely, special forces units providing security at the Olympics participated in the takeover of Crimea.

More obviously, Putin appointed Dmitry Kozak, who had been responsible for organizing the Olympics, as the new curator of Crimean affairs in the Russian government, giving him the goal of supervising the economic development of the region.

The Russian government treated Crimea like another mega-project, seeking to manage it with top-down control, even if the process seemed to be defined more by chaos than competence. While it is hard to predict whether the Kremlin will be able to successfully integrate the Ukrainian province into Russia, it is clear that the task will be extremely expensive at a time when Russia's resources are already tight due to slow economic growth.

In annexing Crimea and starting a war in eastern Ukraine, Putin effectively abandoned the legacy that he had tried to build up through the Sochi Olympics. In order to bolster his own popularity at home, he effectively shifted from a focus on domestic projects to expanding Russia's territory (Wood, 2015, p. 188). The Crimea project proved to be much more effective in boosting Putin's ratings with his own people than the Olympics were.

Crimea presents another parallel with Sochi in that it is a second Black Sea locale, where the local economy is heavily dependent on tourism, and where the Kremlin is taking a strong special interest in its success. The viability of the new infrastructure in Sochi will depend heavily on the arrival of tourists to use the facilities and amenities built at great public expense. But even as it continued to promote Sochi, the Russian government offered strong economic incentives for Russian tourists to travel to Crimea to boost the local economy of the occupied territory.

To some extent, Russia's increasing isolation forced its citizens to stay in-country during their vacations. In 2014, the Kremlin forbid its law enforcement officers to travel abroad, forcing some four million people to remain within Russia's newly enlarged borders. In 2015, the bombing of a Russian jetliner flying back from the Egyptian resort at Sharm el-Sheikh and the hostility between Russia and Turkey after Turkey shot down a Russian bomber that had violated its airspace limited Russians' ability to travel to these once popular destinations. Given the chaos surrounding the Russian takeover of Crimea, however, many fewer tourists travelled there than in the years when it was under Ukrainian control, creating greater possibilities for Sochi, though these were not always realized.

Legacy for the International Olympic Committee

The Sochi Olympics demonstrated that the IOC suffered from many of the same problems as Russia itself, and therefore was in need of comprehensive reform. These traits included a lack of democratic governance, transparency and

120 *The legacy*

accountability; fraudulent voting processes, and ambitions to expand its global power (H.J. Lenskyj, 2014, p. 102). In the wake of the Sochi games, the IOC has taken some steps to address the most glaring consequences of these problems, if not the underlying causes.

On 8 December 2014, less than a year after the Sochi closing ceremony, the IOC approved Olympic Agenda 2020, a large package of reforms that included economic and human rights initiatives. The measures called for cities to host economical games that were in line with their long-term social and economic development plans and encouraged them to make use of existing facilities and temporary structures as well as developing a sustainable legacy. They also addressed human rights provisions that were found wanting in Sochi by making changes in host city contracts and expanding the Olympic Charter to formalize protection of LGBT people, making this the sixth fundamental principle of Olympism (International Olympic Committee, 2014). This change was a big victory for international human rights groups like Human Rights Watch, All Out, and Athlete Ally. According to an e-mail distributed by All Out, the change in rules would 'prevent more anti-gay Olympics'. While the Olympic Charter had banned discrimination, it previously did not specifically ban discrimination of lesbian, gay, bi and trans people. The various international human rights groups successfully used the platform of the Olympics to increase awareness of their issues and protection for members of their communities. Before it was amended, Principle 6 of the Olympic Charter stated, 'Any form of discrimination with regard to a country or a person on grounds of race, religion, politics, gender or otherwise is incompatible with belonging to the Olympic Movement.' The amendment replaced 'otherwise' with more concrete guarantees.

After the 2014 Sochi Olympics, the IOC decided to play it safe in choosing host cities. In September 2013, it awarded the 2020 Summer Olympics to Tokyo over Istanbul and Madrid, avoiding potential Middle East turmoil and unemployment in Europe (Harlan & Svrluga, 2013). Awarding the event to Istanbul would have been the first time a Muslim majority country hosted the games, but IOC voters were worried about the conflict in neighbouring Syria. As noted above, the choice for the winter 2022 games came down to Kazakhstan and China because fewer democratic cities were interested in hosting the games due to the high cost of the spectacle in Beijing 2008 and Sochi 2014. According to David Wallechinsky, the president of the International Society of Olympic Historians:

> In terms of the legacy of Sochi from the point of view of the IOC, the worst possible thing that happened was that it cost them $50 billion, which was almost 500 percent more than the Vancouver Olympics had cost. (Sindelar, 2014)

Doping scandal

Beyond the cost overruns, a wide-ranging doping scandal emerged as a second major headache for the IOC as a result of the Sochi Olympics. In May 2016,

The legacy 121

The New York Times published an extensive report outlining how the Russian authorities had organized a programme over the course of several years to ensure Russian dominance at the games: They provided performance enhancing drugs to Russian athletes and then cleansed their urine samples to cover up the cheating (Ruiz, Lai, Parshina-Kottas, & White, 2016). The newspaper report alleged that participants in the programme included 'Dozens of Russian athletes at the 2014 Winter Olympics in Sochi, including at least 15 medal winners', none of whom had been accused of doping before the allegations appeared. The report was based on the testimony of Grigory Rodchenkov, the head of the Sochi anti-doping laboratory during the 2014 games. Although Putin had awarded him an Order of Friendship award after the games, Rodchenkov subsequently fled Russia for the United States, fearing for his life. Two former leaders of the Russian Anti-Doping Agency, Vyacheslav Sinev and Nikita Kamayev, died in unclear circumstances in February 2016 (Kramer, 2016). Rodchenkov claimed that the Russian athletes had used 'a cocktail of three anabolic steroids–metenolone, trenbolone and oxandrolone' that he had concocted and that he had destroyed 'several thousand' urine samples to cover up the evidence. While athletes typically have to stop using performance enhancing drugs before a competition to avoid detection, hosting the Olympics in Sochi allowed Russian competitors to continue doping because the Russian lab could cover up for them. The journalists charged Russia with 'undermining the integrity of one of the world's most prestigious sporting events'. The Kremlin denied that it had been involved in any wrongdoing.

Rodchenkov told the Times that he took direct orders from Yuri Nagornykh, the deputy of Russian Sports Minister Vitaly Mutko. Each night a letter came from the ministry listing which athlete's samples needed to be replaced. A technician collected the urine samples in a secured area and then passed them through a hole in the wall to a storage space converted into a lab where Rodchenkov and his team worked. Rodchenkov handed the bottles with the supposedly tamper-proof lids to a Federal Security Service official who took them to a nearby building. Hours later the official returned the bottles with their lids open but the seal unbroken to the lab where technicians could discard the tainted urine and replace it with clean samples that had been collected from each athlete before the competition. The technicians then put the clean samples in place to be tested the next day.

The scheme came to light thanks to insiders who sought to alert the World Anti-Doping Agency (WADA) to systematic doping among Russian athletes organized by the Russian state. Russian anti-doping official Vitaliy Stepanov and his wife Yuliya Stepanova, a middle distance runner, provided detailed descriptions to WADA in 2010 of how cheating was endemic to Russian athletes with the complicity of the Russian government and anti-doping agency (Hobson, 2016). In effect, Stepanov was telling WADA that its Russian counterpart, the Russian Anti-Doping Agency (RUSADA), was helping to organize cheating by Russia's Olympic athletes. WADA did not open an investigation, claiming that it did not have the authority to do so until January 2015. However, in early 2014 Jack Robertson, a former US Drug Enforcement Agency agent who had been hired by WADA as an investigator, told Stepanov (who subsequently fled to an undisclosed

122   *The legacy*

location in the United States fearing retribution) to get in touch with Hajo Seppelt, an investigative journalist who worked for German television. Seppelt aired a documentary entitled 'Top-Secret Doping: How Russia Makes Its Winners' in December 2014 on German television which shamed WADA into using its new investigative powers to open an investigation. The result was an explosive report released on 9 November 2015, which found widespread doping among Russian track and field athletes (Pound, McLaren, & Younger, 2015). It also indicated that cheating was rampant in other sports and that government officials were involved, including the central role played by Rodchenkov. That report pointed out that Rodchenkov had destroyed 1,417 samples immediately before the arrival of WADA investigators in the Moscow Anti-Doping Center (Pound *et al.*, 2015, p. 203). Mutko requested that Rodchenkov resign from his position in December 2015. WADA published a second report in January 2016 outlining various criminal charges. On May 8, the US 60 Minutes programme broadcast recorded interviews between Rochenkov and Stepanov claiming that four Russian gold medalists at Sochi had used doping and that the FSB had interfered with the Olympic anti-doping program (Wesolowsky, 2016).

The revelations continued in the run-up to the Rio Summer Olympics when WADA published the independent McLauren Commission report on July 18 (McLaren, 2016). The approximately 100-page report confirmed the allegations made by Rodchenkov of systematic and state-sponsored doping for Russian athletes during the Sochi games as well as in other events. In addition to Russia's sports ministry, the report also implicated the Federal Security Service in the doping scheme and identified Evgeny Blokhin as the security official who played a key role in covering up the positive drug tests. In releasing the report, the WADA Executive Committee noted that there was no evidence that Russia had sought to make changes in its practices or the overall culture in response to previous revelations about its doping program.[2] The results affected a variety of sports at the summer and winter Olympics and raised questions about the actual winners of numerous competitions in the Sochi Olympics. McLaren's research was only partially complete at the time of publication and was expected to continue in the future.

Putin denounced the report as an effort to insert geopolitics into sports.[3] Without addressing the allegations in the report, he claimed, without evidence, that U.S. anti-doping experts had set the tone of the report and sought to question Rodchenkov's character in order to undermine his and the report's credibility.

On the basis of the report, WADA recommended that all Russian Olympic and Paralympic athletes be banned from the Summer 2016 Rio games and that Russian government officials be denied access to international sports competition. The IOC considered banning all Russian athletes from the Rio Olympics, but instead declared that all Russian athletes were guilty of doping unless they could prove otherwise through verifiable testing.[4] The IOC also determined that Yuliya Stepanova could not compete as a neutral athlete at Rio because even though she had served as a whistleblower exposing Russian doping, she had been implicated in the doping system for five years, had tested positive, and therefore did 'not satisfy the ethical requirements for an athlete to enter the Olympic Games'.[5]

The legacy 123

On the eve of the Olympics, the Court of Arbitration for Sport ruled that 271 of Russia's 389 Olympic athletes could compete, while forcing about 120 to sit out the games. The International Association of Athletics Federations banned all track and field athletes from the Rio Olympics except for long jumper Darya Klishina. Ultimately, Russia was fourth in the medal count at the Rio games with 56 medals, 19 of them gold. This result was one of its worst performances ever, but a point of pride for many in the circumstances. Additionally, the entire Russian paralympic team was banned from the competition in Rio. In announcing the penalty, Sir Philip Craven, president of the International Paralympic Committee, said Russia's 'medals over morals mentality disgusts me.'[6] The Court of Arbitration for Sport upheld the ban, noting that Russia did not provide any evidence to contradict the facts on which the decision had been made.

Conclusion

The personalized, centralized, authoritarian and patrimonial political system built by Vladimir Putin since 2000, with its disregard for democracy, formal institutions, transparency and accountability ultimately was responsible for the corruption and mismanagement of the Olympics, the invasion of Ukraine, and the doping scandal that began to explode more than a year after the Sochi games closed. Given the repression of civil society, the disregard for the environment, and the intensification of the strengthening of Russia's security services, the 2014 Sochi Olympics served to heighten many of the tendencies that had long been apparent in Russian society. Ironically, instead of providing an attractive façade for the country, the Olympics simply made the problems surrounding the nature of Russia's regime apparent to the world.

Unfortunately, the Olympics did not bring change to Russia's political or economic system. At the highest levels, the Olympics were ultimately an exercise in redistributing public money to Putin's cronies. Although the economic crisis that began around 2014 has limited Russian spending to some extent, the country continues to rely on mega-projects as a driver for development. Prominent post-Olympic projects included the occupation of Crimea, building a bridge across the Kerch strait to link the captured territory to the Russian mainland, and the 2018 World Cup.

Were the Olympics a success? In some ways, yes. Sochi managed to host 17 days of sports competition without any major problems. The regime built worldclass facilities, though at a high cost. There was no terrorist attack on Sochi, despite the explosions in Volgograd in the run-up to the games. The Olympics successfully took place in a war zone. Since he rose to power in 1999, Putin has been defined by the Caucasus and the wars there. Sochi served as a symbolic affirmation that the wars were over, at least temporarily, and that the Russian leadership had pacified the insurgents. Putin is a populist and Sochi was ultimately part of a deal with the lower middle class. Ordinary Russians who cannot afford to vacation abroad can now go to Sochi and enjoy a transformed cityscape.

To some extent the Olympics were a success for the regime. Many of Putin's closest friends made billions of dollars from the spending surrounding the

124 *The legacy*

preparations for the games. Ordinary Russians had reason to feel proud of their country for hosting the games, though the games themselves did not substantially boost the popularity of the regime.

At the same time, there are clear failures. The games deeply disappointed local environmentalists, who complained that the resort construction ate into protected national parks and the new infrastructure polluted local rivers. Putin and the Kremlin had claimed the best of intentions in striving for a green games, but these promises proved to be either hollow or unfulfillable. The Olympics were defined by extensive corruption even though Putin personally took control of the preparations. The megaproject did little to change the nature of Russia's kleptocracy. And, ultimately, the games did little to boost Russia's image abroad.

However, Sochi's legacy is constantly evolving and it is possible that historians will look back on the games with different eyes. Russian athletes won the most gold medals and the most medals overall, though the subsequent doping scandal has called this achievement into doubt. The questions about cheating have the potential to implicate all of Russian sport with the failure to compete fairly. The International Olympic Committee is being forced to reexamine its relationship with Russia and question whether Russian authorities took advantage of it to win as many medals as possible. Putin and his allies constantly blame the West for seeking ways to humiliate Russia, but ultimately the men who control the Russian state brought upon themselves the most destructive problems due to their authoritarian profiteering.

Notes

1   The number of hotel employees increased from 50,100 (2013) to 56,600 (2014), which was still lower than in 2009 (62,700) and 2010 (57,800).
2   www.wada-ama.org/en/media/news/2016-07/wada-statement-independent-investigation-confirms-russian-state-manipulation-of
3   http://en.kremlin.ru/events/president/news/52537
4   www.olympic.org/news/decision-of-the-ioc-executive-board-concerning-the-participation-of-russian-athletes-in-the-olympic-games-rio-2016
5   www.olympic.org/news/decision-of-the-ioc-executive-board-concerning-the-participation-of-russian-athletes-in-the-olympic-games-rio-2016
6   Editorial: Russia Blames Others for Its Doping Woes, *The New York Times*, 29 August 2016.

References

Andranovich, G., & Burbank, M.J. (2011). Contextualizing Olympic Legacies. *Urban Geography*, *32*(6), 823–44. doi: 10.2747/0272-3638.32.6.823

Anti-Corruption Foundation. (2014). *Sochi 2014: Encyclopedia of spending The Cost of Olympics Report*. Moscow: Anti-Corruption Foundation.

Aptekar', P. (2014, August 12). Rossiia Na Grani Offsaida. *Vedomosti*. Retrieved from www.vedomosti.ru/opinion/articles/2014/08/12/na-grani-ofsajda#/ixzz3AEdfX42X (Accessed 8 October 2016).

Baumann, R., & Matheson, V. (2013). *Infrastructure Investments and Mega-Sports Events: Comparing the Experience of Developing and Industrialized Countries*. College of the

The legacy 125

Holy Cross, Department of Economics Faculty Research Series, Paper no. 13–05. College of the Holy Cross. Worcester, MA.

Blant, M. (2014, February 7). Itogi Nedeli. Kontsentrat Rossiiskikh Realii. *Ej.ru*. Retrieved from www.ej.ru/?a=note&id=24361# (Accessed 8 October 2016).

Bulanov, K. (2016, May 20). Rossiiane Nashli Ideal'nyae Mest dlya Otdykha Vnutri Strany. *RBK*. Retrieved from www.rbc.ru/society/24/05/2016/57443abf9a79472ffa005bb1 (Accessed 8 October 2016).

Cashman, R., & Horne, J. (2013). Managing Legacy. In S. Frawley & D. Adair (Eds), *Managing the Olympics* (pp. 50–65). London: Palgrave Macmillan.

Chappelet, J.L. (2008). Olympic Environmental Concerns as a Legacy of the Winter Games. *The International Journal of the History of Sport*, *25*(14), 1884–1902.

Committee for Russian Economic Freedom. (2016). Olimpiada 2014 v Sochi, dva goda spustia [The 2014 Olimpiade in Sochi, two years on]. http://russianeconomicfreedom.org/ru/2016/03/29/the-2014-sochi-olympics-two-years-on/ (Accessed 8 October 2016).

Cottiero, C., Kucharski, K., Olimpieva, E., & Orttung, R.W. (2015). War of Words: The Impact of Russian State Television on the Russian Internet. *Nationalities Papers*, *43*(4), 533–55.

Dansero, E., & Puttilli, M. (2010). Mega-Events Tourism Legacies: The Case of the Torino 2006 Winter Olympic Games – A Territorialisation Approach. *Leisure Studies*, *29*(3), 321–41.

Darcy, S., & Taylor, T. (2013). Managing Olympic Venues. In S. Frawley & D. Adair (Eds), *Managing the Olympics* (pp. 99–126). London: Palgrave Macmillan.

Demirijian, K. (2015, January 18). Russian Economic Crisis Helps Save Putin's Post-Olympic Dream at Sochi. *Washington Post*. Retrieved from www.washingtonpost.com/world/europe/russian-economic-crisis-helps-save-putins-post-olympic-dream-at-sochi/2015/01/17/d8c7bbd8-92b1-11e4-a66f-0ca5037a597d_story.html (Accessed 8 October 2016).

Diaz, J. (2015, August 2). How Boston Wins by Losing. *San Francisco Chronicle*, p. E2.

Dobrynin, S. (2014, April 22). Posle Sochi. Gorod. *RFE/RL*. Retrieved from www.svoboda.org/content/article/25358677.html

Edds, S. (2012). *Economic Impacts of the Olympic Games through State Comparison*. University of Chicago Honors Thesis.

Federal'noe Agenstvo Po Turizmu. (2015). Svodnye Statisticheskie Dannye (s 2009 po 2014 gody). Retrieved from www.russiatourism.ru/content/8/section/81/detail/4124/ (Accessed 8 October 2016).

Fedorova, M. (2014, December 17). Postolimpiiskii Sindrom [Post-Olympic Syndrome]. *Kommersant*. Retrieved from www.kommersant.ru/projects/sochi (Accessed 8 October 2016).

Felgengauer, T. (2014, February 6). Osoboe Mnenie: Viktor Shenderovich. *Ekho Moskvy*. Retrieved from http://echo.msk.ru/programs/personalno/1252556-echo/(Accessed 8 October 2016).

Gilligan, E. (2016). Smart Sanctions against Russia: Human Rights, Magnitsky and the Ukrainian Crisis. *Demokratizatsiya: The Journal of Post-Soviet Democratization*, *24*(2), 257–77.

Gold, J.R., & Gold, M.M. (2008). Olympic Cities: Regeneration, City Rebranding and Changing Urban Agendas. *Geography Compass*, *2*(1), 300–18.

Golubchikov, O. (2016). The 2014 Sochi Winter Olympics: Who stands to gain? In G. Sweeney (Ed.), *Global Corruption Report: Sport* (pp. 183–91). London: Routledge and Transparency International.

126 *The legacy*

Gribtsova, I., & Tovkailo, M. (2014, July 8). Igornaia Zona V Krasnodarskom Krae Mozhet Ostat'sia Tol'ko Odna. *Vedomosti*. Retrieved from www.vedomosti.ru/com panies/news/2868317l/kazino-tolko-dlya-sochi (Accessed 8 October 2016).

Hale, H.E. (2014). *Patronal Politics: Eurasian Regime Dynamics in Comparative Perspective*. New York: Cambridge University Press.

Harlan, C., & Svrluga, B. (2013, September 8). Tokyo wins bid for 2020 Games. *The Washington Post*.

Hobson, W. (2016, June 3). Alerted to doping in '10, WADA didn't investigate. *The Washington Post*.

International Olympic Committee. (2014). Olympic Agenda 2020: 20+20 Recommendations. www.olympic.org/olympic-agenda-2020 (Accessed 8 October 2016).

International Olympic Committee. (2015). *Factsheet: Sochi 2014 Facts & Figures*. Lausanne, Switzerland: International Olympic Committee.

Jeong, G.H., Jafari, J., & Gartner, W.C. (1990). Expectations of the 1988 Seoul Olympics: A Korean Perspective. *Tourism Recreation Research*, *15*(1), 26–33.

Koch, N., & Valiyev, A. (2015). The Sochi Syndrome Afoot in Central Asia: Spectacle and Speculative Building in Baku, Astana, and Ashgabat. *PONARS Eurasia Policy Memo*, *371*.

Kramer, A.E. (2016, February 15). Nikita Kamayev, Ex-Head of Russian Anti-Doping Agency, Dies. *The New York Times*. Retrieved from www.nytimes.com/2016/02/16/world/europe/nikita-kamayev-ex-head-of-russian-antidoping-agency-dies.html?_r=1 (Accessed 8 October 2016).

Kriviakina, E. (2015, January 12). Medvedev prizval razvivat' novye gornolyzhnye kurorty. *Komsomolskaia pravda*. Retrieved from www.kp.ru/daily/26326.5/3211123/ (Accessed 8 October 2016).

Kryuchkov, I., & Vinokuriv, A. (2016, June 15). Regiony Degradiruyut Pod Kontrolem: Doklad Komiteta Grazhdanskikh Initsiativ Otsenil Nestabil'nost' Regionov Rossii. *Gazeta.ru*. Retrieved from www.gazeta.ru/politics/2016/06/14_a_8308133.shtml (Accessed 8 October 2016).

Kynev, A., Petrov, N., & Titkov, A. (2016). *Index Sotsial'no-Ekonomicheskoi i Politicheskoi Napryazhennosti: Reiting Regional'nykh Riskov Na Nachalo 2016 Goda*. Moscow: Komitet Grazhdanskikh Initsiativ.

Lenskyj, H. (2016). Sports Mega-Event Legacies: From the Beneficial to the Destructive. In G. Sweeney (Ed.), *Global Corruption Report: Sport* (pp. 218–22). London and New York: Routledge and Transparency International.

Lenskyj, H.J. (2014). *Sexual Diversity and the Sochi 2014 Olympics: No More Rainbows*. Basingstoke, UK: Palgrave Macmillian.

Levada Center. (2014, March 3). Itogi Olimpiiskikh Igr v Sochi. Retrieved from www.levada.ru/old/03-03-2014/itogi-olimpiiskikh-igr-v-sochi (Accessed 8 October 2016).

Li, S., & Jago, L. (2012). Evaluating Economic Impacts of International Sports Events. In R. Shipway & A. Fyall (Eds), *International Sports Events: Impacts, experiences, and identities* (pp. 13–26). London: Routledge.

Liauv, B., & Tovkailo, M. (2014, April 21). S Gosudarsvom Ne Postroish. *Vedomosti*. Retrieved from www.vedomosti.ru/newspaper/articles/2014/04/21/s-gosudarstvom-ne-postroish (Accessed 8 October 2016).

Longman, J. (2015, January 8). U.S.O.C. Chooses Boston as Candidate for 2024 Summer Olympics. *The New York Times*. Retrieved from http://nytimes.com/2015/01/09/sports/olympics/boston-to-be-us-bid-city-for-2024-olympics.html (Accessed 8 October 2016).

The legacy   127

McLaren, R. (2016). *The Independent Person Report.* Montreal: World Anti-Doping Agency.

Mangan, J.A. (2008). Prologue: Guarantees of Global Goodwill: Post-Olympic Legacies – Too Many Limping White Elephants? *The International Journal of the History of Sport,* 25(14), 1869–83.

Meduza. (2016, March 9). Chislo Vyezzhayuschikh Za Granitsu Rossiiskikh Turistov Sokratilos' na Tret'. *Meduza.* Retrieved from https://meduza.io/news/2016/03/09/chislo-vyezzhayuschih-za-granitsu-rossiyskih-turistov-sokratilos-na-tret (Accessed 8 October 2016).

Memorial. (2016). *Kontrterror Na Severnom Kavkaze: Vsglyad Pravozaschitnikov. 2014 g. – Pervaya Polovina 2016 g.* Moscow: Memorial.

Moscow Times. (2014, July 4). Crimea and Sochi see future as gambling centers. *The Moscow Times.* Retrieved from www.themoscowtimes.com/business/article/crimea-and-sochi-see-future-as-gambling-centers/503018.html (Accessed 8 October 2016).

Müller, M. (2015). (Im-)Mobile policies: Why Sustainability Went Wrong in the 2014 Olympics in Sochi. *European Urban and Regional Studies,* 22(2), 191–209.

Müller, M. (2016). The Multiple Roles of Mega-Events: Mega-Promises, Mini-Outcomes? In G. Sweeney (Ed.), *Global Corruption Report: Sport* (pp. 133–38). London: Routledge and Transparency International.

Müller, M., & Pickles, J. (2015). Global Games, Local Rules: Megaevents in the Post-Socialist World. *European Urban and Regional Studies,* 22(2), 121–27.

Myers, S.L. (2015). *The New Tsar: The Rise and Reign of Vladimir Putin.* New York: Alfred A. Knopf.

NESru.com. (2015, February 4). Olympiiskii Park Spustia God Posle Igr: Seichas Getto, A Skoro Mozhet Prevratitsia V Banal'nuyu Pomoiku. *NESru.com.* Retrieved from http://realty.newsru.com/article/04feb2015/olimppark (Accessed 8 October 2016).

Olimprus. (2007, September 16). V Sochi K 2014 Godu Budet Sozdano 150–160 tys. Novykh Rabochikh Mest. *Olimprus.* Retrieved from http://olimprus.ru/articles/new150 workplacetoolimp (Accessed 8 October 2016).

Orekh, A. (2015, January 9). Itogi goda. Sport: Zhizn' posle Sochi, ili rubl' kak glavnyi igrok. *Ezhednevnyi zhurnal.* Retrieved from www.ej.ru/?a=note&id=26761 (Accessed 8 October 2016).

Polukhin, A. (2014, August 14). Olimpiard dlia Igora Sechina. *Novaia gazeta.* Retrieved from www.novayagazeta.ru/columns/64839.html (Accessed 8 October 2016).

Popov, Y., & Kiseleva, E. (2015, January 30). Pravitel'stvo Navelo Most K Arkadiyu Rotenbergu. *Kommersant.* Retrieved from http://kommersant.ru/doc/2656318 (Accessed 8 October 2016).

Pound, R.W., McLaren, R.H., & Younger, G. (2015, November 9). The Independent Commission Report #1. Retrieved from www.wada-ama.org/en/resources/world-anti-doping-program/independent-commission-report-1 (Accessed 8 October 2016).

Putin, V. (2014, December 18). News Conference of Vladimir Putin. *Kremlin.ru.* Retrieved from http://en.kremlin.ru/events/president/news/47250 (Accessed 8 October 2016).

Regnum. (2015, February 6). Reiting Vliianiia Glav Sub'ektov Rossiiskoi Federatsii V Yanvare 2015: Agentstvo Politicheskikh i Ekonomicheskikh Kommunikatsii. *Regnum.* Retrieved from https://regnum.ru/news/polit/1892418.html (Accessed 8 October 2016).

Riordan, J. (2007). Sport after the Cold War: Implications for Russia and Eastern Europe. In S. Wagg & D.L. Andrews (Eds), *East Plays West: Sport and the Cold War* (pp. 272–88). London: Routledge.

128 *The legacy*

Rogers, D. (2015). *The Depths of Russia: Oil, Power, and Culture after Socialism*. Ithaca, NY: Cornell University Press.

Rozhdenstvensky, I. a. (2015, February 14). My i Dal'she Budem Idti ot Pobedy k Pobede. *Meduza*. Retrieved from https://meduza.io/feature/2015/02/14/my-i-dalshe-budem-idti-ot-pobedy-k-pobede (Accessed 8 October 2016).

Ruiz, R.R., Lai, K.K.R., Parshina-Kottas, Y., & White, J. (2016, May 13). Russian Doctor Explains How He Helped Beat Doping Tests at the Sochi Olympics. *The New York Times*.

Sindelar, D. (2014, December 23). Sports & Dictators: In 2014, A Match Made In Heaven. *RFE/RL*. Retrieved from www.rferl.org/content/sport-dictators-connections/26759272. html (Accessed 8 October 2016).

Sinitsyn, A. (2015, February 9). Ot Redaktsii: Pamiati Olimpiady. *Vedomosti*. Retrieved from www.vedomosti.ru/opinion/news/39164271/pamyati-olimpiady

Sochi 2014. (2007). Sochi Candidature File 'Sochi 2014 Candidate City: Gateway to the Future'. web.archive.org/web/20100103043040/http://sochi2014.com/sch_questionnaire (Accessed 8 October 2016).

Sokolov, M., & Bigg, C. (2014, June 19). Putin Forever? Russian President's Ratings Skyrocket Over Ukraine. *RFE/RL*. Retrieved from www.rferl.org/content/russia-putin-approval-ratings/25409183.html (Accessed 8 October 2016).

Solsvik, T. (2014, October 1). Norway Withdraws Oslo Bid for 2022 Winter Games. *Reuters*. Retrieved from www.reuters.com/article/2014/10/01/us-olympics-winter-norway-idUSKCN0HQ4QE20141001(Accessed 8 October 2016).

Terent'eva, A., Nikol'sky, A., & Tovkailo, M. (2014, March 6). Olimpiiskie Geroi. *Vedomosti*. Retrieved from www.vedomosti.ru/newspaper/articles/2014/06/03/olimpijskie-geroi#/ixzz35Bslo1KA (Accessed 8 October 2016).

Terret, T. (2008). The Albertville Winter Olympics: Unexpected Legacies – Failed Expectations for Regional Economic Development. *The International Journal of the History of Sport*, 25(14), 1903–21.

Titov, E. (2014, July 21). Sochi sazhaiut na kon. *Novaia gazeta*. Retrieved from www. novayagazeta.ru/economy/64506.html (Accessed 10 October 2016).

Trubina, E. (2015). Mega-events in the context of capitalist modernity: The case of 2014 Sochi Winter Olympics. *Eurasian Geography and Economics*, 55(6), 610–27.

Valov, A. (2015, Feburary 4). Olimpiiskii park. . . god spustia. Retrieved from http://echo. msk.ru/blog/alexandrvalov/1486764-echo/ (Accessed 8 October 2016).

Volkov, D. (2014, December 22). Putin's Ratings: Anomaly or Trend? *Institute of Modern Russia*. Retrieved from http://imrussia.org/en/analysis/nation/2135-putins-ratings-anomaly-or-trend (Accessed 8 October 2016).

Volkov, V. (2014, April 22). Sochi. Taina Belykh Slonov. *Ej.ru*. Retrieved from http://ej.ru/?a=note&id=24980 (Accessed 8 October 2016).

Weir, F. (2016, May 24). In Post-Olympic Sochi, White Elephants – And Improved Daily Life. *Christian Science Monitor*.

Wesolowsky, T. (2016, May 19). As More Doping Allegations Emerge, Russian Sport Braces For Potential Consequences. *RFE/RL*. Retrieved from www.rferl.org/content/russian-sport-braces-doping-allegations-consequences/27745593.html (Accessed 8 October 2016).

Wood, E.A. (2015). A Small Victorious War? The Symbolic Politics of Vladimir Putin. In E.A. Wood, W.E. Pomeranz, E.W. Merry, & M. Trudolyubov (Eds), *Roots of Russia's War in Ukraine* (pp. 164–213). Washington and New York: Woodrow Wilson Center Press and Columbia University Press.

Wurster, S. (2013). Homes for Games: A filmic interpretation of Sochi 2014 and resettlement in Imeretinskaya Bay. *European Urban and Regional Studies*, *22*(2), 210–17.

Wynn, J. (2016, May 12). Why Cities Should Stop Building Museums and Focus on Festivals *The Conversation*. Retrieved from https://theconversation.com/why-cities-should-stop-building-museums-and-focus-on-festivals-57333 (Accessed 8 October 2016).

Zimbalist, A. (2015). *Circus Maximus: The Economic Gamble Behind Hosting the Olympics and the World Cup*. Washington, DC: Brookings Institution Press.

Index

Abkhazia 69–71, 82, 94
Adler 29–30, 48–9, 109
Adygea 83, 87–8, 90
Afanasenkov, Vladimir 41–2
Afghanistan 6, 11, 63, 95
Ahn, Viktor 12
Akhaminova, Elena 91
Al-Qaeda 68
Alekseev, Nikolai 53
Alexander II 86
Alexandra Fyodorovna, czarina 84
Alexandria, fort 84
Altai Republic 109
Anderson, Rocky 71
authoritarianism 106, 111–12, 123–4; and
    accountability 39–41; and corruption
    30, 32, 45; and mega-projects 2, 21;
    and Putin 7–9, 81; and Russia 4, 116
Azerbaijan 94, 111

Bach, Thomas 67
Baltics 93
Bariatinskii, Aleksandr 87
Beijing 109, 117
Belarus 12, 94
Bell, James S. 84–5
Berzek, Dogomuko 84–5
Berzek, Kerantuk 85–7
Bilalov, Akhmed 31
Black Sea 81, 84, 87, 119; and Circassians
    90; and military 66, 69–71, 75; and
    tourism 89, 98
Blokhin, Evgeny 122
Bocharov, Ruchei 88
Bolloev, Taimuraz 29
Bolotnaya Square protests 74
Boston 112
Boston Marathon bombing 62
Bortnikov, Aleksandr 98

boycott 2, 6, 11, 53–4, 82, 94–7
Bradley, Tom 23
Brazil 74–5
Brezhnev, Leonid 6–7
Britain 86, 95; see also England, United
    Kingdom
Brussels 82
Bush, George W. 117
Bychkov, Yegor 5

Cameron, David 54
Canada 43, 63, 89–90
Candemir, Cihan 89
Caucasus Emirate 64–5, 67–8
Caucasus Mountains 66, 105
Caucus, Georgia 96
Chaika, Yury 28, 31
Chechnya 64–5; Russian–Chechen War 64
Chechukh, Mejid 92
Chernobyl 47
Chernyshenko, Dmitri 29
China 5, 8, 12, 30, 43, 64, 81, 111, 120
Chirkunov, Oleg 115
Circassians: 1829 Adrianople Treaty 84;
    1848 Adagum Assembly 85; 1856 Paris
    Treaty 86; Circassian Confederation
    83–6; Circassian issue and containment
    theory 83, 92; Circassian question 15,
    41, 69, 81–94; Natukhai ethnic group
    86; Sashe ethnic 83; Shapsug ethnic
    group 84, 86–7; Ubykh ethnic group
    83–6
civil society 16, 38–41, 50, 54–5, 73, 75,
    105, 123; definition 39–40
Cold War 13, 83, 92, 105
Commonwealth of Independent States 69
Constantinople 85
corruption: anti-corruption 13–14, 24, 26,
    29; as part of Putin's regime 1, 4, 10,

Index 131

21–2, 30–1, 114, 123; during the Sochi games 1–2, 7–8, 13, 15, 21, 25, 27, 29–33, 43, 108, 123–4; and mega-projects 3, 8, 22, 25, 30; in Russia 1–2, 4, 10, 14, 22, 28–9, 31–3, 65, 70, 95; in the USSR 6; in the West 4, 14
Cossacks 74, 89
cost: Olympic games 5, 15, 23, 108, 112, 120; Sochi games 5–6, 14, 21–33, 39, 45, 51, 108–9, 113, 115, 120
counterfactual 10
Craven, Philip 123
Crimea: 1853–1856 Crimean war 85; Russian annexation 1–2, 10, 12–15, 71–2, 74–5, 82–3, 85, 88, 97–9, 106, 109, 113–14, 116–19, 123; vacation resort 88

Dagestan 66–8, 116
Deripaska, Oleg 27, 109, 114
development goals 7–8, 14–15, 26, 32, 39, 47, 56, 105, 110–11, 115–16, 120
doping 1–2, 15, 72, 105–6, 120–4
Dronov, Dmitry 71
Drozdov, Ivan 87
Dziash, Ismail 86

Egypt 119
Elbrus Mt. 88–9
elections: manipulations 8–9, 22, 25, 40, 41–4; Putin's 2012 re-elections 13, 52, 66, 73; Sochi mayoral 39, 41–5; State Duma 45, 73
England 85; *see also* Britain and United Kingdom
environmental issues 5, 9, 14, 26, 38–41, 45–50, 54–5, 105, 110–11, 116, 123–4
Estonia 49, 93
Ernst, Konstantin 91
Euromaidan 108
Europe 54, 82, 85–6, 96–8, 120
European Union 12, 82–3

Fars River 86
Fierstein, Harvey 53
Formula One race 94, 107, 118
France 12, 68, 85

Gaplikov, Sergei 29
Garibashvili, Irakli 95
Gauck, Joachim 54
Gazaryan, Suren 49
Gazprom 4, 26–7, 114

Germany 8, 12, 72, 91, 112
Georgia 43, 61, 69–70, 75, 81, 87, 90–1, 94–5, 97; 2008 Russian–Georgian war 15, 43, 61, 69, 71, 75, 82, 94–6, 117–18; Georgian Olympic Committee 95; recognition of the Circassian genocide 90–1, 94
Goble, Paul 93
Gorbachev, Mikhail 44
Goreslavsky, Sergei 74
Greece 6, 30, 46, 63–4, 70, 106, 112
Greenpeace 48, 117
Gudkov, Lev 113
Gurulev, Andrei 71
Graham, Lindsey (R-SC) 96
Gref, German 109, 114

Hagel, Chuck 96
human rights 10, 15, 38, 49–50, 54, 67–8, 73, 82, 93, 116, 120
Hwan, Chun Doo 38
hybrid regime 22

ideology 2, 7–8, 21, 32, 87
inequality 5
information war 98, 118; *see also* propaganda
Ingushetia 65–6, 116
International Olympic Committee (IOC) 5–6, 23, 27–8, 45, 47, 64, 69–71, 81–2, 88, 95–6, 104–6, 119–20, 122; Olympic reforms 15, 105, 119–20; and Sochi 3, 10; and spending 6
Interros 27, 114
ISIS 68
Islam 65, 67, 84, 93, 116; Salafi 65–7
Israel 62, 90–1
Istanbul 89, 91, 120
Italy 12, 73
Ivanov, Sergei 98

Jordan 89

Kabardino-Balkaria 65, 87–8, 91
Kaliningrad 109
Kamayev, Nikita 121
Karachay-Cherkessia 66, 87–8
Kardanov, Murat 91
Kavkazskaya Riviera 87
Kazakhstan 12, 94, 111, 120
Kazan 4, 24, 26
Kebekov, Aliaskhab 68
Kerry, John 96
Khakim, David 49

132 *Index*

Khapai, Arambi 88
Khatuov, Dzhambulat (not Jambulat) 42, 52
Khloponin, Alexander 31
Khodorkovsky, Mikhail 117
Khrekov, Anton 44
Khrushchev, Nikita 6
Khushtov, Aslanbek 91
Kirzhinov, Mukharbi 91
kleptocracy 9, 124
Klishina, Darya 123
Kolesnik, Vadim 71
Kolodyazhnyi, Viktor 29, 41
Kondratyev, Veniamin 116
Kozak, Dmitry 28, 31, 42, 50, 52–3, 98, 108–9, 119
Krakow 111
Krasnaya Polyana resort 29–31, 48–9, 83, 87, 109; and Circassian genocide 83, 87
Krasnodar 109
Krasnodar Krai 30–1, 41, 49, 51–2, 83, 87, 107–9, 115–16
Krastev, Ivan 8
Krymstroy 98
Kuashev, Timur 93
Kudepsta 50
Kyiv 13
Kyrgyzstan 94

Lago-Naki resort 88
Lavrov, Sergey 61, 96
Lazarev, Mikhail 87
Lazarevskoe 87
Lebedev, Alexander 44
LGBT 10–11, 14–15, 39, 41, 52–5, 81, 96–7, 117, 120; vs traditional values 10–11, 52, 54, 97
Litvinenko, Alexander 44, 95
Leningrad oblast 66
Lithuania 93
London 30, 44, 86, 95
Longworth, John A. 84
Lugovoi Andrei 44
Lviv 112

Madrid 120
Magnitogorsk 6
Magnitsky List 95
Magnitsky, Sergei 95, 117
Mecca 85
medals 11–12, 91, 95, 121–4
Medvedev, Dmitry 13, 28–9, 31, 41, 66–7, 70, 107
mega-events definition 2–3, 21, 25, 38–9

mega-projects 4; annexation of Crimea 119, 123; consequences 7, 9, 32–3, 69, 98, 104, 106, 110–11, 11–19; corruption 24, 30; definition 3, 21–2, 25
Memorial 49, 63, 66–7, 116
Merkel, Angela 97, 117
Middle East 120
Migrant labor/workers 11, 64
Mikhail Nikolaevich, Prince 87
Miller, Alexei 114
Milov, Vladimir 43
Milyutin, Dmitry 86
Minnikhanov, Rustam 24
Moldova 94
Morozov, Valery 32
Moscow 4, 6, 13, 32, 45, 49, 65, 72–3, 92, 107, 115, 122
Moscow military district 71
Muller, Martin 24, 26
Munich 27, 62, 91, 112
Mutko, Vitaly 99, 121–2

Nagornykh, Yuri 121
Nalchik 91, 93–4
NATO 13, 70, 82, 98
Navaginsky Fort 84
Navalny, Alexey 24, 26, 29–30, 45, 114
Nemtsov, Boris 29–30, 42–5
New Jersey 89–90
New York 63, 89, 91
The New York Times 53, 86–7, 98, 121
Nicolas I 84–5
Nizhny Tagil 5
North Caucasus region 14–15, 31, 43, 47–50, 63–9, 71, 75, 83, 87–9, 94, 116, 123; anti-Russian insurgency 15, 64–5, 67–8, 75, 94, 116, 123; Russian conquest 83–87
North Caucasus Federal District 64, 66, 68
North Ossetia 87
Norway 12, 112
Novorossiisk 71

Obama, Barack 11, 54, 96–7, 117
Oblagu, Ali 84
Ochamchira 71
Olympic Charter 23, 74, 104, 120
Olympic games: 1908 London 106; 1936 Berlin 7, 36; 1964 Tokyo 5, 8, 23; 1972 Munich 8, 27, 62, 91; 1976 Montreal 23, 106; 1980 Moscow 4, 6, 11, 23, 43, 64, 91, 95, 98, 104; 1984 Innsbruck 12; 1984 Los Angeles 23, 48, 95;1988

Index 133

Calgary; 1988 Seoul 38, 112; 1992 Albertville 45; 1992 Barcelona 5, 106; 1996 Atlanta 8, 48, 62; 1996 Lillehammer 45; 2000 Sydney 46, 81, 90–1; 2000 Sydney and First nations issue 81, 90; 2002 Salt Lake City 30, 48, 72–3; 2004 Athens 6, 46, 63, 106; 2006 Torino 46; 2008 Beijing 5, 8, 23, 46, 51, 63–4, 81, 91, 109, 111, 117, 120; 2008 Beijing and Tibet issue 81; 2010 Vancouver 63, 81, 89–90, 120; 2010 Vancouver and First nations issue 81, 90; 2012 London 25, 63–4, 71, 106; 2016 Rio 74–5, 122–3; 2020 Tokyo 112, 120
Olympstroy 14, 25, 28–30, 49, 51, 98, 108
opposition 9–10, 14, 24, 29, 38–45, 93, 112
Orthodox Church 52, 87, 107
Oslo 112
Ovechkin, Alexei 11

Pakhomov, Anatoly 42, 44–5, 52, 54
paralympic games 12, 66, 71, 122–3
Patrushev, Nikolai 98
patrimonialism 4
patronal regime 10, 116
Poland 12, 86, 93, 112
Pomerantsev, Peter 4
Potanin, Vladimir 6, 27, 114
Primorskii Krai 109
propaganda 11, 98, 113–14, 118; *see also* information war
protests: Circassian movement 41, 84, 89, 91–3; Olympics 38, 47; Putin 9, 45, 52, 73; in Russia 9, 14–15, 29, 40–1, 45; Sochi games 14–15, 40, 45, 50, 52, 73–4, 82, 91
public opinion 2, 47–8, 96
Pussy Riot 74, 117
Putin, Vladimir: authoritarianism 1, 4, 30, 45, 81, 112, 116, 123–4; Circassian question 81, 87–8, 92; containment theory 83, 92; corruption 1, 4, 10, 21–2, 30–1, 114, 123; civil rights 8, 38–40, 61–2, 123; civil society 8, 14, 54–5, 73, 75; cronies 4, 8, 30, 105, 114–15, 123; elections 8, 13, 22, 25, 52, 64, 66, 70, 73; inner circle 22, 82, 115; kleptocracy 9–10, 124; Ozero dacha group 115; political protests 9, 45, 52, 73; popularity, rating 11, 13, 112–14, 119, 124; Putinism 22; regime 8–11, 22, 30,

32, 40–1, 45, 55, 87, 106, 112, 116, 123–4; terrorism 61–62, 67
Putina, Lyudmila 6
Pyatigorsk 11, 67

regional development 5, 7, 15, 28, 108–9
Reilian, Yury 110
Renova 114
rent distribution 9, 32
Rice, Condoleezza 69
Richmond, Walter 87
Robertson, Jack 121
Rodchenkov, Grigori 121–2
Romania 93
Rosneft 113
Rosoboronexport 74
Rostov oblast 109
Rotenberg, Arkady 30, 114
Rotenberg, Boris 30
Rudolph, Eric 62
Rudomakha, Andrei 49
Russia: civil society 1–2, 7–8, 14, 16, 29, 38–40, 48, 54–5, 73, 75, 105, 123; concept of return to the world stage 62, 64, 69, 98; corruption 1–2, 4, 10, 14, 22, 28–9, 31–3, 65, 70, 95; economic crisis after the Sochi Olympics 42–3, 116, 123; foreign agents law 50, 53, 73; foreign policy crisis after the Sochi Olympics 13, 83; military reform 14, 61–2, 75, 118; Russian counter-sanctions against U.S and EU 118; western sanctions 30, 74, 83, 95, 98, 106, 113, 117–18
Russian Olympic Committee 29, 31, 49, 90–1
Russian Railroads company 26, 30, 49, 114–15

Saakashvili, Mikheil 69–70, 94
Salzberg 46
Savage, Dan 53
Saurin, Alexander 52
Sberbank 27, 109, 114
Schwartz, Allyson (D-PA) 96
Sechin, Igor 113
security services 9, 50, 65–8, 98, 121–3; FSB 64–6, 67, 71–2, 122; KGB 44, 66, 82–3, 89, 95; siloviki 9; state organized doping 121–2
Senezh 72
Seppelt, Hajo 122
Sevastopol 71
Shazzo, Aslan 93

134 *Index*

Shenderovich, Viktor 113
Shoigu, Sergei 72, 96, 98
Shukhov, Boris 91
Shuster, Bill (R-PA) 96
Sinev, Vyacheslav 121
Skolkovo 4
Slyunyaev, Igor 28
Snimschikova, Galina 44
snow issue 6, 11, 46
Snowden, Edward 81, 96
Sobchak, Anatoly 6
Sochi: 1918 Georgian annexation of Sochi
  87; capital of Circassia 81, 83–87;
  Circassian genocide 69; mayor elections
  39, 41–2, 44–5, 52, 54; resort 3, 6, 11,
  27, 29, 31, 42–3, 87–9, 98, 105–10,
  124; Russian military 61–4, 69–70;
  security 61–9; Sochi Police Department
  65; terrorism 62–9, 106; tourism 3–4, 7,
  27, 43, 89, 105–11, 119
Sochi games: boycott 2, 53–4, 82, 94–7;
  budget (cost) 2, 4–5, 8, 14, 21, 23–33,
  45, 51, 108, 113–15, 120; corruption
  1–2, 7–8, 13, 15, 21, 25, 27, 29–33, 43,
  108, 123–4; doping 1–2, 15, 72, 105–6,
  120–4; environmental issues 9, 14, 26,
  38–41, 45–50, 54–5, 105, 110–11, 116,
  123–4; migrant workers 11, 64; protests
  14–15, 40, 45, 50, 52, 73–4, 82, 91;
  Russia's invasion in Crimea 1–2, 7, 10,
  13, 15–16, 30, 61, 70–2, 75, 82–3, 98,
  105, 113, 117, 123; security 9, 11, 13,
  15, 61–3, 67–9, 74–5, 123; Sochi
  Syndrome 111
Sokolov, Alexandr 29
Solberg, Erna 112
Spectator pass 66, 73; Tessera del Tifoso
  73
Stalin, Joseph 6–7, 87–8, 98
Starikov, Ivan 43
state corporations 9, 14, 25–9, 32, 38–40,
  45, 49, 51, 54, 98, 108
Stavropol Krai 87
Stepanov, Vitaly 121–2
Stepanova, Yuliya 121–2
Stockholm 112
South Ossetia 69, 82, 94
Southern Federal District 64–9
Surkov, Vladislav 44
sustainability 104–5, 111, 120; urban 5
St. Moritz 112
St. Petersburg 4, 6, 65–6, 107
Stavropol Krai 67, 87
Sweden 12, 112

Switzerland 12, 112
Syria 7, 61, 68, 70, 72, 74–5, 87, 89,
  120
Syromolotov, Oleg 61, 66, 68

Tbilisi 69, 82, 94–5
television 2, 7, 9, 22, 25, 38, 44, 94, 122
terrorism: 9/11 terrorist attack 62–3;
  anti-terrorism 15, 61–2, 64–7, 75;
  2013 Boston Marathon terrorist attack
  62; in Russia 15, 61–2, 65, 67–8;
  Olympics 8, 61–2; Sochi games 9, 11,
  13, 15, 61–3, 67–9, 74–5, 123; soft
  power methods 66–7, 116; state terror
  64, 67, 72, 116
Teuvazhev, Beslan 92
Timchenko, Gennady 30, 114
Tkachev, Aleksandr 6, 41, 51, 107, 109,
  115
Transnistria 94
Tornau, Fyodor 84
Tuapse 84–5
Turkey 74, 83, 86–7, 89, 91, 119; Ottoman
  Empire 83–4, 89
Turkmenistan 111

Ukraine 88, 93, 112; and the 2004 Orange
  revolution 13; the 2014 Euromaidan
  revolution 12–14, 75, 82, 97, 116–18;
  Donbas conflict 14, 97, 106, 107, 117,
  119; Russia's after-Olympics invasion
  in Crimea 1–2, 7, 10, 13, 15–16, 30, 61,
  70–2, 75, 82–3, 98, 105, 113, 117, 123;
  Russia's annexation of Crimea 14–15,
  97, 106, 117, 119
Umarov, Doku 65, 67–8
UNESCO 47–8
United Kingdom 12, 63–4; *see also*
  England, Britain
United Nations 13, 95
urban development 5, 14, 21, 24, 32, 39,
  46, 105–6, 111, 116
Urquhart, David 86
USA 63, 81, 83, 89–91, 94
US Congress 96
USSR (also Soviet Union) 4, 6–7, 11, 21,
  42–3, 44, 47, 51, 71, 87–8, 92–3, 95,
  98, 104, 106

Vainshtok, Semyon 29
Vekselberg, Viktor 114
Vitishko, Yevgenii 49
Vladivostok 4–5
Volga-Urals military district 71

Index 135

Volgograd 11, 67–8, 75, 123
Volochkova, Anastasia 44

WADA 72, 106, 121–2
Wallechinsky, David 120
Walsh, Marty 112
World Cup 2, 16, 32, 43, 74–5, 104, 109, 113, 123
World War II 1, 8, 71, 92, 98
Washington, DC 63, 96
Washington, George 84–5

Wild, Vic 11–2
Wilson, Andrew 10

Yakunin, Vladimir 30, 114–15
Yanukovych, Viktor 10, 12–13, 97, 108
Yeltsin, Boris 6, 42
Yerevan 94

Zazabor'e 71
Zhukov, Aleksandr 29, 48

Taylor & Francis eBooks

Helping you to choose the right eBooks for your Library

Add Routledge titles to your library's digital collection today. Taylor and Francis ebooks contains over 50,000 titles in the Humanities, Social Sciences, Behavioural Sciences, Built Environment and Law.

Choose from a range of subject packages or create your own!

Benefits for you
- Free MARC records
- COUNTER-compliant usage statistics
- Flexible purchase and pricing options
- All titles DRM-free.

Benefits for your user
- Off-site, anytime access via Athens or referring URL
- Print or copy pages or chapters
- Full content search
- Bookmark, highlight and annotate text
- Access to thousands of pages of quality research at the click of a button.

REQUEST YOUR FREE INSTITUTIONAL TRIAL TODAY

Free Trials Available
We offer free trials to qualifying academic, corporate and government customers.

eCollections – Choose from over 30 subject eCollections, including:

Archaeology	Language Learning
Architecture	Law
Asian Studies	Literature
Business & Management	Media & Communication
Classical Studies	Middle East Studies
Construction	Music
Creative & Media Arts	Philosophy
Criminology & Criminal Justice	Planning
Economics	Politics
Education	Psychology & Mental Health
Energy	Religion
Engineering	Security
English Language & Linguistics	Social Work
Environment & Sustainability	Sociology
Geography	Sport
Health Studies	Theatre & Performance
History	Tourism, Hospitality & Events

For more information, pricing enquiries or to order a free trial, please contact your local sales team:
www.tandfebooks.com/page/sales

The home of Routledge books

www.tandfebooks.com